The
Beckett Studies
Reader

Edited by

S. E. Gontarski

D1527164

University Press of Florida

Gainesville/Tallahassee/Tampa

Boca Raton/Pensacola/Orlando

Miami/Jacksonville

Copyright © 1993 by the Board of Regents of the State of Florida
Printed in the U.S. on acid-free paper
All Rights Reserved

Library of Congress Cataloging-in-Publication Data

The Beckett studies reader (1976–1991) / edited by S. E. Gontarski.
p.   cm.
Includes bibliographical references and index.
ISBN 0-8130-1197-3
1. Beckett, Samuel, 1906–   —Criticism and interpretation.
I. Gontarski, S. E.
PR6003.E282Z5719   1993
848'.91409—dc20   92-39423

Frontispiece: Samuel Beckett, 1979. Photograph courtesy of the
Goodman Theatre, Chicago.

The University Press of Florida is the scholarly publishing agency
for the State University System of Florida, comprised of Florida
A & M University, Florida Atlantic University, Florida International
University, Florida State University, University of Central Florida,
University of Florida, University of North Florida, University of
South Florida, University of West Florida.

University Press of Florida
15 Northwest 15th Street
Gainesville, Florida 32611

For John Calder,
the last publisher

Contents

The *Journal of Beckett Studies,*
The First Fifteen Years:
An Introduction

S. E. Gontarski

This volume gathers, and so makes readily available for the first time, a selection of essays from the *Journal of Beckett Studies'* first fifteen years, 1976–91. *The Reader* is designed to supplement existing books and anthologies by concentrating on that portion of Beckett's *oeuvre* only lightly or incompletely explored by scholars and critics, and by focusing on the interconnections among Beckett's works. The critics gathered here have consistently demonstrated remarkable continuity between works less well known (Beckett's mimes, the short stories "What a Misfortune" and "Imagination Dead Imagine," the radio play *Embers,* and the prose tribute, "La Falaise," for instance) and those more widely known (*Murphy, Watt, Molloy,* and *Waiting for Godot*). *The Beckett Studies Reader,* then, is designed to fill two gaps in current Beckett studies; it brings to a wider audience essays on Beckett's work that have never achieved the distribution and readership they merit, and it supplements (in the Derridean sense as well) existing books and anthologies by focusing on works and critical perspectives less than thoroughly explored in the bulk of Beckett criticism.

The History

Founded in 1976 by James Knowlson (founder as well of the Samuel Beckett Archive at the University of Reading in 1971), the *Journal of Beckett*

Studies was published until 1991 by John Calder (Publishers) Ltd. That special relationship between the English publisher of Beckett's fiction and the Samuel Beckett Archive at the University of Reading enabled the *Journal of Beckett Studies* to feature previously unpublished drama, fiction, poetry, and a specially commissioned tribute from Beckett in its first six issues.[1] Consequently, those early issues of the *Journal of Beckett Studies* have been eagerly sought by scholars and collectors.[2]

As an unsubsidized commercial enterprise, however, the *Journal* was subject to the economic vicissitudes of John Calder (Publishers) Ltd., and so it has appeared irregularly, only eleven times in its fifteen-year history. Although John Calder remained steadfastly committed to publishing—and keeping in print—not only all of Beckett's prose fiction, poetry, and criticism but to publishing a scholarly journal devoted to Samuel Beckett and his circle, the economic realities of his independent publishing house permitted publication only as money could be found. The possibilities of continued publication by John Calder ended with the demise of John Calder (Publishers) Ltd. in 1991, and the publication of the *Journal* was taken over by Florida State University with a new series in 1992. *The Beckett Studies Reader,* then, brings to a close that first phase of the *Journal*'s history by making available high-quality essays[3] that have never received the distribution they deserve either because the *Journal,* due to its irregularity, has had only limited circulation in the past, even among research libraries, or because the essays were not book chapters.

Despite publication interruptions of up to two years, the *Journal of Beckett Studies* has attracted and retained the loyalty of major scholars in the field; thus, publication standards have remained consistently high even as contributors faced prolonged publication delays. Its erratic publication schedule notwithstanding, the *Journal of Beckett Studies* has remained a major force in the field due to its ability to attract prominent scholars, among them Enoch Brater, Ruby Cohn, Martin Esslin, James Knowlson, John Pilling (himself a former editor of the *Journal*), Rubin Rabinovitz, and Katharine Worth, as well as the best of the newer scholars. As the accompanying alumni bibliography suggests, essays that originally appeared in the *Journal,* such as Cohn's "Beckett's German *Godot*" (No. 1, Winter 1976), have later appeared in significant books and so have already achieved substantial distribution—in Cohn's case in her superb *Just Play: Beckett's Theater* (Princeton, NJ: Princeton University Press, 1980). Three of Rabinovitz's *Journal of Beckett Studies* essays (in Nos. 2, Summer 1977; 5, Autumn 1979; and 11/12, Spring 1989) have been incorporated into his *Innovation in Samuel Beckett's Fiction* (Urbana, Il: University of Illinois Press, 1992). Other influential essays, like Walter Asmus's "Rehearsal Notes for the German Première of *That Time* and *Footfalls*" (No. 2, Summer 1982), are readily available in widely distributed anthologies—in my own *On Beckett: Essays and Criticism* (New York: Grove Press, 1986) in this case. *The Beckett Studies Reader* concentrates instead on those essays of exceptional merit that are not readily available on library shelves.

The Essays

The collection opens with an essay on Beckett's second book,[4] *Proust,* written in 1930 and published in 1931 while Beckett entertained his short-lived aspiration for an academic career.[5] John Pilling is one of the few critics to examine fully Samuel Beckett's one and only book of literary criticism less as an anticipation of the fiction Beckett himself was to write than as a critique of Proust.[6] Pilling, moreover, makes extensive use of Beckett's personal, annotated copy of *A la recherche du temps perdu,* "the abominable edition of the *Nouvelle Revue Française,* in sixteen volumes," according to Beckett, that is now on deposit at the University of Reading's Beckett Archive. As Pilling notes, "It would be going too far to state that Beckett's marginal comments are more important than any of the available critical commentaries . . . but there can be no doubt that our understanding of the remarkable mental and emotional apparatus that has given us such great masterpieces as *Molloy* and *Waiting for Godot* is immeasurably enriched by them."

Jeri Kroll may concentrate on a single story, "What a Misfortune," from the collection of Beckett's "apprentice" fiction, *More Pricks than Kicks,* but her reading reaches out to all the stories of the volume, the relation of those stories to their long-suppressed source, *Dream of Fair to Middling Women,*[7] and the transition of its hero Belacqua Shuah to the eponymous hero of *Murphy.* In examining Beckett's alter ego, Belacqua Shuah, a radical celibate with castration fantasies, in his roles as artist and lover, Kroll explores how the "theme of spiritual and physical conflict is mediated by an array of female characters. . . ." In what is surely one of the finest essays dealing with the role of women in Beckett's work, Kroll examines the "bungled romantic encounters" of Belacqua Shuah and concludes that ". . . when Beckett squarely faces what Belacqua avoids (the irrationality of the human experience), women cease to function as symbols of the dilemma." "Beckett's development," she concludes, "of all the characters from Belacqua to the Unnamable testifies to the continuing search for a way to cope with human dichotomies, treading a fine line between sanity and insanity."

My own study refocuses attention on another of the neglected works in the Beckett canon, the short mime *Act Without Words I,* and develops an existentialist reading for this surprisingly complex but rarely performed theater work. Within this paradigmatic tale of Everyman's humiliation and demise, thrust as he is into a system designed to thwart him, the unnamed protagonist manages an act of defiance in the manner of Albert Camus's rebel: "The climactic ending of the mime may signify not a pathetic defeat, but a conscious rebellion, man's deliberate refusal to obey." One hopes, as well, that the essay encourages readers to revisit the rest of Beckett's mimes, as well as those works that feature strong mimetic elements, such as *Endgame, Krapp's Last Tape, That Time, Film,* and *Ohio Impromptu.*

When major works, like *Watt, Murphy, Molloy,* and *Waiting for Godot,* are treated, the approaches tend to be tightly focused on fundamental issues. Thus, Thomas J. Cousineau's analysis of "the illusory nature of consciousness" in the 1945 novel *Watt* uses Jacques Lacan's paradigm of the "mirror stage" in the development of human consciousness and Paul Ricoeur's dialectic of destruction and renewal. Himself a musician, Heath Lees brings a specialist's ear to the musical complexities of Beckett's *diminuendo al niente, Watt,* whose main character, like the eponymous Murphy, fails to achieve "attunement." Using manuscripts and typescripts on deposit at the University of Texas Humanities Research Center, Lees corrects those critics who "fall into the trap of crediting Beckett (or themselves) with only a limited understanding of music and thus fail to appreciate how strongly and pervasively the musical themes are exploited in the novel." "Had Watt learned to respond to the non-literal language of music," Lees concludes, "his mental catastrophe might have been avoided" (see as well the failure of Orphic song in Katherine Kelly's analysis of *Not I,* and the twin failures at life and love in J. D. O'Hara's analysis of the Jungian *Molloy*).

James Acheson catalogs Beckett's satirical treatment in *Murphy* of the metaphysics of Leibniz, Geulincx, and Schopenhauer as well as the psychology of William James and the gestalt of Solomon Asch and Oswald Külpe. Acheson details the conarium-shrunken Murphy's attempts to reconcile the poles of determinism and freedom in his doomed struggle toward will-lessness through the transcendence of desire. J. D. O'Hara analyzes the Jungian subconscious operating thematically and structurally in what many consider Samuel Beckett's most significant and influential novel,

Molloy. As O'Hara notes, Molloy's "basic problem is to find his mother—not the 'personal mother' but the mother within him, as a primary variant of his anima." The conflicts of animus and anima, of Logos and the Wise Old Woman remain irresolute, and, O'Hara concludes, "Beckett uses Jungian psychology to present Molloy as failing at life because he fails at love."

The essay further suggests how incompletely critics have examined Beckett's relationship to Carl Jung, even though we know that Beckett attended at least one of Jung's Tavistock Clinic lectures in London in 1935 and was enormously influenced by a story Jung told of a woman who had "never been born entirely." One of the addenda to *Watt*, for instance, notes simply, "never been properly born." Beckett discussed the theme in the mid-1960s with the critic whom many consider Beckett's first biographer, Lawrence E. Harvey. Beckett spoke, according to Harvey, of "a presence, embryonic, underdeveloped, of a self that might have been but *never* got born, an *être manqué.*" Beckett used the concept again a decade later during the German rehearsals of *Footfalls* to describe the character of May to actress Hildegard Schmahl (see also Lawley, n. 23).

Anne C. Murch focuses on a production of—or rather a variation on—*Waiting for Godot* that undoubtedly made Beckett at least uncomfortable—André Engel's Strasbourg theaterwork *Ils allaient obscurs sous la nuit solitaire,* subtitled *D'après 'En attendant Godot' de Samuel Beckett.* For Murch and Engel, Beckett's two tramps "have rapidly left the narrow precincts of art to become, perhaps subliminally, part of the collective imagination of our time." As such, *Godot* can be not only played but played with, "quoted," to use Murch's term, to form a new work, "'neither an adaptation nor a new staging of Beckett's play, but rather a work for the stage grafted on to extracts from Beckett's text,'" according to Dramaturg Bernard Pautrat. Although much of Beckett studies is still preoccupied with authorized or "correct" stagings of Beckett's texts, Murch's essay offers a *soupçon* of the future, what may be the next phase in the evolution of Beckett's theater, post-postmodern stagings.

Paul Lawley takes up another of the neglected works in the Beckett canon, and his analysis of *Embers* is a concentrated, Freudian explication of Beckett's transitional radio play, written between *All that Fall* and *Words and Music.* "One might say," notes Lawley, "that the symbolic structure of *Embers* (which is also Henry's own imaginative structure) is built on the punning relation of eye-I to see-sea." But the radio play is more than just "play as dramatic poem." Beckett's play with language suggests "the possibility that the whole 'geography' of the play is a fiction of the central consciousness rather than just an evocative background for the 'action.'" Katherine Kelly returns to the issue of Beckett and myth as she explores the failure of Orphic power in Beckett's drama of the dismembered Orpheus, *Not I.* "The failure of the lyric, intelligibly and melodically, to sum up the singer's life is the equivalent of the failure of Orphic power in this piece," notes Kelly; "Burdened with her story, the function of expression has, for [Mouth], lost its ancient connection with prayer and power as well as its romantic association with truth and beauty."

Among the most theoretically informed of the essays in this volume, the two by James Hansford examine "the narrative consciousness 'half in' and 'half out' of the imagined world" in both "Imagination Dead Imagine" and "La Falaise." Written as an homage to painter and friend Bram van Velde, "La Falaise" is a work that links not only Beckett's criticism to the (late) fiction but offers fresh insights into the relationship between painting and fiction in Beckett's art. Hansford's essays, moreover, provide as succinct an analysis of Beckett's "negative aesthetics" as one is likely to find (see Lawley on this issue as well). The volume ends as appropriately as it begins, with philosopher Ileana Marcoulesco's comprehensive survey of a— if not *the*—central question in Beckett studies, Beckett's relationship to the philosophical tradition of solipsism, which she locates in Bishop Berkeley, and its aesthetic equivalent, minimalism, which she defines as "the conscious progression, in his art, toward experiencing the minimal structures still able to account for an aesthetic effect." "By uncluttering the natural landscape," notes Marcoulesco, "the artist arrives at bare figures and scarce colors; successive eliminations, far from hurting the mysterious meanings, let them shine through." Further, Marcoulesco reexamines the notion of the "absurd" in Beckett's work that "lies at the centre of Beckett's dramaticules, not as sheer *non sequiturs,* nonsense and flat denials of meaning, but as the logical paradox [of solipsism] which moves the writing hand out of its inertia."

Collectively, the essays gathered here have themselves something of a through-line; they comprise a set of variations on the themes of consciousness and perception, particularly the persistent interplay and irresolution of dualities. Almost every commentator on Beckett's work has offered some analysis of the Cartesian split of mind and body, self and other, developed by Beckett most explicitly in *Murphy,* or, as Jeri Kroll notes, "the conflict between the physical and the spiritual" in the fiction that precedes *Murphy.* Increasingly, critics are examining the Manichean tension of light and dark that pervades Beckett's work and that Beckett himself has acknowledged was at work at least in *Krapp's Last Tape.*[8] The principle of structural and thematic opposition is evident as well even in titles of such critical studies as Vivian Mercier's quirky *Beckett/Beckett* (1977) and Enoch Brater's (ed.) *Beckett at 80/Beckett in Context* (1988). The critical perspective is outlined succinctly by David Hesla in *The Shape of Chaos: An Interpretation of the Art of Samuel Beckett* (1971): Beckett's "art is . . . energized precisely by the dialectical interplay of opposites—body and mind, the self and the other, speech and silence, life and death, hope and despair, being and non-being, yes and no" (pp. 10–11). The essays here offer a fresh look at those tensions, dialectics, antinomies, or syzygies that "energize" Beckett's art: sexually, in the male/female opposition (Kroll); psychoanalytically, in the animus/anima (O'Hara), true self/surrogate self (Cousineau), and hallucination/reality (Lawley) interplay; cosmically, in the submission/defiance confluence (Gontarski); philosophically, in the actual/virtual flux (Acheson); musically, in the tuning/untuning tension (Lees); spatially, in the inside/outside paradox (Hansford); aesthetically and phenomenologically, in the relationship between illusion and reality (Lawley), art and reality (Murch, Lawley), and consciousness and the external world (Pilling, Kroll, Lawley, Hansford, Gontarski, and Marcoulesco); and theatrically, in the exposure/concealment paradox (Kroll and Kelly). The *Godot* "quoted" in Murch's analysis of André Engel's intertextual theater work is, moreover, simultaneously present and absent, material skeleton and diaphanous aura.

In addition, then, to celebrating the first fifteen years of the *Journal of Beckett Studies,* this volume is designed as a substantial contribution to Beckett studies itself. It supplements the plethora of books on Samuel Beckett by making available significant and lively essays that have received less than deserved distribution; by spotlighting those works too often slighted in other studies; and finally by offering fresh perspectives on some very fundamental themes in the work of a writer whom many consider the chief figure in post–World War II English and European literature.

Hampstead, London

Notes

1. The teleplay *Ghost Trio* appeared in the *Journal of Beckett Studies* No. 1, a tribute to George Reavey in No. 2, the prose works, "All Strange Away" in No. 3, "Heard in the Dark, 2" in No. 5, "One Evening" in No. 6, and the poem "Neither" in No. 4.

2. George Robert Minkoff, Inc., Rare Books, for instance, has recently offered

the *Journal of Beckett Studies,* No. 1, inscribed "For Calvin Israel from Sam. Beckett," for $200.00.

3. Six of the fourteen essays were lead essays in their respective issues: Pilling (No. 1), Kroll (No. 3), Cousineau (No. 4), Acheson (No. 5), Lawley (No. 6), Lees (No. 9).

4. Beckett's long poem *Whoroscope* was published in Paris by Nancy Cunard's The Hours Press in 1930.

5. Beckett resigned his teaching post from Trinity College, Dublin in December 1931.

6. See also Nicholas Zurbrugg, *Beckett and Proust* (Totowa, NJ: Barnes and Noble Books, 1988).

7. Monkstown, Dublin: Black Cat Press, 1992.

8. See particularly James Knowlson, *Light and Darkness in the Theatre of Samuel Beckett* (London: Turret Books, 1972).

2

Beckett's *Proust*

███

John Pilling

Beckett's *Proust* (1931) is not just a critical monograph by a young academic of ability, but much more a creative encounter between one great writer and another. It has, of course, been liberally plundered, with more or less justification, by those commentators on Beckett who have admired the economy and pertinacity with which he lays bare his deepest and most intimate fears and obsessions, but, until recent years, it was tacitly ignored by academic critics of *Proust* as an aberration not to be encouraged. That the book is mandarin in tone and sometimes dense in its discriminations cannot be denied; it is not a model to be unreservedly recommended to freshmen. It is as much intellectual biography, perhaps, as literary criticism, an adventure of the mind as much as a foray into *belles-lettres*. The book is written *con amore,* with the passionate engagement and excitement of discovery that distinguish all true criticism. But at the same time it also bears the occasional marks of being a task, a hard job, a commission that has come his way, through good fortune and the friendship of Richard Aldington.[1]

With the "abominable" edition of the *Nouvelle revue française* which Beckett used now available to scholars,[2] we are in a unique position to study the transmission and genesis of the *Proust* volume, and to clarify some of the problems that the book, not entirely innocently, has caused to arise. It would be going too far to say that Beckett's marginal comments are more important than any of the available critical commentaries, or even that they are more important than the *Proust* monograph, but there can be no doubt that our understanding of the remarkable mental and emotional apparatus that was to give us such great masterpieces as *Molloy* and *Waiting for Godot* is immeasurably enriched by them.

The first thing that needs to be said of the *Proust* volume is that, in Beckett's eyes at least, it was a genuine attempt to say something about Proust. He did not enter into the commission with any intention of clothing his metaphysical speculations and spiritual dilemmas in a mask of academic obliquity. This is no doubt precisely why the book reads nakedly at times, as if the writer is suffering mysterious agonies whose origins are unclear to him, or as if the ostensible subject of the discourse has had to give way in the face of something more intransigent and menacing. But Beckett remained adamant that the book was intended as a critical introduction to Proust, on which he hoped to base an academic career that might lead to similar commissions being placed in his path.[3] The fact that he "gave up," as he puts it, his summer vacation of 1930 to rereading the sixteen volumes of Proust twice, apart from testifying to Beckett's scholarly diligence, lends color to his claim that it was an academic production first and foremost. It is precisely what a scholar would do, especially a scholar faced with the two-edged prospect of a first book.

Hard as it is to bring oneself to say it, the book is, by academic standards, only a partial success. Despite its remarkable acuteness, at a time when there was little really informed commentary on Proust, at any rate in English, it is not the best available introduction to Proust, nor is it even the most accurate guide to the themes and structures of Proust's work. The absence of an index and a bibliography can scarcely be blamed on Beckett, however, since the only comparable volume in the series in which it appears—Thomas MacGreevy's *T. S. Eliot* (1931)—also lacks these aids. MacGreevy's essay, praised later by Beckett as a model of what criticism should be, shows some resemblances to Beckett's, in both manner and matter, and the two men were often together at this time. A more serious lack is that both essays also lack footnotes identifying the precise location of quotations used in the text, a much more crippling deficiency in Beckett's essay than in MacGreevy's, not simply because of Proust's bulk as compared with Eliot's, but because Beckett seems to have read almost every important contribution to the cultural history of the West and to have most of this material at his fingertips in a way not even a seasoned polymath could emulate.

It is not, therefore, a book that observes the academic pieties. It disdains the established strategies (occasionally even the subtleties) of traditional discursive prose. This is clearest perhaps at the delightful moment when Beckett "cordially" invites his reader to omit what is basically a paraphrase of what Beckett considers, interestingly enough, "perhaps the greatest passage that Proust ever wrote."[4] We may infer from this that he is no more interested in criticism as paraphrase than in literature as book-keeping.[5] It is a dramatic and no doubt partly unconscious illustration of a premise which later on he attributes to Proust; we may, altering the wording slightly, say of Beckett that "the copiable he does not wish to see."[6] That the reader who obeyed Beckett's injunction would miss a splendidly economical summary analysis rounded off with a brilliantly serpentine sentence of Proustian length perhaps hardly needs saying; we are familiar with such self-canceling gestures, not meant to be acceded to, in Beckett's novels and plays of the 'fifties and 'sixties. However, the strain of being on his best behavior is clearly, at this and moments like it, irksome to Beckett, and he must have realized while writing it that the academic life was not for him. Certainly, within a few months of the book's publication, he had left the academy for good.[7]

Perhaps we may legitimately wonder, at first encounter, how Beckett forced himself to finish the task at all. He frequently proceeds, for several paragraphs, at a high level of generality not sufficiently argued to form the basis of a philosophy, but with enough resonance and bite to be considered more than wordly-wise rumination. Beckett clearly considered that criticism's main claim on our time was its truth-telling faculty; it was nothing less than a kind of wisdom. And as wisdom, it would sanction and benefit from hermetic and arcane modes of expression. This goes some way to explaining some of the archness and pomposity of Beckett's prose, but the now familiar irony which we find throughout his other creative writing is an important qualifying feature. He can puncture his own pretensions with a devastating and irresistible panache:

> Whatever opinion we may be pleased to hold on the subject of death, we may be sure that it is meaningless and valueless. Death has not required us to keep a day free. The art of publicity has been revolutionized by a similar consideration. Thus I am exhorted, not merely to try the aperient of the Shepherd, but to try it at seven o'clock.[8]

Here the presence of utter seriousness, baffled in the face of an extraordinary world, is what guarantees and informs the humor. Humor becomes the justified instrument of the critical surgery that lays bare a wound.

In *Proust* it is clearly, as the above quotation suggests, something like a work of art that we are faced with. Without going so far as to pretend that Beckett was intending every part of the jigsaw to cast reflective light on every other part, there is considerable, even excessive artfulness expended between the abrupt and brisk beginning—"The Proustian equation is never simple"—and the weary and distressed Latin with which the piece concludes—*defunctus*. Between these two poles the book takes shape, a shape Beckett periodically adverts to lest we lose in the flurry of what is happening on the surface the overall sense of a developing argument. Time, Habit, Memory, and Salvation are the topics of the first four sections, divided by the triangular asterisks of Chatto's English translation of Proust. The interpolated illustration—the paraphrase already mentioned—marks the point at which the structure appears to begin to disintegrate, and the transition to Albertine and the nature of love is not so much clumsy as nonexistent. But the effect, whether successful or not, is clearly intended, since the next section, a brilliant account of the afternoon party at the Guermantes' with which Proust's novel closes, is begun in similar fashion, and it is obviously Beckett's awakened sense of juxtaposition which is the most important factor in his decision to end one section with the devastating quote from Calderón (but really from Schopenhauer)[9] and to begin the next with a seemingly unengaged, but in fact emotionally turbid, piece of writing not far removed from the paraphrastic manner implicitly criticized earlier. One does not need to look far for Beckett's model here; it is obviously Proust himself. Beckett is, with some deliberation and perhaps a good deal of unconscious reverence, taking on the color of the author about whom he is writing, and the apparent loose ends, the seemingly gratuitous excursions from the point, and the carefully weighted preliminaries leading to a clinching and resonant conclusion are indisputably Proustian.

In the final section, in many ways the densest of all, Beckett attempts to summarize his conclusions but, finding himself on the verge of repetition, he concludes instead with a number of fascinating discussions on styles, influences, and genres which are in many ways the most revealing of all Beckett's comments. As an index of Beckett's own stylistic sensitivity, and before turning to the origins of Beckett's monograph, we might notice the self-conscious escalation of verbs at the beginning of the account of Albertine's disappearance: "The Albertine tragedy is prepared during the narrator's first stay at Balbec, involved by their relations in Paris, consolidated during his second stay at Balbec, and consummated by her imprisonment in Paris"[10] or the balanced antithesis ("the boredom of living . . . the suffering of being"[11]) and gnomic apophthegms which are everywhere apparent, and perhaps not entirely admirable. The rhetorically frenetic conclusion to section one, the dazzling phrase ("voluntary memory is Shadwell, and of Irish extraction";[12] "a neuralgia rather than a theme"[13]), and the studied put downs (of Constant, Cocteau, and Romantic writers generally)—all these are a measure of the book's idiosyncratic originality.

Beckett's copy of Proust bears witness to how intensive his reading had been, each volume being heavily scored in the margins, with any number of crucial individual words underlined, often very heavily, in ink or crayon or pencil. From the evidence one might have supposed him to have read the whole work many more times than twice; obviously certain parts were read many times. Beckett's scorings tend to occur in clusters, but perhaps this tells us as much, if not more, about Proust's method as about Beckett's, for even the most devoted Proustian would admit that there are dull stretches on the long road we have to travel. Beckett refrains from such evidence of frustration as one is used to from his notebooks—the squiggles of Byzantine complexity, the doodles that throw up weird human figures—but there are a number of rather blank periods, especially in *Le côté de Guermantes* but also in "Un amour de Swann" (except for the section concerned with music) and quite frequently in *Sodome et Gomorrhe* where Beckett has obviously found little to interest him. The absence from the monograph of any real consideration of what society meant for Proust might have led one to predict this, but it is surprising to find so few scorings in, for instance, the third volume of *A l'ombre des jeunes filles en fleurs,* or the first volume of *Le temps retrouvé.* Not that any easy correlation between the number of marginal marks and the importance of particular volumes can be established, for the two volumes of *Albertine disparue,* which are proportionately the most heavily marked, contain little extra marginal comment of importance and fewer "block" scorings (i.e., marking of whole episodes covering two or more pages) than is customary. Of course, in the case of *Du côté de chez Swann 1* and *Le temps retrouvé 2,* the most heavily scored individual volumes, there obviously is a distinct correlation between the intensity of Beckett's attention, the importance of these areas of Proust for his thesis, and indeed the generally accepted high-water marks of Proust's genius. It would, nevertheless, be true to say that, in the last analysis, it was the latter rather than the former—the mature man on the point of becoming a writer rather than the suffering child—who dominated the monograph Beckett was writing. As an introductory *explication* of *Le temps retrouvé,* indeed, the *Proust* book to some extent disarms such criticisms as were offered earlier on its stature as a straightforward piece of literary criticism.

It would be pointless and unhelpful to itemize every passage that impressed Beckett, and especially tedious to talk at length about what is sufficiently obvious from the published work, such as how he came to choose his quotations (not, by present-day standards, very numerous). Many of the marginal comments are largely *aides-mémoires* in the face of a work of sprawling complexity, or straightforward comparisons of one passage with another. Beckett remains sufficiently wide awake to catch Proust repeating a whole sentence verbatim,[14] but his approach is, in this respect, not unlike that of any intelligent reader. The same might be said of the heavy scoring that accompanies the instances of what Beckett calls the "process . . . of intellectualized animism, the eleven *moments privilégiés*"—elsewhere numbered "twelve or thirteen"[15] with a mock-flippant, if understandable, disregard for detail. But the eagerness with which Beckett seizes on points of cultural reference, especially the allusions to works of art, indicates a rather more special cast of mind, very much the young intellectual who is revealed in Beckett's other critical writings of the late twenties and early thirties. This is in no sense to sneer at the very important "educational" force that is exerted on any reader of Proust, for the numerous passages describing the paintings and music of both real and fictitious people are not only among the most dramatic and illuminating threads through Proust's labyrinth, but as informative and stimulating as any amount of professional art criticism. Beckett was obviously impressed by Proust's ability to make everything, even his most intimate contemporaries, part of the art work, thus making its retroactive grip on life indissolubly strong, and the experience of reading it about as unnovelistic as any novel ever.

Beckett is generally content to follow or silently digest Proust's cultural references, without adding any comparisons of his own. But there are two interesting exceptions to this, one in *Swann 1,* where the reflections concluding "Combray" are scored "Base senses (Kant)"—(whom he had doubtless just been reading[16]) and the other in *A l'ombre 2,* where a passage discussing the workings of memory is triumphantly marked "utterly non-Joycian" in what amounts to a brilliant, if undeveloped, distinction which one ignores at one's peril.[17] Proust is talking about how the mind comes once again upon material which, having no use for it, it had rejected; and he goes on to elaborate, beautifully, on how this material fades and how irretrievable it can seem. Beckett recognizes that Joyce is, in this respect as in others, quintessentially different from Proust. Joyce operates on the principle that everything is relevant and does not therefore need to engage on a quest in search of what has been forgotten. Joyce is "working with omniscience, omnipotence," and by comparison with him the nervous Proust is a hesitant and shambling figure, what Beckett would call "a non-can-er."[18]

What is clearly most important is to situate the exact nature of the relationship between Proust and Beckett. Beckett's tangible debt to Proust resides mainly in the area of ideas, but we should always remember that even where there are clear points of convergence it is perfectly possible that Beckett had discovered the ideas independently and found them confirmed by his reading of Proust. Since, however, some of these ideas are, either implicitly or explicitly, radically new, Beckett must have been gratified to encounter a kindred spirit who had fearlessly pursued the unconventional, and nowhere, perhaps, is this more true than in the matter of what constitutes a person's essential being, which is central to Beckett's work, and is the goal of Proust's quest also. Both writers investigate the matter through the question of personality, and it is above all here that Proust's example was important to Beckett. Proust asserts (and supports the assertion by demonstration) that personal identity is not a matter of stable, fixed, one-to-one correspondences, but a confused and occasionally volatile chaos brought about by oscillations in the relationship between the inner self and the outer world. For Beckett, plagued throughout his life with periodic moments of "absence" from the apparently normal world,[19] this coincidence of vision must have been of the utmost importance. But whereas it is, in a sense, Beckett's premise, on which his subsequent arguments depend in more or less disarray, it is in Proust's case more the conclusion to reams and reams of analysis that has everywhere suggested it. "Peut-être est-ce le néant qui est le vrai et tout notre rêve est-il inexistant," writes Proust early in the work.[20]

In his monograph Beckett deals with this topic through the medium of Albertine, not because he favors the criticism that isolates character (which would tend to destroy Proust's point), but because it is through Albertine that Proust is most dramatically brought to realize how ineluctably shifting our reality is. Indeed the absence of any real discussion of such interesting personalities as Bloch, or Charlus, or more particularly Gilberte, is symptomatic of Beckett's whole approach,[21] and it is fair to say that he does not so much misrepresent Proust's insight into personality as give it a one-sided emphasis that falls into line with his own thinking. The fact that Beckett tends to "become" Proust, or at least spokesman for him, indicates neither a spurious identification of their different aims, nor a dishonest attempt at concealing himself, chameleon-fashion, which is a retreat his other criticism disdains. It is clearly done partly in order that he may say what he must say in the small space allotted to him, but also because he has been profoundly impressed by Proust's statement of his own predicament. This explains why so much of the essay is "lifted" from Proust, and yet why it is nonetheless an utterly original essay. Reading Proust was tantamount to reading about himself; how could writing about him be other than self-revelatory?

However, since the self is problematic, what tools can we employ in its elucidation? Beckett, as a young intellectual, obviously began by choosing the intellect. But the intellect, as he soon realized, leads up a blind alley into a quicksand of paradoxes. Proust here once again offered a way of solution, for, throughout his novel, he unsparingly charts the futility of mere intellect and seeks constantly for the wonderful tranquillity that can be felt in the mind once the intellect has been recognized for what it is. Again and again reading Beckett's copy of Proust we find him scornful of minor characters who rely on "timid pure logic"[22] to get them out of their predicament, and again and again Proust's recommended cultivation of the inner faculties—what Beckett calls the "immersive necessity" as distinct from the "emersive tendency"[23]—engages Beckett's deepest interest. Proust's solitude is not simply the physical fact of retirement behind the cork walls of his apartment in the Boulevard Haussmann. The more important retirement is into the mind, where one's solitude can be peopled. As Proust says, "Ma solitude [est] une vie de salon mentale."[24] This clearly coincided with Beckett's thinking, and we may say that Proust's realization that the real Gilberte is within the heart and mind of Marcel is as important for A la recherche as Moran's recognition that the real Molloy is his mental projection is crucial to the second part of Molloy.[25] Indeed, the number of Beckett characters who find themselves peopled with a host of apparently dissimilar personalities is almost incalculable. But Beckett stops short of Proust's rationalization of this state of affairs. The idea which Proust is prepared to entertain, that there may be "une seule intelligence dont tout le monde est co-locataire"[26] is one which is rather too mystical for Beckett to accept, and too much a conventionally novelistic attitude to be entirely satisfactory. Beckett admittedly scores the sentence in which Proust speculates on whether the resurrection of the soul after death is a phenomenon of memory, but he ignores earlier explorations of the idea,[27] and is content with a cursory remark about Proust's "intellectualized animism" in the monograph.[28] Proust's basic insight into the centrifugal tendency of the human mind,[29] however, is everywhere confirmed in Beckett's own writings later.

It follows from Proust's discovery of the workings of the mind that "la vérité n'a pas besoin d'être dite pour être manifestée,"[30] but in practice this is a faith that proves hard to keep. Beckett's marginalia show that he is intrigued by Proust's oscillations between his impressions of the outer world and his relentless burrowing analyses into what these impressions are in essence.[31] Proust's own description of his state, "anxieuse inertie,"[32] could hardly be improved upon, and it is a condition that so fascinated Beckett that the description could be extended, without distortion, to his own state of mind, as revealed in his own imaginative writing later. In fact, Beckett's prose, very different though it is from Proust's, is similar in the way it is at one moment seemingly content with gratuitous irrelevance, and at the next pressing suddenly onward with tremendous thrust and impetus toward ultimate clarity. It is obviously the sundering of cause and effect—many of Beckett's marginalia are devoted to this theme[33]—which has disturbed the surface of the prose that emanates from the creative mind. But Beckett, like Proust, stresses that it is the self which is the real originator of disorder,[34] and that it is the responsibility of the self to put some kind of shape in its place, if for no other reason than that the external world continues to exist, however much the inner consciousness constructs a refuge for itself.[35] Rather than settle the issue one way or the other ("I take no sides" was what he would say), Beckett, in his fiction and drama, explores the changing relationship of the two elements that, though sundered, still miraculously interact. He lacks, however, Proust's single-mindedness, the single-mindedness that enabled Proust ultimately to collect all his effort into one enormous outpouring. But he is fascinated by the shapes and patterns that Proust tries out and, as it were, rejects along the way, and many of Proust's solutions to the problem of inner self and outer world reappear in Beckett's own creative work later. There is, for instance, the reaction that seeks to cut out the stimulus from the outside world: Beckett scores a passage in which Proust compares love with shutting one's ears to sound, and we cannot but be aware of how often and how unsuccessfully he tries this remedy through the plays (especially the radio plays) and prose fictions of the postwar period.[36] Malone's two unforgettable days of which nothing will ever be known are of this kind, and the idea may well be an unconscious extension of Proust's narrator's chagrin that seven hours of Albertine's time are irretrievably lost to him.[37]

A second possible reaction is to concentrate on the distortions that seemingly disfigure ordinary reality, but which contain priceless clues about what is real. Proust repeatedly asserts that there is a screen between the self and the world, and his work is full of images of partition and separation which Beckett often takes over wholesale. Especially interesting screens, from Proust's point of view, are such modern inventions as the telephone, the camera, the motorcar, and the airplane, and it is interesting to see how Beckett shares this fascination to the point of being keen to take it further. The telephone call is not, for Beckett, simply a stick with which to beat Cocteau,[38] nor even simply a way of leading up to the splendid paradox that Marcel is present at his own absence.[39] It is a coincidence of human voice and impersonal mechanism which reaches full fruition in the tape recorder of *Krapp's Last Tape,* the microphonic voice of *Not I,* and the voices which throng the radio plays. Like Proust, he is prepared to encounter apparent deformations head-on in an attempt to clarify the nature of the reality he is living through.

Obviously, the most readily available medium in which to do this is that of speech, which is made up of innumerable idiolects that are all deformations of one sort or another. Beckett's citation of *Les intermittences du coeur* as perhaps the greatest passage Proust ever wrote is interesting not least because it contains the most concentrated exploration of verbal deformation in the whole work. Beckett's scoring of Proust's reflections on the word "Syncope" uttered by the hotel manager—"qui m'aurait peut-être, s'appliquant à d'autres, paru ridicule, mais qui . . . resta longtemps ce qui était capable d'éveiller en moi les sensations plus douloureuses"[40]—is really the progenitor of those haunting verbal collisions that make Beckett's people unable to share information with any certainty. The relationship between Sam and Watt is memorably punctuated by such distortions. Indeed, in view of the very extreme distortions Watt introduces into his narrative—including the ultimate distortion of reading it backwards—one Proustian admission is of particular interest: "Parfois l'écriture où je déchiffrais les mensonges d'Albertine, sans être idéographique avait simplement besoin d'être lue à rebours."[41] And it is difficult not to feel that his explanation of why his novel has an occasionally fuzzy quality was not in Beckett's mind when he composed Sam's self-exculpation in *Watt.*[42] Beckett's sensitivity to sound is in fact almost as neurasthenic as Proust's, but Proust's total sensory equipment is arguably more nervously tense even than Beckett's. It is interesting, therefore, to see how Beckett tends to score not those passages that deal with peculiarities of visual perception but, almost exclusively, those dealing with strange and unexpected sounds.[43] Proust's work also contains many examples of eyes meeting eyes, which becomes in Beckett's later work an obsessive image, but the obsessiveness is so extreme as to suggest this is something he did not need Proust to isolate for him to be aware of it. However, Beckett, or at least his characters (the Mr. Rooney of *All that Fall* most obviously perhaps), would surely wholeheartedly endorse Proust's insight that "le besoin de parler n'empêche pas seulement d'écouter, mais de voir,"[44] and it is the strength of Beckett's work, as of Proust's, that one cannot isolate, even for critical purposes, one sense from another.

The optical distortion has extra importance for Proust because his affection for paintings looms so large in his work, and because he is concerned about defending the symbolism of painting as a means of attaining truth. Beckett doubly scores, and was obviously impressed by, the sentence in which Proust explains that in Giotto's allegorical painting symbols are "non comme une symbole puisque la pensée symbolisée n'était pas exprimée, mais comme réel, comme effectivement subi ou matériellement manié."[45] He shows himself here, as later on in his career, to be on the side of reality rather than simplified or schematized codifications of it. But realism *tout court,* or at least the literary variant of realism, is far too plodding and circumstantial to appeal to someone who has identified—after a brush with Curtius—the quality of Proust's "impressionism."[46] It is an impressionism that informs both the deliquescent and euphoric passages on childhood, and the more gnarled and grotesque images that are part of growing up. Proust responds fully to Giotto's grotesqueries, and later shows himself as not inferior in this regard, for example in the descriptions of the Marquis de Palancy and the dying Swann.[47] The fact that Beckett does not score these passages means only that he rested content with the early set piece as a possible illustration; like the description of Françoise killing the chicken, and the wry nature notes on the burrowing wasp,[48] the subsequent passages are full of elements that Beckett would admire. The puppetlike Legrandin is, for instance, a forerunner of the Watt who has such difficulty advancing due east, and close optical scrutiny of the kind Proust employs here remained with Beckett throughout his writing life.

Not that Proust's world may be said to be inhabited by such a gallery of moribunds as Beckett's, except perhaps at the afternoon party of Madame de Guermantes in the last volume. This is perhaps because the art of grotesque involves a preliminary detachment not unlike that of the caricaturist, and for Proust "cette indifférence aux souffrances qu'on cause . . . est la forme terrible et permanente de la cruauté." At the same time, however, he identified "le visage . . . sublime de la vraie bonté" as one in which "[on] ne se lit aucune commisération,"[49] and it is true of both Beckett and Proust that they are severe and unsparing writers who see little point in sentimental indulgence. Beckett's marginal notes are throughout unemotional, and only occasionally—as in the case of Marcel's reflections on seeing Gilberte with the young man or at the moment when Mme. de Villeparisis's carriage drives away from a pretty girl—does Beckett use the word "tragic."[50] Despite this, the published monograph contains an important section on tragedy, in which humanity's need to bear witness to its corporate guilt is the crucial feature,[51] and Marcel's analyses of Racine's tragic drama *Phèdre* (one of the literary works Beckett most admired) are, predictably, among the most comprehensively scored. Beckett may, throughout his work, be said to practice diligently the faculty of philosophic resignation which makes tragedy possible, and which earned Proust's undying approval.[52]

In Beckett's case, it might be said that his tendency to philosophic resignation can sometimes become inhuman coldness, and that his work sometimes shows the absence of human feelings that made Beckett say to Peggy Guggenheim, in the 'thirties, that he was "dead." It is certainly true that Beckett's excoriations of human folly and knavery are more thoroughgoing than Proust's, no doubt partly because his sense of his own identity is so much more intermittent than Proust's. Beckett is much more uncertain about the advantages of oblivion than Proust because he inhabits this vacuity more frequently. For Proust, the moments of obliteration are basically pleasant, and they are even important milestones on his quest, as in his contemplation of the blue blind prior to reading the letters of Madame de Sévigné.[53] This important moment could scarcely have been lost on Beckett, since he was similarly haunted by blue, and also associated it with contemplation (or the fruit of contemplation). However, the blue in his writing is rarely an unmixed blessing; it is subject to occasional white lacunae, like the summer day he speaks of in the first section of *How It Is*. We may say that the satisfactions, even of contemplation, are more remote for Beckett, more irretrievable. Proust speaks of the "sense of being at rest that one has when one shuts one's eyes" in a manner that Malone, among others (for few are in a more Proustian situation than him) would partially agree with; but he, like other Beckett figures, is only too aware that the problems do not cease by operating such a simple mechanism.[54] In a structurally parallel reflection, much later in his work, Proust reveals how profoundly aware he is of the fact that even when we remain silent—which is another mechanism we can operate, as Malone knows—we are nevertheless inscribing the hieroglyphics of reality on our brain.[55] Proust's prose at this point is far less fraught than Beckett's, since Beckett finds this kind of idea little short of horrifying, and he does not score it. It is not, however, surprising that most of Proust's long discussion on the oblivion that time ultimately brings interested Beckett considerably, although he does not record what he thought of the moment in *A l'ombre* where Proust, exceptionally, longs for the oblivion of death.[56] The infinity of space he discovers in his heart is one Beckett's characters have no option but to traverse.

Proust's main remedy, in the face of the confusing flux of living, is either to seek out a still object, or to construct for himself a situation in which he, at least, can remain immobile.[57] Although Proust never connects this need with his attitude to sounds, it is basically analogous to his feeling that an author "n'est qu'un instinct réligieusement écouté au milieu du silence."[58] Beckett is to be distinguished from Proust here, especially in view of the fact that it is the connection between soundlessness, stillness, and silence that he sets himself to explore, but also no doubt because, though these moments of stillness often occur in Proust, Proust is mainly dependent on movements (either self-induced or involuntary) and sounds outside himself, for the elucidation of his problems.[59] Proust, indeed, changes his mind on this question of immobility later in the work, recognizing that it may mean sterility, in a manner that Beckett would hardly condone. Much more remarkable, at least for Beckettians, is the passage in *Swann* which Beckett scored and underlined, and which is almost a description of the area, and indeed the procedures, that Beckett will spend his life exploring. Swann feels himself:

transformé en une créature étrangère à l'humanité, aveugle, dépourvue de facultés logiques, presque une fantastique licorne, une créature chimérique ne percevant le monde que par l'ouïe. Et comme dans la petite phrase il cherchait cependant un sens où son intelligence ne pouvait descendre, quelle étrange ivresse il avait à dépouiller son âme la plus intérieure de tous les secours du raisonnement et à la faire passer seule dans le couloir, dans le filtre obscur du son.[60]

If immobility cannot be said to help much, there is no doubt that sheer involuntary insensibility offers more tangible rewards. Once again Proust and Beckett diverge. Proust, not so much because of his *snobisme* but because of the high value he placed on sensibility, notes of his long-suffering maid, Françoise, that "to know nothing is to understand nothing." It is true that Beckett's world is, in some ways, even more a world of masters and servants than Proust's, but it is striking that the pitifully limited Worm, whose plight is similar to Françoise's, should earn one of Beckett's greatest encomiums: "Worm, to say he does not know what he is, where he is, what is happening, is to underestimate him. What he does not know is that there is anything to know." Proust speaks, in one of his most pessimistic moments, of how "the sole remedy which we do not seek is to be ignorant of everything, so as to have no desire for further knowledge," and it is clear that Worm has not only achieved, but has transcended, this state. In view of his interests, which included gardening and anything that would keep him from thinking, Beckett's scoring of a passage earlier in

La prisonnière—"Il vaut mieux ne pas savoir, penser le moins possible . . ." is nothing more than we should expect.[61]

As the above account suggests, there are often great divergences between Proust and Beckett, which is surely no surprise when we think of the differences between their backgrounds and writing careers. When we find Beckett scoring the moment when Proust suggests that we should fear the past as much as the future,[62] it is understandable if specters of existential angst not entirely relevant to Proust should momentarily dazzle us. Beckett admitted to me, "Perhaps I overstated Proust's pessimism a little," and his copy is littered with marginal marks not important in themselves, but cumulatively suggesting that Proust's universe is as desolated and desiccated as his own will one day be. At the same time he obviously agrees with Proust that "des vrais maîtres," whose company he would modestly disclaim, are "ceux qui se sont maîtrisés"[63] and it is obvious that Beckett learned a great deal from standing back and looking at Proust from a distance, which ultimately bore fruit in his own creative explorations. First and foremost, he learned that Proust's "complète absence de sens moral" did not prevent him from being a great writer, and that the "plagiarism of oneself" was not only not to be condemned but actually to be encouraged and embraced as unavoidable.[64] Beckett's works are full of self-plagiarisms and sudden reappearances of characters *à la* Balzac, none more striking, perhaps, than that of Watt at the end of *Mercier and Camier*. Admittedly Beckett made no attempt at creating the massive single work in which such self-plagiarism is seen to be an essential part of the whole, but his whole writing life illustrates the truth enunciated by Proust to Albertine that "les grands littérateurs n'ont jamais que réfracté à travers des milieux divers une même beauté qu'ils apportent au monde."[65] He also shared Proust's faith that art is "symbolical" of reality and the most profound of real things, "réels sans être actuels, idéaux sans être abstraits."[66] He shared, too, Proust's concern for style (which is more a question of total vision than mere technique), and for art's reception at the hands of ignorant critics.[67] He also learned from Proust that art does not need to be, and cannot hope to be, a matter of total success, that one of its properties is to disappoint its audience, but that this should not affect the writer's sense of vocation.[68] Beckett was clearly impressed by Proust's openness to experience, his readiness to make discoveries no less precious than Pascal's *Pensées* in an advertisement for soap, discoveries which are a direct result of "the power of the human imagination" and which guarantee the "pleasure of the imagination"—both phrases used by Beckett in his marginal notes.[69] Finally, on the level of generality, it was impossible for Beckett, after reading Proust, to harbor any illusions about the art work toward which there has been so much striving, on Proust's part: Proust's realization—"un livre est un grand cimetière"—is perhaps the most unanswerable of all the sentences underlined by Beckett.[70]

If the matter were not so important, especially in view of the pervasive and misleading tendency in early Beckett criticism that attempted to derive Beckett from Joyce, one might be content to leave the parallel there. But it is an index of how deeply Proust had penetrated his consciousness, and in no sense a limitation of Beckett's originality, that we find so many individual elements in Beckett that are derived, in one way or another, from Proust. His only attempt at a Proustian party scene in "A Wet Night" (in *More Pricks than Kicks*) can hardly be considered a success, and it is arguable that had Beckett's attention not wandered a little while reading the party scenes in Proust (the nine great society scenes are mostly barren of marginalia) he might have produced a more focused story. But this kind of thing was clearly alien to his genius, and may have been a deliberately experimental venture anyway. In fact, typically Proustian situations, except for the inherently highly charged image of the man writing in bed (like Malone), did not exert much influence. That *Play* might be based on a chance remark—"les vases clos et sans communication entre eux d'après-midi différents"[71]—seems a little unlikely, when that work can be explained by the Beckett dramas that have preceded it. However, whether Watt's difficulties with the word "pot" can be entirely divorced from the appalling word that horrifies Marcel is open to doubt.[72] It seems likely that Proustian images were slightly more influential, although Beckett's images are so universal that it would be dangerous to offer only one source, or indeed any source, and there is no real sign of him pursuing a particular image or cluster of images through a work which is astonishingly rich in this area. The one exception is the image of a barrier which occurs first when Proust is discussing the nature of the screen we unconsciously place between ourselves and our percepts, in *Du côté de chez Swann* 1.[73] Beckett does not mark every occurrence of this image, but is particularly impressed by Proust's use of the word "cloison" (once at 7, p. 227, then again at 8, p. 366),[74] a word he himself uses in the first line of his French poem "Ascension," written in the late 1930s.[75] Beckett is also particularly sensitive to Proust's occasional use of a religious vocabulary,[76] but no doubt reading Joyce's *Portrait of the Artist as a Young Man* had sharpened his senses for such things, and Beckett's own interest in religion goes a good deal deeper than Proust's. In view of the way a word like "cloison" can be seen to have stayed in his mind, albeit unconsciously, for about a decade, it is particularly intriguing to see how the word "lest" (which means ballast and forms the basis for Beckett's startling phrase, "Habit is the ballast that chains the dog to his vomit," *Proust,* p. 19), crops up again in the third of Beckett's *Quatre poèmes,* written about twenty years later.[77] It is precisely an individual instance like this which reveals how deep and long-lasting an influence can be.

It is clear, also, that Proust's stylistic habits obviously went deeper with Beckett than is commonly imagined, though Beckett certainly never made any serious attempt to emulate the serpentine and elongated sentences for which Proust is notorious. He almost certainly learned much about the art of the short sentence from Proust, which he would find used with exemplary skill in "Un amour de Swann," and at almost any one of the great moments of drama that break upon the stunned Marcel. He could hardly have been unmoved by the manner in which Proust, by slightly changing his focus of vision, increases his happiness, if only momentarily, without ever lulling to sleep the carping unhappiness that necessitated the change of focus in the first place. This is so much a staple of Proust's work that almost any example would do, but the subsequent one is especially close to Beckett's mode: "Et je trouvais, comme tous ceux qui souffrent, que ma triste situation aurait pu être pire. Car ayant libre entrée dans la demeure où habitait Gilberte, je me disais toujours, bien que décidé à ne pas user de cette faculté, que si jamais ma douleur était trop vive, je pourrais la faire cesser. Je n'étais malheureux qu'au jour le jour. Et c'est trop dire encore."[78]

Equally, the occasional moments of *hauteur* that are at the furthest remove from this quavering uncertainty, but which Proust finds indispensable to his quest for the truth, are not entirely absent from Beckett's prose. The tone of the erstwhile university lecturer can be detected behind many sentences in the trilogy, and Beckett seems almost to be administering a shrewd self-criticism in *How It Is,* at the extraordinary moment when the narrator forgets his suffering long enough to begin a disquisition on sponges: "some reflections none the less while waiting for things to improve on the fragility of euphoria among the different orders of the animal kingdom beginning with the sponges. . . ."[79] Without seeking a precise Proustian analogue, it is clear that this kind of device can only be used by someone sufficiently all-embracing to bring together Pascal's *Pensées* and a soap advertisement.

Proust's occasional irritation with his own loquaciousness[80] is, of course, nothing like so thoroughgoing as Beckett's and need not be thought of as lying behind the innumerable moments of disgust registered by Beckett's narrators at the garbage they are being forced to utter. In much the same way, Proust's digression and conversation with an imaginary interlocutor, though scored by Beckett, far from being a source for Beckettian audience assaults, shares a common origin with them in Sterne.[81] However, the moments when Proust forgets his Cartesian dualism, and admits a conjunction of mind and body—in such phrases as "une mémoire involontaire des membres" (which Beckett underlines)—provide the basis for such characteristically Beckettian strategies as "so given am I to thinking with my blood," which he adopts in desperation at the failure of the Cartesian dichotomy.[82] A not dissimilar Proustian trick is to employ a cliché either to make more readily accessible an unfamiliar idea or to imitate the complexity of reality by means of one of its commonest items. A phrase like "cette route battue des heures," which occurs in a sentence scored by Beckett, must have given him confidence in his own intrepid resuscitation of dead metaphor that retrieves, for The Unnamable, such gems as "tracks as beaten as the day is long and no ordinary last straw."[83]

Beckett's own writing is so individual that it cannot be diminished by the discovery of deep-seated parallels such as these. Part of the attractiveness of the Proust monograph resides precisely in the way Beckett dissociates himself, in the Foreword most memorably but throughout the main body of the text also, from many of Proust's more equivocal and less attractive postures. The seeds of this can be seen late in the final volume where Beckett shrewdly points out how Proust's understanding of the significance of his writing conflicts with much of what he has been saying. Proust did not, of course, live to correct the text of Le temps retrouvé, and the passage in which he rather simple-mindedly limits his achievement to that of holding up a magnifying glass to nature is roundly glossed "Balls"[84] by Beckett.

Exclamation marks dot the text, not just where the text is plainly incorrect (it is full of printing errors and thoroughly deserves the opprobrium heaped on it by Beckett, however difficult Proust's intentions may have been to decipher), but at such lapses of taste (in Beckett's eyes) as Proust's liking for the poet Anna de Noailles. The monograph benefits from moments of high spirits like this, and it will outlast many more stuffy commentaries; the mixture may be heady, but it is invigorating. It may not be impeccable history of ideas but it is as exciting as Proust's own excursions into that field.[85] The Proust monograph, together with the special insights revealed by the copy Beckett was working from, is nothing less than essential to any full understanding of the man already on the way to becoming the major postwar writer in the world.[86]

Notes

1. See Raymond Federman and John Fletcher, *Samuel Beckett: His Works and His Critics* (Berkeley: University of California Press, 1970), 9.

2. As part of the Reading University Beckett Archive. The texts Beckett used were: *Du côté de chez Swann* 1 and 2, 107th ed., 1923; *A l'ombre des jeunes filles en fleurs* 2 and 3, 119th ed., 1929; *Le côté de Guermantes* 1 and 2, 63rd ed., 1927; *Sodome et Gomorrhe* 1, 54th ed., 1921; 2, 71st ed., 1922; *La prisonnière* 1 and 2, 46th ed., 1927; *Albertine disparue*, 45th ed., 1926; *Le temps retrouvé* 1 and 2, 36th ed., 1929. *A l'ombre des jeunes filles en fleurs* 1 is missing. In the notes the following abbreviations are used: *Swann, JF, CG, SG, P, AD,* and *TR,* with the appropriate volume number.

3. "There was never any thought of becoming a writer," Ruby Cohn, "Beckett for Comparatists," *Comparative Literature Studies* 3:4 (1966): 451.

4. *Proust* (London: Chatto and Windus, 1931), 25. The omission of the Leopardi epigraph (which gave such pleasure to Joyce because it could be turned into a multilingual mirror-image—"immonde" for "il mondo") in the 1965 reprint is much to be regretted.

5. "Dante . . . Bruno . Vico . . Joyce," *Our Exagmination Round His Factification for Incamination of Work in Progress* (1929; London: Faber and Faber, 1936), 4.

6. *Proust*, 63.

7. He resigned his teaching post at Trinity College, Dublin, in December 1931, nine months after the book's appearance.

8. *Proust*, 6.

9. Ibid., 49. See Arthur Schopenhauer's *The World as Will and Idea*, trans. Haldane and Kemp, (London, 1896), 1:321. See ibid., p. 239, for the phrase quoted on p. 66 of *Proust*, pp. 246 and 331 for the phrases quoted on p. 70 of *Proust*, and pp. 333–44 for the background to the discussion on p. 71 of *Proust*.

10. Ibid., 30–31.

11. Ibid., 8.

12. Ibid., 20.

13. Ibid., 22, adapting *P 1*, 217 (underlined by Beckett).

14. *SG 2*, iii, 52; cf. *JF 2*, 165.

15. *Proust*, 23, 21.

16. Ludovic Janvier, *Beckett par lui-même* (Paris, Éditions du Seuil, 1969), [12], dates his reading of Kant to 1930, but his lecture "Le concentrisme" refers to Kant and may well be earlier.

17. See, e.g., Melvin J. Friedman, "The Novels of Samuel Beckett: An Amalgam of Joyce and Proust," *Comparative Literature* 12 (1960): 47–58.

18. See the interview with Israel Shenker, *New York Times*, sec. 2, May 6, 1956, pp. x, 1, 3.

19. See Lawrence Harvey, *Samuel Beckett: Poet and Critic* (Princeton, NJ: Princeton University Press, 1970), 247–50.

20. *Swann* 2, 191.

21. Other areas of the work, either not scored at all, or only lightly scored, are the death of Bergotte, the first picture of Elstir, and the sections "Place Names: The Name" and "Place Names: The Place," at least the early part.

22. *Swann* 2, 14; *JF* 2, 105; *JF* 3, 155; *SG* 2, ii, 178.

23. *Swann* 1, 124.

24. *JF* 1, 139.

25. *JF* 2, 39; cf. *Three Novels* (London: John Calder, 1959), 115ff.

26. *JF* 1, 129.

27. *CG* 1, 79.

28. *Proust*, 23.

29. *JF* 2, 81.

30. *CG* 1, 59.

31. *Swann* 1, 33, 200, 201–3.

32. *SG* 2, i, 107.

33. E.g., "relativism multiplies cause" (*AD* 2, 96) and "1 cause 2 results" (*AD* 2, 173).

34. *JF* 1, 139; cf. Harvey, *Samuel Beckett*, 435: "Being is constantly putting form in danger."

35. *JF* 2, 88, 92.

36. *CG* 1, 68. Beckett's prose text "Sounds" explores it further.

37. *Three Novels*, 222; *P* 1, 180.

38. *Proust*, 14.

39. Ibid., 15.

40. *SG* 2, i, 208.

41. *P* 1, 122.

42. *P* 2, 199; cf. *Watt*, (London: John Calder, 1963), 72.

43. E.g., 1, 112.

44. *CG* 2, 213–14; cf. *All That Fall* (London: Faber and Faber, 1965), 28: "Once and for all do not ask me to speak and move at the same time."

45. *Swann* 1, 120–121.

46. *SG* 2, i, 215. His disagreement with Curtius (*Proust*, 85) is based on his marginal note to *JF* 3, 151.

47. *CG* 1, 39; *SG* 2, i, 85.

48. *Swann* 1, 177–78, 180.

49. Ibid., 237, 122.

50. *JF* 2, 19–20; 156 (altered to "pessimist"); *JF* 2, 36, is similarly marked.

51. *Proust*, 49. Beckett is especially sensitive to Proust's use of the word "témoin" (e.g., *Swann* 1, 70–71); cf. Mr. Knott's need for a "witness" in *Watt*.

52. *JF* 2, 16.

53. Ibid., 73.

54. Ibid., 165; cf. Mr. Kelly in *Murphy*. Malone may get his finicky formal sense from Proust. There is something Malone-like in Marcel's absurdly porten-

tous promise that the subject of the Profanation of the Mother "deserves a chapter to itself."

55. *AD 1*, 28.

56. Ibid., 63–65. Beckett does, however, mark *TR 2*, 68, which speaks of death as the only deliverance from irremediable suffering.

57. See the second volume of *La prisonnière* for Proust's interest in paralytic illnesses, shared (especially in *The Unnamable*—Mahood's condition being the logical terminus of a Proustian tendency) by the even more medically aware Beckett.

58. *TR 2*, 46. (Beckett underlines the sentence.)

59. See, e.g., *CG 2*, 37, 40, and *AD 1*, 126.

60. *Swann 2*, 34.

61. *P 1*, 31–32, *Three Novels*, 349.

62. *P 1*, 116–17.

63. *SG 2*, ii, 23.

64. *P 2*, 119; *AD 1*, 34.

65. *P 2*, 235.

66. Ibid., 234; *TR 2*, 15.

67. *TR 2*, 251.

68. *CG 1*, 44ff.; *Swann 1*, 256ff; cf. Beckett's later aesthetics of failure.

69. *AD 1*, 203; *CG 1*, 144; *CG 2*, 77.

70. *TR 2*, 59.

71. *Swann 1*, 196.

72. *P 2*, 189.

73. Cf. the cage images of *JF 2*, 92, 137; *P 2*, 200; and *Proust*, 12.

74. *SG 2*, i, 186; iii, 219.

75. See *Poèmes* (Paris: Éditions de Minuit, 1968).

76. *Swann 2*, 187; *P 2*, 72.

77. *P 2*, 208. See *Poems in English* (London: John Calder, 1961), 50.

78. *JF 1*, 149–50.

79. *How It Is* (London: John Calder, 1964), 43.

80. E.g., *JF 3*, 153.

81. *SG 2*, i, 31–33. It is a pity the missing volume of the set deprives us of Beckett's attitude to Proust's subtle self-criticism at the hands of M. de Norpois.

82. *TR 1*, 8–9; cf. *CG 1*, 266; "Text VII" of *Texts for Nothing*, in *No's Knife* (London: Calder and Boyars, 1967), later changed to "so given am I to thinking with my breath."

83. *JF 2*, 13.

84. *TR 2*, 240.

85. Beckett has written on the back page of the last volume: "Arabian Nights of the mind" and "Thought—*jellyfish* of Spirit."

86. See, for an especially illuminating discussion, John Fletcher's "Beckett et Proust," *Caliban* 1 (janvier 1964): 89–100. Beckett's other scholarly contribution on Proust was "Proust in Pieces" (reprinted in *Disjecta*).

3

"Birth Astride of a Grave": Samuel Beckett's *Act Without Words I*

██████

S. E. Gontarski

". . . where there are no words
there is less to spoil."

WILLIAM BUTLER YEATS,
The Death of Cuchulain

Samuel Beckett's first published mime, *Act Without Words I,* which Beckett has called "in some obscure way, a codicil to *End-Game (sic),*"[1] remains one of the few slighted works in the Beckett canon. Often ignored, the play has generally not fared well even among those critics who have treated it. Ruby Cohn has dismissed it as "almost too explicit,"[2] and Ihab Hassan has similarly suggested that the mime seems "a little too obvious and pat."[3] John Spurling concurs: compared to *Godot,* "*Act Without Words I* is . . . over-explicit, over-emphasized and even, unless redeemed by its performer, so unparticularized as to verge on the banal."[4] Annamaria Sportelli observes that the mime "crudely discloses a dumb ritual. . . ."[5] And even Beckett himself has referred to it as "primitive theatre."

The mime's directness has prompted some forced interpretation as well. Martin Esslin, for one, has argued that the protagonist "is drawn to the pursuit of illusory objectives. . . ."[6] Ruby Cohn echoes the view, suggesting that the "sustenance and tools are man's own invention, and his frustration the result of the impossibility of ever being able to reach what may be a mirage."[7] But the objects are certainly substantial enough for the protagonist to stand on the cubes and yank on the chord in a tug-of-war with a force outside himself, presumably the same force which *threw* him onto the stage. The scissors and rope may be human invention, but they are nonetheless substantial, real. If they were not, the exterior force would have little reason to confiscate them. Rather than an obvious, unparticularized mime about illusion or mirage, Beckett has created here one of his most subtle and compact images of the birth of existential humanity, of the existential artist, with all the ironies inherent in the coincidence of birth and death. If the mime is "primitive theater," as Beckett suggests, it is "primitive" in the sense of Nietzsche's Dionysian theater or Artaud's "theater of cruelty." While Samuel Beckett grew increasingly uncomfortable with the influence of Artaud on the modern drama, an emphasis which devalued the author in favor of the director, *Act Without Words I* may finally represent the "unperverted pantomime" which Artaud yearned for in "Metaphysics and the *Mise en Scène*," a theater of "pure theatrical language which does without words, a language of signs, gestures and attitudes having an ideographic value. . . ."[8] This is Artaud's "direct" mime where:

> . . . gestures . . . represent ideas, attitudes of mind, aspects of nature, all in an effective, concrete manner, i.e., by constantly evoking objects or natural details, like that Oriental language which represents night by a tree on which a bird that has already closed one eye is beginning to close another. . . . It is plain that these signs constitute true hieroglyphs, in which man, to the extent that he contributes to their formation, is only a form like the rest, yet to which, because of his double nature, he adds a singular prestige.[9]

Admittedly, *Act Without Words I* has struck some critics as more obvious allegory than inscrutable Oriental hieroglyph. On casual reading it appears to be a behavioristic experiment within the framework of a classic myth. The protagonist (Adam, Tantalus, Everyman?) is thrown,[10] forced, born into a hostile environment from which he cannot exit and in which he cannot succeed. What nature exists is apart from and hostile to him, the curse of thistles and thorns. From the first the protagonist is a thinker, but inadequately created or adapted to deal with hostile environmental forces. He is pathetic; born, indeed created to fail, a caged rat frustrated by an inept or malicious handler. He examines his hands, his primary tools; his prehensile thumbs oppose the fingers. Armed with two systemic tools, mind and hands, those features which separate him from lower orders of animals, he tries to survive, to secure some water in the desert. The mind works, at least in part. He learns—small cube on large.[11] He invents, or is given inventions—scissors, cubes, ropes. But when he learns to use his tools freely, to exit the scene, so to speak, they are confiscated: the scissors, when he reasons that in addition to cutting his fingernails, he might cut his throat as well; the blocks and rope, when he discovers that they might make a gallows. So far, a rather obvious allegory: Tantalus punished, the offense uncertain. G. C. Barnard argues the prevalent interpretation of the ending. The protagonist does not move because he is simply crushed: "the man remains, defeated, having opted out of the struggle, lying on the empty desert."[12]

The play, however, contains anomalies which suggest a departure from the usual Beckettian world. No words, for one. Or more precisely, one elemental word, "water," but written not spoken.[13] While much has been made of the names of Beckett's characters, especially his Ms, this protagonist is nameless and finally perhaps unnamable. Although Beckett considers him "human meat—or bones," he associates him as well with Clov: "thinking and stumbling and sweating, under our noses, like Clov about Hamm, but gone from refuge."[14] But the protagonist remains through most of the play active, healthy, even athletic, not an avatar of Belacqua, Murphy, or Watt, nor one of the paraplegics, nor even a bowed Clov. Although he regresses toward characteristic Beckettian immobility, he suffers no further physical deterioration. His immobility seems, finally, willed. Unlike *Waiting for Godot,* moreover, where we are never sure of Godot's existence,[15] here a force outside humanity certainly exists. The protagonist, like Jacob, wrestles with it to confirm its substance, its fundamental materiality. Finally, the action of the mime is linear, apparently terminal, not the unusual Beckettian circle. Critics like Linda Ben-Zvi have ignored such anomalies and so have got the mime wrong at both ends. Of the opening she suggests that "Like all Beckett plays, the action in *Act Without Words I* begins in the middle." And she forces a cyclical pattern onto the end: "The mime ends with the man still looking at his hands, suspended—as are Estragon and Vladimir, Hamm and Clov—between cessation and the next round."[16] But clearly birth (or being "thrown" into "being") is a point of origination, and it takes a Procrustean reading of the ending to fit the mime into the circular patterns of *Waiting for Godot* or *Endgame.* Its futility is finally of another, quite linear order.

In the end the superior force apparently defeats the inferior, rather predictable, pathetic stuff. With this climax, the play appears more traditional and didactic than anything else in the Beckett canon. The mime seems to lack Beckett's characteristic irony and doubling, for instance. But Beckett finally plays against this obvious, traditional ending, for the real play begins with its terminus. The climactic ending of the mime may signify not pathetic defeat, but conscious rebellion, a deliberate, willful refusal to obey. Lucky has finally turned on Pozzo, not with brute force, however, but humanely, by refusing to validate him, as Clov does to Hamm in the closing tableau of *Endgame*. Ironically then, the protagonist is most active, most potent when inert, and his life acquires meaning as it closes. In this refusal, this cutting of the umbilical rope, a second birth occurs, the birth of Man. The protagonist has finally acquired, earned, a name, Mankind or hu-Manity (another M, in any case). As he refuses the bidding of the outside force, as he refuses to act predictably, in his own self-interest, as he refuses the struggle for the most elemental of man's needs, he breaks free of need the way Murphy never could. Man, in a frenzy of (in)activity, is born—free. If at first we saw man created by another, we end with Man creating himself. In his refusal to be driven by need, to devote himself to physical existence, solely to survival and pleasure (shade, water, the off-stage womb, for instance), the protagonist has created a free, separate, individual self. He has said with Camus' rebel, so far and no further.

Rebellion is, of course, dangerous activity. The rebellious slave may indeed be physically destroyed by the master. In the final dramatic image of *Act Without Words I*, the moments of birth and death virtually coincide in an echo of blind Pozzo's insight: "They give birth astride of a grave." Dramatic action is here produced by inaction, a corollary to the tension produced by the prolonged silences and tableaux in the wordplays.

In addition to an ending that is at least ambiguous, a series of brilliant visual allusions adds to the richness of this "primitive," "unperverted" mime. The protagonist's similarities to Tantalus, the patriarch of the troubled house of Atreus, and Jacob, the patriarch of Israel, have already been suggested. And the former myth provides most of the dramatic framework for the play, not unlike, on a miniaturized scale, Joyce's use of the Odyssean myth to shape *Ulysses*. Moreover, the playlet contains several additional Joycean echoes. The struggle between the protagonist and the more powerful outside force suggests not only Jacob's wrestling with an angel, but Joyce's quest (at least in Beckett's eyes) for artistic omniscience and omnipotence. The protagonist of the mime, like Stephen Dedalus, finally says *non serviam*. The figure paring his fingernails further suggests (and perhaps parodies along with Joyce) Stephen's aesthetic theories. Like Dedalus, the protagonist in *Act Without Words I* is an inventor and consequently an artist, a "fabulous artificer." If the inventions fail, that failure is inevitable and consistent with Beckett's attitude toward art. As Beckett suggested to Israel Shenker, it is Joyce who is "tending toward omniscience and omnipotence as an artist. I'm working with impotence, ignorance."[17] The artistic associations of the protagonist are further reinforced with reference to the tailor's scissors. The tailor is himself a craftsman, a maker, and the scissors call to mind Nagg's story of the Englishman and the tailor from *Endgame,* the point of which is the imperfection of the world compared to human creations. The scissors then may be one of the "obscure" ways in which *Act Without Words I* acts as a "codicil" to *Endgame,* the play which precedes it in French and English editions alike.

Act Without Words I then is not the banal dramatic image of defeat some critics have suggested, but a powerful if futile image of rebellion, of artistic rebellion as well, of Sartre's man freeing himself from outside forces which may be god, instinct, tradition, mythology, human nature, or basic need, and the struggle is punctuated with a series of visual images that suggest the artist's plight. As the mime closes, humans are free of their instinct for survival, free of the limitation of acting according to their nature. The freedom may only be the spiteful freedom of Dostoyevsky's "underground man," and the victory, as Thomas Barbour suggests, "may be hollow."[18] But in an antiheroic age perhaps there are no meaningful victories. The ending is an existential and artistic triumph, for whatever those are worth in the waning days of the twentieth century. *Act Without Words I* may finally be Beckett's own portrait of the artist—as a young (man, dog) rat.

Notes

1. In a letter of August 27, 1957, to his American publisher, Barney Rosset. The letter is published as a frontispiece to Clas Zilliacus, *Beckett and Broadcasting: A Study of the Works of Samuel Beckett for and in Radio and Television* (Abo, Finland: Abo Akademie, 1976). Subsequent Beckett quotations are to this letter.

2. Ruby Cohn, *Samuel Beckett: The Comic Gamut* (New Brunswick, NJ: Rutgers University Press, 1962), 247.

3. Ihab Hassan, *The Literature of Silence: Henry Miller and Samuel Beckett* (New York: Alfred A. Knopf, 1967), 192.

4. John Fletcher and John Spurling, *Beckett: A Study of His Plays* (New York: Hill and Wang, 1972), 118.

5. "'Make Sense Who May,' a Study of *Catastrophe* and *What Where,*" in

"Make Sense Who May": Essays on Samuel Beckett's Later Work, ed. Robin J. Davis and Lance St. John Butler (Totowa, NJ: Barnes and Noble Books), 124.

6. Martin Esslin, *The Theatre of the Absurd* (New York: Doubleday and Company, 1961), 38.

7. *The Comic Gamut,* 247.

8. Antonin Artaud, *The Theater and Its Double,* trans. Mary Caroline Richards (New York: Grove Press, 1958), 39.

9. Ibid., 39–40.

10. See Lance St. John Butler's discussion of Heidegger's concept of *Geworfenheit* or "throwness" and *Dasein* or "being" in *Samuel Beckett and the Meaning of Being: A Study in Ontological Parable* (New York: St. Martin's Press, 1984), 36–38.

11. Much of the plot for the mime seems to have been suggested by a series of experiments on the learning abilities of apes that Gestalt psychologist Wolfgang Köhler conducted on the island of Teneriffe during Word War I and published as *The Mental Activity of Apes* (English translation, 1925). That Beckett knew of the experiments seems evident from *Murphy,* "And then. . . . Back to Teneriffe and the apes?" (p. 5). See Rubin Rabinovitz, *The Development of Samuel Beckett's Fiction* (Urbana, IL: University of Illinois Press, 1984), 97–98, n. 14.

12. *Samuel Beckett: A New Approach* (New York: Dodd, Mead, and Company, 1970), 109.

13. Here the mime suggests Roger Vitrac's surrealist theater piece "Poison, drame sans paroles," published originally in *Littérature* 8 (January 1923), in which, although no words are spoken, a poem is written out and signed Hector de JESUS. See Marcel Jean, *The Autobiography of Surrealism* (New York: Viking Press, 1980), 96–97 for the English translation.

14. This also from the letter to Barney Rosset of April 27, 1957.

15. The existence of Godot is more certain in the early drafts of *Godot* since Didi and Gogo actually have a note from him. In revision, the note is excised and so the existence of Godot open to further question. See chap. 3, "Genesis and Composition," in *En attendant Godot: Pièce en deux actes,* ed. Colin Duckworth (London: Harrap, 1966), xlv–lxxv, reprinted in *Casebook on "Waiting for Godot,"* ed. Ruby Cohn (New York: Grove Press, 1967), 89–100.

16. *Samuel Beckett* (Boston: Twayne Publishers, 1986), 150–51.

17. Israel Shenker, "A Portrait of Samuel Beckett, Author of the Puzzling *Waiting for Godot,*" *New York Times,* May 6, 1956, sec. 2, pp. 1, 3.

18. "Beckett and Ionesco," *Hudson Review* 11 (Summer 1958): 273.

4

Belacqua as Artist and Lover: "What a Misfortune"

Jeri L. Kroll

Belacqua, paying pious suit to the hem of her garment and
gutting his raptures . . . at a safe remove, represented precisely
the ineffable long-distance paramour. . . .[1]

The bourgeois Protestant hero of *Dream of Fair to Middling Women* and
More Pricks than Kicks is almost immediately defined for the reader as
student, artist, and lover: a lover of Dante, a student of the bohemian
pose, and a creator of his own beatific image of his beloved. Rambling
from Ireland to the Continent and back again, however, Belacqua has
difficulty in maintaining the identities which he has fabricated for himself. In each new abode, consequently, he takes the precaution of setting
up sufficient defenses against the macrocosm: "this to break not so much
the flow of people and things to him as the ebb of him to people and
things."[2] The intercourse which he allows between his consciousness and
the external world, particularly in *Dream,* is designed to keep his artistic
soul content and stocked with material, and his human relationships under
control. This self-imposed psychic incarceration is pictured as withdrawal
into the cup of his mind, from which he enjoys throwing out lines to the
macrocosm. These "velleities of radiation" (*Dream,* p. 38) hook onto
sources of inspiration; "they would trickle back and replenish his rumination as marriage the earth and virginity paradise . . . he could release the
boomerangs of his fantasy on all sides unanxiously, that one by one they
would return with the trophy of an echo" (*Dream,* p. 38).

Belacqua Shuah conceives of himself first as an artist, and then as a lover, but he has trouble conceiving of others as anything more than "other." They are individuals in the sense of being separate from Belacqua, but he prefers to relate to the human race in general, and to his lady friends in particular, as if they were projections of his own psyche; or, he does not even wish to worry about their mode of existence, and accepts them merely as "given." Unfortunately, Belacqua cannot maintain a consistent position, and his rambunctious body gets him involved in love affairs where his sweethearts eventually contradict his vision of reality; they refuse to act as if they issued from his imagination. Belacqua would like the lover in him to be disciplined by the artist. There is, therefore, a lack of total commitment on Belacqua's part, either to his internal world or to the meditative life. It is the indecision that makes him declare, "Give me chastity . . . and continence, only not yet" (*Dream*, p. 166), which now demands our attention.

The image of Belacqua's mind being fertilized or restocked by the external world, as marriage replenishes the earth and virginity paradise, suggests a central reason for his vacillation. Belacqua cannot deal with sexual experience because it reminds him that he is, in fact, a creature composed of two seemingly contradictory elements: mind and body. Further, this reluctance to confront the paradox, or his fear of investigating it, lead him to project his own dissatisfactions onto women, in particular the diverse group of ladies with whom he becomes consistently and comically involved. An understanding of Belacqua's perplexed psyche, evidenced by his bungled romantic encounters, is crucial in understanding the problems that Beckett as author has with Belacqua, and, as we shall see, what these artistic difficulties ultimately reveal about Beckett's own conception of himself as a young artist.

An examination, therefore, of Belacqua, the first hero in the English prose, and his relationship with women, will elucidate the critical puzzles in what can be termed Beckett's apprentice fiction, and will suggest why these difficulties do not appear in the mature French work. The questions which now occur, which must be answered, and which no one seems to have asked before, are: why does Belacqua become involved in imbroglios with women; how and why are women treated in a significant way in the early work; what do women then represent for both Beckett and Belacqua; and what, if anything, do the conclusions which can be drawn about Beckett, Belacqua, and women tell us about the development of theme and structure in Beckett's art as a whole? I would like to suggest that Belacqua is no longer useful to Beckett when Beckett himself has solved certain problems in defining the nature of his subject and, consequently, in refining his technique. In other words, when Beckett squarely faces what Belacqua avoids (the irrationality of human experience), women cease to function as symbols of the dilemma. The later characters are not particularly interested in or differentiated by their sex. There are jokes about the dangers of riding a bicycle, given Molloy's anatomical peculiarities, of course, or about whether his true love was male or female, but generally sex is irrelevant in demonstrating Beckett's cardinal themes. In the later novels and plays, men and women are treated in much the same manner.

The most effective way of approaching a topic of this magnitude is to undertake a textual analysis of one of the most perplexing and yet critical stories in *More Pricks than Kicks,* "What a Misfortune," which concerns Belacqua's ambiguous attitudes towards love, art, and society. The story graphically illustrates the enigma of Belacqua's personality by being an enigma itself, which is appropriate for a hero who is obsessed with quodlibets and esoteric jargon (Belacqua is the type of person who sits in a bar doing the *Times* crossword puzzle in ink). But Beckett the creator technically practices what his creature Belacqua only plays with. "What a Misfortune" revolves around question and answer, innuendo and allusion, and ends with a conundrum. Before embarking on an explication of this tale, however, we must clarify our initial questions about Belacqua in both novel and stories by making some observations about the relationship between Beckett's treatment of women in the majority of his early fiction and the reasons for Belacqua's romantic miscarriages.

It seems that most of Beckett's readers take for granted the humorous criticism or satire of his female characters. By refusing to examine this treatment, by accepting it as normal, even predictable, given a tradition that encompasses the history of Western literature, from Helen of Troy, to the Wyf of Bath, to Molly Bloom, they avoid confronting the issue of what Beckett is actually about in his portrayal of women. There is, of course, an obvious explanation based on Belacqua's role as a traditional hero himself. Since he is still an immature and (occasionally) randy young man, attached in some degree to conventional society and its mores, he is conditioned at least to consider courtship and marriage. Even as a poet, he can consider women in a traditional way as catalysts for artistic inspiration—as Muses. But Beckett attempts, most critics agree, more in his apprentice work than simply a repetition of the Kunstlerroman. We have a fundamental paradox, then, involved in critical response to Beckett's heroes and heroines that has never been quite defined: why would Beckett exploit a traditional portrayal of women, women as essentially physical beings or at least as inherently contradictory creatures (the Weib vs. the Madonna), when he so distrusted conventional literary practice? True, much of what could be called traditional material is presented ironically, but this explanation does not encompass all the material. Beckett presents Belacqua, for example, clearly as both a serious and a satiric figure.

The answer seems to lie in Beckett's difficulty in finding something to replace what he considered outmoded literary form. He had no difficulty in criticizing these forms (in fact he frequently does so with great verve) or the "clockwork cabbage" figures and chloroformed world of "Balzac, for example, and the divine Jane and many others" (*Dream*, p. 106). Finding a technique to supersede that of the "greats" and a main character who would be a successful illustration of this as yet hypothetical new technique, was another matter. Belacqua, therefore, serves a dual purpose— a character who embodies Beckett's aesthetic views and a surrogate for the author who consciously analyzes these views (at least in the body of *Dream*). We see Belacqua in the novel on board a ship ruminating about writing, developing principles to govern the work that he intends to write. Beckett's uncertainty at this stage in his career led him, however, to keep the products of Belacqua's aesthetic theory out of the sight of the reader almost entirely. We have a rare example of Belacqua's poetic genius in *Dream* in the "Sonnet to the Smeraldina" (addressed to Belacqua's Teutonic paramour), which we only hear about in *More Pricks than Kicks,* along with the poet's "Hypothalamion." According to Lawrence Harvey in his comprehensive study of Beckett's poetry,[3] Beckett may have originally composed the sonnet seriously, for he did actually have an attachment to a girl in Germany at about this time. Beckett, however, palms the sonnet off as Belacqua's, perhaps an effective way of shielding the self-mocking writer who fears for "clumsy artistry" (in a 1931 poem, "Casket of Pralinen," which concerns the Smeraldina, too), which might not measure up to what he wants to say, or might say too much, thus making him vulnerable. In fact, in *More Pricks than Kicks,* Beckett goes so far as to palm off the novel *Dream* on Walter Draffin, the effeminate bureaucrat cum writer cum cicisbeo of "What a Misfortune," and includes an ironic (and rather accurate) description of his macaronic early prose style.

Belacqua is, consequently, both a serious and a satiric figure, which accounts for a situation where Beckett, perhaps half-consciously, intends to forestall criticism of both book and author. If Belacqua's theories in *Dream,* though humorously presented, are found intriguing by the reader, then all is well. If they are not, the author's defense is that Belacqua is obviously being ridiculed. Beckett clearly was not satisfied as far as the novel was concerned, whatever the ultimate reasons, for only the extracts "Text" and "Sedendo et Quiesciendo" were ever printed until 1992.

Beckett, then, did not wish to be trapped either by someone else's perceptions of reality or by the hackneyed style used to express them. In these circumstances, a logical first step is to point out the flaws in previous literary and philosophical theories in order to develop fresh ones. On one level, both *Dream* and *More Pricks than Kicks* are meant to be parodies of conventional fiction and its hero (or "principal boy" as Beckett jocularly calls his protagonist). On another level, though, these two works comprise Beckett's portrait of the artist as a young bourgeois intellectual, while Beckett is still a young artist himself. Developing his own opinions about society, about the body and the spirit, and about humanity's attempts to cope with its irrational environment, is inseparable for Beckett from discovering what kind of character will be an appropriate vehicle for expressing these views.

It is most evident from the confusion in *Dream,* and to a lesser extent in *More Pricks than Kicks,* that Beckett is not yet sure how much he really is Belacqua.[4] This confusion is paralleled by Belacqua's inability to decide how much he owes to the world at large, and how much he owes to himself (his little world). This inability or refusal to discriminate between various modes of reality (mind, body, external world) or the wish, if he does discriminate, to impose absolute value judgments on each mode of being, is dramatically illustrated by Belacqua's responses to women (as, perhaps, discrete minds and certainly different bodies in the macrocosm). If Belacqua cannot cope with women successfully, it may be because he (or Beckett) cannot adequately conceive of them. This bewildering state of affairs demands clarification, and two possibilities now suggest themselves. Is it only women as specific examples of contradictory human nature (the quandary of one body and mind relating to another) in which Beckett is interested, or is there something more about women in particular that complicates the issue?

In Beckett's early fiction, women can sometimes pose the same questions as men about the paradoxical nature of human life, but they usually function more as a symbol of the predicament than anything else. "Assumption" (*transition* 16–17 [Spring–Summer, 1929]), the story which opens Beckett's exploration of mystical experience and the way in which women may function as catalytic agents in artistic inspiration or catharsis, details the enigmatic influence "the Woman" has on the protagonist. She simultaneously affects his physical and mental being (the body weakens, the mind expands). This initial formulation of Beckett's conception of women as givers of life and, by implication, death, the thought that perhaps they can bridge the gap from womb to tomb, develops into Belacqua's ideas about his "wombtomb" in *Dream,* and his attempts at suicide with Ruby in *More Pricks than Kicks* ("she should connive at his felo de se" [p. 95]).[5] The pseudoartist in "Assumption" achieves an isolated apotheosis, as he is burst asunder by sound, his psyche scattered to the farthest reaches of the universe in a kind of pantheistic climax. Beckett's first rather shabby Beatrice surrogate is left alone caressing the dead hero and, one presumes, somewhat bewildered. In both novel and story Belacqua fantasizes about physical encounters (or observes other couple's springtime frolics in the woods) in order to allow complete and unsullied spiritual intercourse with his beloved. Belacqua has a psychic orgasm that flows out to the far shores of his spirit, while the Smeraldina is left high and dry under a tree.

Sexual experience for Belacqua is not, therefore, simply avoided because it depletes his energy. It is symptomatic of the agonizing division that he feels is nevertheless a part of his nature. Physical activity and mental activity exist in a continuum and maintain a constant tension whereby one gains at the other's expense. The effect that "the Woman" has on the hero of "Assumption" also has affinities with the effect that Celia will have on Murphy. After Murphy's death, Celia explains with painful hindsight, "that I was a piece out of him that he could not go on without, no matter what I did. . . . I was the last exile."[6] Hoping for a birth into oblivion or nirvana, Beckett's heroes are foiled and the forceps aren't needed.[7]

Although Belacqua eventually gives up on literal death as a means of spiritual fulfillment, his conception of mystic experience remains tinged with the timelessness and obscurity of death. Trying to express his prewedding sentiments to his friend Hairy in "What a Misfortune," Belacqua observes: "If what I love . . . were only in Australia. . . . Whereas what I am on the lookout for . . . is nowhere as far as I can see" (p. 146). The hero's search for a nowhere in which to merge his "Ego maximus, little me" (p. 42) is too often disturbed by external circumstances requiring him to be somewhere. His love, alas, is not in Australia but waiting for her groom at St. Tamar's. Belacqua is brought back to reality from his momentary enlightenment about himself: "A cloud obscured the sun, the room grew dark, the light ebbed from the pier-glass and Belacqua, feeling his eyes moist, turned away from the blurred image of himself" (p. 146). But Beckett's first hero does not distinctly see either the source of his own anguish or the fact that other isolate souls may feel the same way. This almost ontological confusion is demonstrated on a literal level in the comic tale of Belacqua's second marriage, "What a Misfortune."

At this point, a brief discussion of the plot of *Dream* and *More Pricks than Kicks* is necessary, especially since the first work is not only unfinished, but has only just been published. In addition, a good deal of the material in the novel is indispensable in elucidating many of the obscure passages in the short stories. It will then be easier to examine "What a Misfortune" in detail, so that we can see exactly how the story presents, in a highly complex form, the initial obstacles which Beckett had to overcome in developing his principal issues.

Ostensibly, *Dream* and *More Pricks than Kicks* involve a fledgling writer's social, intellectual, and emotional escapades, and under the impression that we are about to plunge into another Kunstlerroman (albeit ironic), we begin to discover the hero's interconnected preoccupations with the womb, death, nirvana, and art. These obsessions of Belacqua's crystallize into Beckett's initial fictional treatment of the conflict between the physical and the spiritual, somehow miraculously coexisting in human beings. The primary chapters of *Dream* ("Two" and "Three") explore this tension in their treatment of Belacqua's two paramours, the Smeraldina-Rima (a buxom Teutonic Weib) and the Alba (a pale, aesthetic creature whose name enchants Belacqua before he has even met her). The Smeraldina-Rima in her frustration at her supposed lover's negligence finally "rapes" the hero in *Dream;* the Alba remains content with a platonic relationship, though there are innuendoes that she, too, becomes a bit irritated by Belacqua's puerile behavior.

In *More Pricks than Kicks,* the series of short stories which are partially based on Belacqua's adventures in *Dream,* this theme of spiritual and physical conflict is mediated by an array of female characters, including the Smeraldina and the Alba. It becomes evident that Belacqua, as artist, wants to believe in the spirituality of women, and in a mystic communion that transcends death. These romantic clichés protect the anxious Belacqua from the world as it really is (whatever that may be; but Belacqua isn't concerned). Disgusted with his effete peers in Dublin, he concludes that their affectation is partly the result of their money and education, so he rebels by adopting a bohemian pose as a way of differentiating himself— the lone-wolf intellectual sits in a lower-class pub immersed in an upper-class newspaper. Similarly, Belacqua does not want to indulge in romantic entanglements patterned after society's versions of the male-female relationship. Like the hero of *Dream,* he dislikes those whom he calls stallions, men who have no difficulty in pursuing relationships with the opposite sex. They either do not perceive women as spiritual partners, or they do not feel that one type of communication necessarily precludes another.

Though Belacqua's affairs, consequently, may be conducted with the superficial trappings of conventional romance (such as courtship and marriage), lurking behind this "normal" version of things is his "ideal" version. Part of the comedy of *More Pricks than Kicks* derives from the poet's efforts first to conceal and then gradually to reveal his true nature to his paramours. It is Belacqua's private vision of reality, then, that prevents active interchange with members of society at large, and with individuals on an intimate basis. His social alienation and his personal alienation are a result of his aesthetics—the artist remains isolated within society.

Two instances in the story "A Wet Night," which appears early in *More Pricks than Kicks,* admirably illustrate Belacqua the artist's behavior and will allow us to recognize similar responses when they occur on a more complex level later in "What a Misfortune." First, in the opening of the tale, the hero displays his penchant for reading reality in terms of art as he wanders around Dublin, losing himself anonymously in Pearse Street's "simple cantilena in his mind" (p. 54). In his consciousness, present, past, and the timeless realm of art interpenetrate to produce a kind of Proustian transfiguration, where mundane buildings in Dublin recall more impressive buildings in Florence. Belacqua tries to involve his new wife in this type of psychological metamorphosis in "What a Misfortune." Second, and more significant in "A Wet Night," the artist in Belacqua agonizes over the fact that his platonic lover, the Alba, intends to go to a party in a dress that might be backless:

> Not that he had any doubts as to the back thus bared being a sight for sore eyes. The omoplates would be well defined. . . . In repose they would be the blades of an anchor, the delicate furrow of the spine its stem. . . . He saw it as a flower-de-luce, a spatulate leaf with segments angled back, like the wings of a butterfly sucking a blossom, from their common hinge. Then fetching from further afield, as an obelisk, a cross-potent, pain and death, still death, a bird crucified on a wall. This flesh and bones swathed in scarlet, this heart of washed flesh draped in scarlet. . . . (pp. 58–59)

As a catalyst for his fantasy, the Alba's unbared back sends him off proliferating similes and metaphors; but to be confronted by her back in the flesh, no matter how enticing, would be to rob it of its mystery, and the infinite permutations, artistic and mystic, which it possesses in Belacqua's imagination. Worse, it could flatly contradict him. Reality never measures up to his far-ranging dreams. Luckily for the hero, the maid can report: "'It buttons ups behind, sir, with the help of God'. . . . 'Praise be to God' said Belacqua, 'and his blissful Mother'" (p. 59). But Belacqua is not so lucky with later heroines, who obviously want the kind of physical relationship that the Alba deplores. Although adept at wriggling out of threatening situations, even Belacqua finds it hard to convince Thelma, his bride of a day, that they can be united as one in separate beds.

If Belacqua would like to appeal to women primarily as an artist, Beckett does do him the justice of showing the reader that he has encouragement. The narrator of More Pricks than Kicks makes it clear that the hero's attractiveness to women as a lover is intimately connected to his preferred identity as artist—or at least to his pose as sensitive, "suffering" man. In fact, his female admirers are beguiled by some ineffable quality that less sympathetic observers fail to notice, for the hero is pale, fat, limps, and frequently suffers from impetigo. The narrator pinpoints Belacqua's special charm in "What a Misfortune," by explaining her fiancé's fascination for Thelma. Belacqua, apparently, has "soul."

A poet is indeed a very nubile creature, dowered, don't you know, with the love of love, like La Rochefoucauld's woman from her second passion on. So nubile that women, God bless them, can't resist them. Except of course those intended merely for breeding and innocent of soul, who prefer, as less likely to upset them, the more balanced and punctual raptures of a chartered accountant or a publisher's reader. Now Thelma, however much she left to be desired, was not a brood-maiden. (p. 128)

This description of the poet is obviously ironic in Belacqua's case, since he expresses his "love of love" by a decidedly "keycold embrace" (p. 129). And though Thelma is no brood-maiden, she still desires after her wedding night not to be a maiden.

"What a Misfortune" emphasizes Belacqua's wish for spiritual communion and his concomitant instinct for self-preservation. On one level a satire of middle-class matrimony, the story as a whole is a neat exposition of Belacqua's artistically determined autoeroticism. More clearly than anywhere else in More Pricks than Kicks, Beckett reveals how Belacqua's spirituality influences his sexuality, and why he finds his desires so difficult to fulfill.

Structurally, "What a Misfortune" is knit together by a series of sexual and spiritual motifs. First of all, we encounter the bride's father, Otto Olaf bboggs, a man who has risen from the depths of his profession; he is in plumbing and toilet requisites.[8] Otto Olaf's interest in sex, dating from "his self-made sanitary phase" (p. 128), is so meager that he more than welcomes his jejune wife's affair with Walter Draffin, the effeminate bureaucrat, since it saves him considerable trouble. Belacqua would have envied this ideal arrangement. Otto Olaf allows his wife's former cicisbeo (the affair having petered out) to consider their house and liquor supply as his own. Bridie bboggs seems to be such a nonentity and the adulterous liaison so low key, that it is difficult to believe that Thelma ever resulted from such a union: "Bridie bboggs was nothing at all, neither as wife, as Otto Olaf had been careful to ascertain before he made her one, nor as mistress, which suited Walter's taste for moderation in all things" (p. 131). Belacqua's beloved, nevertheless, is the product of this vapid pair. Ironically, Thelma's demise during her honeymoon suggests that she did not inherit her mother's passionless personality.

Beckett suggests just what kind of a mate the onanistic Belacqua has chosen by giving her an appropriate name. Thelma comes from the Greek for "nursling," but also means "air-maiden." The narrator has stated that she is decidedly "not a brood-maiden . . . while as for soul, sparkling or still, as preferred, it was her speciality" (pp. 128–129). Belacqua's bride's name also derives from the Greek *thalamos,* a woman's apartment or bridal chamber, in which the poet is afraid of being trapped. Directly before the ceremony, the groom has feelings of panic, expressed by images of incarceration: "Belacqua's heart made a hopeless dash against the wall of its box, the church suddenly cruciform cage, the bulldogs of heaven holding the chancel . . . the transepts culs-de-sac. The organist darted into his loft like an assassin" (p. 148).

In addition to Thelma's parents (all three who claim her allegiance), another incongruous couple serve as romantic foils. Hermione Nautzsche, "a powerfully built nymphomaniac panting in black and mauve between shipped crutches" (p. 148), and "Jimmy the Duck Skyrm, an aged cretin, outrageous in pepper and salt" (p. 148), find each other in a burst of senile passion in the pews of St. Tamar's. The female "moot struldbrug's" surname, Nautzsche, emphasizes her bizarre sexuality. "Nautch" refers to "sensuous Indian dancers known as 'nautch girls'" (Harvey, p. 148). If the crippled Hermione cannot exactly entice her new lover,[9] her presence nevertheless seems to have a profound effect, and Jimmy the Skyrm gnashes his teeth, touched beyond measure. At last she has found "her missing sexual hemisphere" (p. 148). This grotesque pair prefigures later ancient couples, particularly Moll and McMann, who find love when they can barely consummate it.

Belacqua, about to be married, is in much better physical shape than his aged relatives, but the reader begins to suspect that the bridegroom shuns what they would welcome. His attraction to Thelma, "a divine frenzy . . . none of your lewd passions" (p. 126), depends on her "promissory wad" (p. 127) and her speciality, soul. She was "so definitely not beautiful that once she was seen she was with difficulty forgotten, which is more than can be said for, say, the Venus Callipyge" (p. 127–Callipyge: having shapely buttocks). Belacqua's best man, Hairy Capper Quin, understands his friend's artistic and erotic peculiarities. Dressing for the wedding, the groom laments to Hairy: "It's a small thing . . . separates lovers" (p. 146). Nothing so grandiose as mountains, or as pedestrian as city walls, it is sex that intrudes in the hero's romantic liaisons. Though decidedly nonverbal, Capper Quin somehow manages to rise to the occasion of explaining his comrade's attitudes to a friend named Sproule, and "dilated with splendid incoherence on the contradiction involved in the idea of a happy Belacqua and on the impertinence of desiring that he should derogate into such an anomaly. 'Fornication' he vociferated 'before the Shekinah'" (p. 142).

In *Dream,* the hero had claimed that "the true Shekinah . . . is Woman" (p. 94); that is, a manifestation of God in the world, "a revelation of the holy in the midst of the profane,"[10] and this is probably how Belacqua would like to view Thelma. One interpretation definitely classifies Shekinah as a feminine principle, reflecting the divine masculine light as the moon reflects the sun. Beckett observes of his character's religious expectations before the wedding: "Without going so far as to say that Belacqua felt God or Thelma the sum of the Apostolic series, still there was in some indeterminate way communicated to the solemnization a kind or sort of mystical radiance that Joseph Smith would have found touching" (p. 149). The appeal to Joseph Smith's hypothetical judgment underlines the equivocal nature of Belacqua's attitude toward women. Supposedly experiencing a divine revelation during which he acquired the tablets of Mormon Law, Smith founded a religion originally maintaining certain practices, such as polygamy, which led critics to accuse him of lechery. As demonstrated in other stories, Belacqua is not free from concupiscent thoughts about the true Shekinah. His approach to women, however, is hopelessly confused by his attempts to achieve mystic fulfillment and his desire to perfect artistic expression.

Belacqua's efforts to reach a timeless and volitionless realm through the earthly radiance of his beloved (with Lucy [light], the Alba [white, dawn], and then Thelma), is clarified by a more detailed consideration of Shekinah, which has various meanings in Biblical tradition. In "rabbinic literature . . . the Shekinah is God viewed in spatio-temporal terms as a presence, particularly in a this-worldly context: when He sanctifies a place, an object, an individual, or a whole people" (*Judaica*, pp. 1349–50). An example of Shekinah in this sense is the burning bush. In Jewish thought, the Shekinah also signified the proximity of God to suffering humanity. Developing this concept and personalizing it, certain Jewish philosophers equated the Shekinah with "the glory of God, which served as an intermediary between God and man during the prophetic experience . . . and which sometimes takes on human form" (*Judaica*, p. 1352). The dilemma, at least for Belacqua, seems to lie in his belief that women not only can serve as inspirations for art, but that they can somehow lead to a reunification of man with his essential nature or source (which may, unfortunately and ironically for someone like Belacqua, render art irrelevant). One goal of the religious experience, then, is to heal the breach between masculine and feminine principles and to reinstate unity.[11] The Shekinah, thus, is "the first goal of the mystic who tries to achieve direct communion with divine powers" (*Judaica*, p. 1354). Belacqua's efforts to keep both himself and his paramours chaste probably stem from his wish to redeem both their fallen spirits and to release them from the tainted body into a nirvanalike peace.

What Belacqua does not question (and what Beckett as narrator does not make explicit) is why he should turn toward women for the answer to spiritual malaise or metaphysical anguish in the first place. (It is worth emphasizing that Belacqua does not seek to lose himself in women to avoid facing the problem, but to solve it.) The difficulty lies in the inherently paradoxical nature of the quest—to reunite the infinite with the finite is only a more general way of seeking to understand or affirm contact between the mind and the body. Various philosophers have conceived of a human being (at least since Descartes) as a "thing which thinks," a spirit tied to an often recalcitrant physical being. As early as his 1929 story "Assumption," Beckett's heroes have been grappling with a way to release their spirits from the quotidian world and from their unruly bodies in particular. One way Belacqua seeks release is by intense contemplation of a woman's eyes, deep pools which open up into a bottomless reality. It is made clear, particularly in *Dream*, that this dark, amorphous reality suggests the womb. Agents of birth, possible agents of death (and, thus, release), women draw the expectant hero into the spirit's "wombtomb." The name of Belacqua's second wife is Thelma bboggs, and the microcosm of the Irish solipsist in *Dream*[12] had been described as "an unsurveyed marsh of sloth" (*Dream*, p. 108). At least initially, Belacqua has hopes of establishing a mystico-religious rapport with Thelma's own spiritual bog. Along these same lines, Beckett further suggests throughout *More Pricks than Kicks* the relationship between love, art, and death—"l'Amour et la Mort n'est qu'une même chose." It is Ronsard, albeit a bit distorted, who closes the ironic story "Love and Lethe." We can also recall in this connection the seventeenth-century pun on "die." Furthermore, sexual procreation and artistic creation can be similarly expressed. According to Freud, they may also maintain inverse relations; i.e., sublimation leads to creation.[13]

The questionable nature of Thelma's and Belacqua's relationship is further amplified by the name Beckett chooses for the place where the wedding occurs. They are to be married in a nonexistent Dublin Church, St. Tamar's, "pointed almost to the point of indecency" (p. 147). This phallic allusion which seems, at first glance, a feeble matrimonial joke, actually points to the femaleness and self-imposed impotence (or autoeroticism) of the hero. (Harvey points out that Belacqua is called a "compound of ephebe and old woman" [p. 189] in "Draff.") There is no Saint Tamar in the Bible, but in Genesis there is a Tamar who is the daughter-in-law of Judah. Originally the Canaanite wife of his eldest son, Er, she is the same woman who married her brother-in-law, Onan, at Judah's insistence. She represents the rejected woman since Onan scattered his seed on the ground, refusing to consummate their marriage (he was slain by God for this sin). The implications of the union of Tamar and Onan are further developed in the closing scene. The success of Belacqua's honeymoon[14] appears questionable, since the bridegroom's veronica had "wormed its stem out of the slit, fallen to the ground and been trodden underfoot" (p. 160).

Belacqua's fantasies and his fascination with myth and legend, some of which he wants to incorporate into his life, have been communicated to Thelma in a minimal way. She is being primed, as it were, before her marriage, for the fuller revelation of her husband's temperament after her marriage. One of the first things that he has told her he wishes to do on their honeymoon in Connemara is to reenact an historical event. His enthusiasm has infected his fiancée, who finds it difficult to keep her mind on the wedding preparations.

For Thelma's thoughts, truant to the complicated manoeuvres required of a snow-white bride, had flown on the usual wings to Galway, Gate of Connaught and dream of stone, and more precisely to the Church of Saint Nicholas whither Belacqua projected, if it were not closed when they arrived, to repair without delay and kneel, with her on his right hand at last for a pleasant change, and invoke, in pursuance of a vow of long standing, the spirits of Crusoe and Columbus, who had knelt there before him. Then no doubt, as they returned by the harbor to integrate their room in the Great Southern, she would see the sun sink in the sea. How was it possible to give them her attention with such a prospect opening up before her? Oh well is thee, and happy shalt thou be. (pp. 135–136)

In point of fact, there is a Church of St. Nicolas in Galway, and a Great Southern Hotel which, from the advertisements in contemporary travel books, looks as if it were once fashionable. St. Nicolas (the same saint who was corrupted into Santa Claus) is the patron saint of sailors and captives, especially in the East, and of children in the West. Galway for some time had been the gateway to trade and travel to the West, and it is natural that a seaport town should erect a church in his honor. Most interesting is the fact that Columbus, according to a longstanding Galway tradition, supposedly knelt in the church before embarking in the *Santa María* on his voyage to discover a northwest passage to the Indies and the Orient.[15] Columbus may have captured Belacqua's imagination in his role as Western explorer, who has undertaken a seemingly impossible task (i.e., to find a passage to the East by going west). Transposing the Italian's literal voyage, Belacqua wishes to bless his metaphysical voyage toward nirvana (or the East) and spiritual fulfillment, or even death (the West). The literal and metaphorical connotations of West are specifically exploited at the end of the story, when the honeymoon couple journey westward, and reflect back on the meaning of Columbus's paradoxical journey for the hero.

As for Crusoe, the protagonist must be referring to Defoe's literary character, a rebel of sorts who refused the conventional life that his father had mapped out for him and chose to become a sailor in order to explore the world himself.[16] Galway was often the jumping-off point for trips to the East, and Crusoe's adventures were inspired by the account of an actual sailor, Alexander Selkirk. Crusoe's voyage and consequent estrangement from society on an uninhabited island, where he was totally isolated until Friday appeared, made him completely dependent on his own resources. Crusoe, typically handy and stoic in his British way, created his own one-man society on the island in order to survive physically; to survive psychologically he had to depend on the strength of his internal world. In both senses, Crusoe's isle functioned as a self-contained, insular microcosm.

The motifs suggesting erotic eccentricity by mocking sexual relationships and pointing to impotence lead up to the strange closing scene, where Beckett parodies the happy couple disappearing west into the sunset. In an indirect manner, Belacqua's plans for his marriage are revealed, but since they are habitually cast by the hero in the form of legend and riddle, the reader is forced to identify the allusions. What emerges is Belacqua's vision of himself as priest or devotee before his spiritual partner, also priestess and participant in the mysteries that lead to mystical union, and his contrary fear that his Shekinah may turn into a destructive Circe.

Before the wedding, the protagonist, like acolyte or novice, had prepared himself by entering a period of "inertia, which proceeded partly . . . from the need for self-purification" (p. 138). But once the retreat and the nuptials are over, Belacqua fears that the time has come to unravel his fantasies to Thelma. The memory of his late wife ("Lucy was atra cura in the dicky the best part of the way down to Galway" [p. 160])[17] reminds him that he may have certain problems with Thelma that were precluded by Lucy's crippling accident. Oblivious to his predicament, Thelma "begins to insist that she was Mrs. Shuah, making his little heart go pit-a-pat" (p. 160). Belacqua summons up his courage, nevertheless, assumes an expression which Thelma has never seen before, and begins the sounding-out process:

> "Do you ever hear tell of a babylan?" he said.
> Now Thelma was a brave girl.
> "A what did you say?" she said.
> Belacqua went to the trouble of spelling the strange word.
> "Never" she said. "What is it? Something to eat?"
> "Oh" he said "you're thinking of a baba."
> "Well then" she said. (p. 160)

Although Belacqua corrects Thelma, she is still waiting for him to spell out the answer, not just the word. Instead of resolving this stalemate, the bridegroom retreats and begins to fantasize:

> His eyes were parched, he closed them and saw, clearer than ever before, the mule, up to its knees in mire, and astride its back a beaver, flogging it with a wooden sword.

But she was not merely brave, she was discreet as well.

"Your veronica" she said "that I wanted so much, where is it gone?"

He clapped his hand to the place. Alas! the tassel had drooped, wormed its stem out of the slit, fallen to the ground and been trodden underfoot.

"Gone west" he said.

They went further. (p. 160)

The complex of allusions and word-play in this passage create a comprehensive picture of Belacqua's sexual preferences and fears. "Babylan," the test word for the bride, refers, according to Harvey, to "a pagan priest, priestess, or medium in the central and south Philippines" (p. 258). If this reading is correct, the word calls to mind exotic Eastern ritual. In primitive communities where women function as shamans, they oversee birth, marriage, death, and the laws of their society in general.[18] These female shamans often found their vocation after a dream or vision, and after this summons were instructed by their predecessors in the kind of knowledge appropriate to their calling; healing and midwifery specifically were part of this knowledge. A related factor, which bears on Beckett's treatment of women (whether or not "babylan" refers to priest or priestess), is primitive understanding of the reproductive process. Frequently, the relationship between sexual intercourse and birth was obscure; in fact, all the processes of the female reproductive system were the object of awe and taboo. Women could miraculously give life—so what about death? Thelma, as Shekinah or babylan, and Belacqua, as humble worshipper or interpreter of the mystery, are supposed to strive together for assumption, at least as far as Belacqua is concerned.

Unfortunately, Thelma's associations are not spiritual but physical. She thinks of a baba au rhum, which may play into her husband's sexual fears of being devoured by female physicality. (In *Dream,* the voluptuous Smeraldina's refrain when she doesn't understand a word that Belacqua uses is: "What's that? . . . something to eat?" [p. 85].)

Given Belacqua's sexual predicament, however, it seems that babylan must refer to "*Babilanisme* (mot italien),"[19] as Stendhal describes it in a letter to Prosper Mérimée concerning his novel *Armance.* Stendhal's hero, Octave, suffers from a hidden physical disability that causes him to hold back from society, a society which he already sees as generally amoral and vicious. In a world of philistines, this disability inevitability complicates his relationships with women. Stendhal explains Octave's dilemma which apparently, is not unique, or eunique, in Paris: "Il y a beaucoup plus d'impuissants qu'on ne croit" (*Correspondance*, p. 290). Though Belacqua is not really impotent, to all intents and purposes he wishes to behave as if he were in "What a Misfortune."[20]

Stendhal raises a point in his letter that reflects on Belacqua's decision to marry Thelma in the first place. Stendhal feels that his readers might justly question why a babilan would marry at all. In the case of Octave, his desire to marry is bound up with the sincere affection that he feels for Armance—wedlock would ensure that they could always be together, which has not always been possible in the course of the novel. Social decorum and problems with relatives have made it advisable that they formalize their relations. Octave then becomes her protector. Belacqua wants something similar with his paramours. He often suggests, however, what Stendhal specifically rejects for his hero—a cicisbeo (specifically in the case of his fiancée, Lucy, in "Walking Out").

Stendhal then examines the problem of the babilan as deceiver and the babilan as cuckold. Significantly, he uses Jonathan Swift as an example of the babilan who keeps his secret: *"Le Dean Swift* ne voulait pas se marier pour ne pas faire l'aveu: il se maria, sollicité par sa maîtresse mais jamais ne la vit *en tête-a-tête,* pas plus après qu'avant" (p. 291).[21] If Stendhal is correct, Stella obviously did not object to this arrangement, whereby she never saw Swift alone. In order to clarify his analogy, Stendhal goes on to analyze what might have occurred between his pair of lovers if he had not decided to have Octave kill himself in the novel. Octave's marriage to Armance might have succeeded, he speculates, for four reasons. First, Armance is shy; second, she loves Octave; third, like most babilans, her husband is an adept at substitute methods of satisfaction; and fourth, the majority of women do not really understand what the physical side of marriage entails (at least according to Stendhal). With Belacqua's wife, Thelma, however, the case appears to be different. The aura of confusion that surrounds the babilan's dealings with women reflects on her bewilderment about Belacqua and on her vague anticipation for the honeymoon, when she and her husband will "integrate" their room on the wedding night.

Finally, the problem of how the babilan deals with the object of his affections, either as beloved or as wife, explains why Belacqua uses this indirect question-and-answer method with Thelma. Stendhal himself first chose the name Olivier for his protagonist (after another impotent hero) in order to avoid a direct mention of this delicate subject. Polite, hypocritical society was not yet ready for the direct approach: "Mais cette vérité est du nombre de celles que la peinture *par du noir et du blanc,* la peinture par l'imagination du spectateur ne peut pas rendre. Que de choses vraies qui sortent des moyens de l'art! . . . Le genre noir sur du blanc, ne me permet pas de suivre la vérité" (p. 291). Belacqua, then, is like sensitive Octave: "songe-creux, homme d'esprit, élève . . ." (p. 292). This comparison, however, finally reinforces the indolent Belacqua's character as poseur, since his impotence is self-imposed. A passage in *Dream* clarifies this distinction, since it at once specifically identifies Belacqua with and differentiates him from Octave.

Beckett is describing the hero's relationship with the Syra-Cusa, a Parisian femme fatale whom Belacqua admires. Beckett reveals that she is "as impotently besotted on Belacqua babylan, fiasco incarnate, Limbese, as the moon on Endymion. When it was patent, and increasingly so, that he was more Octave of Malivert [Stendhal's village] than Valmont and more of a Limbo barnacle than either, mollecone . . . honing after the dark" (*Dream,* p. 44). The Syra-Cusa's futile passion imitates the moon's hapless passion for the mortal Endymion. The narrator, however, goes on to qualify this comparison. Belacqua is, finally, more interested in immersion in his own consciousness, his Limbo (his identity as the Florentine Belacqua), where inactivity and impotence are specifically sought after as a release from the emotional tangles of the external world. The hero's difficulties are, therefore, largely fabricated, and the fiascoes in which he becomes involved are due to his inability either to maintain his impotence or to achieve a mature sexuality.

Belacqua may still possess some of the characteristics of the hero of *Dream* but his efforts to carry out his "narcissistic manoeuvres" to deceive his paramours do not work as effectively. In *Dream,* Beckett had also used "babylan" to identify the bohemian poet as fake or fraud: "He found him naif and a dull vain dog and a patent babylan" (p. 80). Both these related identities (babylan as fraud and babylan as covert impotent) bode ill for Thelma's happiness. The hero's onanism and narcissism (the Limbese aspect of his personality) and the frustration of woman in the face of an unattainable love object (also see Stendhal on love) are responsible for this romantic miscarriage. The mention of Endymion and the moon in *Dream* as counterpoints for Belacqua and the Syra-Cusa amplifies this sense of mismatch, and underlines what Harvey has elsewhere, in a related context, called the theme of "non-consummation."

These allusions to a confused sexual identity lead into the bridegroom's castration fantasy. He momentarily retreats from his new wife, to take breath, as it were, before possibly trying again to enlighten her about his desire to reify his dearest dreams. The ultimate failure of this project is implied because the apparently recurring castration fable appears to him "clearer than ever before" (p. 160). Belacqua recalls the tradition that beavers were sought for their testicles, which were useful in manufacturing perfume or medicine. In an attempt to avoid death, the beaver would bite or cut off its own testicles and give them to the hunters, who would then be satisfied and spare the animal's life. According to T. H. White's medieval *Bestiary,* "The creature is called a Beaver (Castor) because of the castration."[22] The fact that the sword in Belacqua's fantasy is wooden, a sword used for training and not for actual battle, indicates his cowardice, his ambiguous sexual inclinations, and perhaps even his masochism. Significantly, the protagonist envisages the beaver in his reverie astride a mule, stuck in the mire, and Thelma's name is a play on bogs, so prevalent in the Irish countryside. Furthermore, the mule is a hybrid animal, sterile by nature. Belacqua is obviously afraid of being lost in the physical being of his new wife, instead of being lost in her spiritual being, "those windows onto better world's that Lucy's big black eyes had been" (p. 126).

Neither the beaver, nor Belacqua, are brave (unlike Thelma, as we learn shortly after). What appears from the outside as a momentary pause in the conversation, or even an impasse, is, in reality, Belacqua's struggle to maintain control. But he panics within. The approach-avoidance reaction Belacqua has toward sex is illustrated by this frantic response to stubbornness. The tableau is a metaphor for his conflict. The mule stands knee-deep in mud, and Belacqua can't get away, like someone trapped in a nightmare, terror-stricken, paralyzed, unable to flee. If he is caught, the wooden sword, which doesn't seem to be doing much good as a goad for the animal, won't go to waste.

Although Harvey notes the beaver myth, the nature of the mule, and Thelma as bog in his discussion of Belacqua, he fails to mention a passage in *Dream* which clarifies the beaver allusion and which strengthens the identification of babylan as impotent rather than solely as priest or priestess. Sick in bed in Paris, the hero is debating how to respond to the irate telegram of the Smeraldina's mother, ordering him to be up and away to his beloved in Vienna. Belacqua already has strong inclinations to drop the affair and this menacing note reinforces his wish to escape: "But the moment passed . . . and he opened wide the lids of the mind and let in the glare. The beaver bites his off, he said, I know, that he may live. That was a very persuasive chapter of Natural History. But he lost no time in reminding himself that, far from being a beaver or the least likely to sympathize with its aspirations, he was no less a person than the lover of the

Belacqua Jesus and a very inward man" (p. 56). So the hero gives in, despite hepatic colic, and takes himself off to the panting Smeraldina in Vienna.

Belacqua's anxiety about castration in "What a Misfortune" is amplified directly after the beaver reverie. The narrator ironically says that Thelma is not only brave but discreet. In an effort possibly to placate her husband, who closes his eyes and withdraws, and to distract attention from the fact that she is ignorant about babylans, she changes the subject, or so she thinks. Earlier, Thelma had requested his veronica as a wedding memento. As in the case of babylan, veronica suggests both physical and spiritual realms, referring to both the slender flower and the handkerchief impressed with Christ's features. Thelma wants his veronica terribly, and it is his sexual inviolability (in order to ensure his spiritual inviolability) that Belacqua is determined to preserve. His energetic response ("He clapped his hand to the place. Alas!") displays his concern. Gone limp, it has vanished. Somber omens for the hero.

The title, "What a Misfortune," completes this portrait of sexual fear and confusion. Significantly, Beckett had previously used the Italian version of this title on an undergraduate satire about contraceptives, "Che sciagura," which appeared in *T.C.D.: A College Miscellany* (November 14, 1929). The expression originates in Voltaire's *Candide*. In chapters eleven and twelve (chapters ordinarily excluded from anthologized versions of the novel to protect the impressionable), the Old Woman, once the proud and beautiful daughter of a pope, busily details the miseries of her life to the hero and Cunégonde. She had been kidnapped by pirates and raped; then she had witnessed a massacre in Morocco where her mother along with thousands of others had been cut to pieces. Covered with blood herself, she had stumbled into a faint by a stream, and recovered only to hear a voice saying in her native tongue: "O che sciagura d'essere senza c[oglioni]!"²³—Oh what a misfortune to be without balls!—on which note chapter eleven concludes. It is revealed in chapter twelve that the handsome Italian is one of the castrati, and he reiterates his regret in the same terms when faced with this beautiful, but for him impenetrable, creature. Beckett implies in his satire, "Che sciagura," that for those unfortunate Irishmen with large families, who were denied contraceptive information because of Irish provincialism, the young Italian's plight in *Candide* might not be such a misfortune (compare Swift's "A Modest Proposal"). Belacqua, however, would prefer to remain physically intact in order to indulge his onanism when the mood takes him; those moods get him into some ridiculous scrapes in *More Pricks than Kicks* (e.g., his Peeping-Tom expedition in "Walking Out").

Beckett intimates, therefore, that the newlyweds' relationship will be a great misfortune for both of them. Later in "Draff," the narrator informs us that "Thelma née bboggs perished of sunset and honeymoon that time in Connemara" (p. 189). Before her wedding, she had fantasized on the strength of her lover's portrayal of their trip, when they would pray together in church and then "integrate" their bridal chamber. The implication is that Belacqua's erotic aberrations have had something to do with Thelma's death, sunset and honeymoon not usually being fatal. The light sinking in the west, the unorthodox poet may have explained how he wanted to die "a rapturous strange death" ("Sonnet to the Smeraldina")[24] with his beloved. Perhaps he suggested a cicisbeo to the innocent bride, as he had before marriage to Lucy in "Walking Out," fearing embarrassment or emasculation. Already, an attempt at mystical communion via death had literally misfired and turned into a physical communion with Ruby in "Love and Lethe," though Belacqua fought his impulses until Scotch and Ruby's knickers got the better of him. There have in fact been several abortive affairs[25] in *More Pricks than Kicks* before the poet marries Thelma, a healthy, solvent woman. "What a Misfortune" thus portrays the comic start of an obviously (and swiftly) doomed relationship. The social fiasco of the wedding prefigures the emotional and physical fiasco to come.

The order of the stories in *More Pricks than Kicks,* finally, reinforces our impression not only of Belacqua's sexual inadequacy, but of a much more crucial kind of inadequacy, which allows us to see why Beckett ultimately rejects his hero. The second, more general weakness, Belacqua's failure of integrity, relates inversely to his sexuality—in other words, the less equivocal Belacqua feels about women, the better he functions socially and sexually, the worse he behaves, as far as the narrator is concerned: "I gave him up in the end because he was not serious" (p. 41). But since the two weaknesses are intimately connected, let us first dispense with the more particular problem of the hero's sexuality.

After "What a Misfortune," the reader is immediately plunged into "The Smeraldina's Billet Doux." Juxtaposed as it is with that tale of abortive marriage, "The Billet Doux," which details the rampant physicality of its supposed writer (soon to be Belacqua's third wife), is consummately ironic. Her dreams about her lover, so much more intense than Thelma's, are at once hilarious and ominous. Yet the Belacqua of *More Pricks than Kicks,* unlike the hero of *Dream,* finds by the end of the collection that he can apparently cope with her energy—for he marries her. Although we never find out whether their union is a disaster, the Smeraldina has triumphed in a way. She survives, not only the honeymoon, but the hero. Yet passion and impatience, even if they are "quasi-Gorgonesque" (p. 190), cannot sufficiently account for Belacqua's capitulation.[26]

One explanation of the poet's behavior lies in Beckett's final evaluation of him in the last two stories. In "Yellow" and "Draff," we see that the first hero is not strong enough to help the young "Mr. Beckett" as author untangle the grounds of his art. Belacqua's inchoate personality, ultimately, did not allow a scrupulous analysis of the complex themes that already concerned his creator. When we encounter Belacqua alive for the last time in "Yellow," he is fretting over how his relatives will receive the news of his cowardice if he breaks down in tears before the operation, and over how he can impress the attractive or otherwise intimidating nurses who have become guardians of his body. The "misfortune" now is not an inconclusive judgment about wholehearted dedication to mind or body; the misfortune now, more for Beckett the creator than for Belacqua the creature, is that his Dublin rambler has allowed the world to infiltrate and sully his consciousness. Belacqua gives in to what Beckett specifically rejects in a 1936 satire about censorship in the world of the philistines: "the common sense mean."[27] His progressive socialization in the stories, which leads him to flirt, to court, and finally to marry—which leads him, in other words, to relish the world (p. 39)—inevitably means a betrayal of integrity. Belacqua is fraternizing with the enemy, his body as well as women. If this loss of purpose and potency is the effect of living in society on the man, the effect on the artist is even more paramount for Beckett. Conventional beliefs should never influence the writer's direction. "This is getting dangerously close to the opinion . . . that for the artist as for the restaurateur, the customer is always right" ("Censorship in the Saorstat," p. 85). Perhaps Belacqua's adventures in *Dream* and *More Pricks than Kicks* provided a test case for Beckett. A character fails either because his creator fails unwittingly in his portrayal, or because his creator consciously wills that failure in order to test specific hypotheses. Beckett makes his hero behave according to a domino theory of integrity. Once Belacqua gives in to one primary convention (marriage, not once but three times), he seems to be on the way to giving in to them all. But before he can, Beckett spares himself and the reader by eliminating his hero precipitately on the operating table.

In his apprentice work, then, Beckett moves toward the creation of a character who can accept responsibility, even though Beckett, as a young writer, does not know exactly what kind of responsibility he wants his character to accept. The initial situations facing his protagonists embrace the problem of options—what options are available to human beings in general and to artists in particular; how can we function effectively given the spiritual and emotional poverty of contemporary culture? Mind and body, man and woman, society and the individual all seem at odds, struggling to achieve some sort of harmony. All of Beckett's apprentice work, therefore, is a search. He seeks to plot the dimensions of his subject—humanity's fragmentation—and to discover his own unique mode of expression.[28]

Beckett's problems with his first character, Belacqua, have to do, consequently, with his attempt to define for himself what being a writer is—why one writes, what one should write about, and what one can hope to achieve. Beckett singled out courage and tenacity (among other affinities) to emulate in those thinkers that he admired—courage to experiment with language, tenacity to persevere despite ridicule and criticism. But Beckett lacked the requisite faith in art (Joyce and Proust), and faith in God (Dante and Descartes). This lack is one reason why his first artist-hero feels torn constantly between allegiance to the macrocosm, which offers human, if not divine, love, and the microcosm, which promises self-love and peace. In either realm, as it turns out, the individual as artist, or merely as sensitive being, is threatened. He finds sources of inspiration in the external world (particularly woman as aesthetic object and woman as muse), but he also finds himself distracted by obstacles that hinder artistic production (woman as physical object and woman as Circe). In the internal world, of course, the consciousness is free of physical vexations. And yet even in this retreat, the hero is not completely at ease. Once in the lowest depths (for example, Belacqua's "wombtomb," Murphy's "third zone," Molloy's "ruins"), the artist's will may be engulfed by the volitionless pull of a primeval flux, which makes no distinction between thoughts and images, and where composition and decomposition occur simultaneously. This tension between microcosm and macrocosm becomes more pronounced and complex as Beckett develops. The personae are threatened by their "vice-existers" (their creations, masculine as well as feminine) and by their relentless hypothetical imperatives in a more terrifying way than they were ever threatened by the world outside (women included). The stakes of the game now are elemental—the persona is fighting for his voice; in other words, for his very existence.

The crucial difference in the later work, then, is the honesty and integrity with which the human condition is faced; though sometimes, paradoxically, Beckett allows honesty to yield to what will help a character to survive, to endure. Emotion can be a double-edged sword. In *Happy Days,* for example, Winnie keeps up a brave front by talking enthusiastically, as the sands slowly climb higher and higher and the sun beats down. Willie, for his part, hides silently, no more effective than she. Yet his presence comforts her. Game playing in the mature work alternates with acerbic flashes of truth. Relationships between the sexes take their place along with other games people play to avoid recognizing their insuperable isolation. And yet those relationships hover about like religious and cultural ghosts—divine love, human love, once they were supposed to mean something. Nagg and Nell can still remember Lake Como; Krapp, despite his cynical groans, cannot forget that tape recorded in his thirty-ninth year, that incident on the lake with his lover. Women, thus, when they do appear as central characters in Beckett's later novels and plays, are no more ridiculous or noble than men. The more traditional portrayal of female character, patronizing or satiric, has generally been exorcised along with Beckett's reliance on traditional form and style.[29] The voice in the dark, or the lone figure on the stage, is sometimes a man and sometimes a woman; and sometimes it is difficult to tell—the anguish is all that counts.

In the apprentice fiction, then, Beckett does not make the women who try to seduce Belacqua (or whom he tries to seduce) the real culprits. They are often deceived systematically by the poet's arcane methods of lovemaking and are no more ludicrous than he. Beckett's treatment of women soon after in his first complete novel, *Murphy,* is particularly instructive. He takes Belacqua's reluctance about sex and transforms it in Murphy's character. The second hero's paramour, Celia, is certainly a victim of the physical world as much as her lover, and she in fact becomes his spiritual heir. If Murphy had not died, she might have been able to explore with him their perplexing common humanity. She has always known about the comfort of the bed; she learns about the comfort of the rocking-chair. She could then, perhaps, have offered the hero "music music music" with Celia, the golden-haired Irish prostitute; and "music music music" with Celia, the namesake of St. Cecilia.[30] She begins to question her identity as Mr. Willoughby Kelly questions her name: "S'il y a" (*Murphy,* p. 115).

But although Belacqua fails with women as Murphy does not fail, his initial reactions to failure set the pattern for his successor's reactions. We can see this connection in the outcome of Belacqua's amorous schemes in "Love and Lethe" and "What a Misfortune," which epitomize the outcome of all of his artistic-erotic plans. His "temporarily sane" (p. 102) attempts to fulfill both his mystic and artistic nature by integrating himself with the true Shekinah of his choice (except in the case of the cripple Lucy) lead to fiasco, frustration, or flight. His behavior early in *More Pricks than Kicks,* in "Fingal" in particular, before he learns to relish the world, points to a solution favored by his successors. Belacqua disappears from his current girlfriend Winnie in a "square bawnless tower" (p. 30)[31] for isolated self-communion, for "sursum corda" according to his God. He prays that he were back in the caul. When all else fails, immersion in the cogito provides some measure of compensation; in other words, when all else fails, the Beckett hero longs for madness.

Belacqua's attitudes toward sex, then, which clarify his desire to return to the womb and his budding solipsism, lead into Beckett's initial exploration of insanity, too. But Belacqua is left on the threshold of madness, as he is left on the threshold of everything else. He only occasionally visits Portrane Lunatic Asylum; he only briefly finds "l'amour and la mort" in the ling with Ruby; he only fleetingly enjoys sunset and honeymoon in Connemara. Belacqua's comic exit from the macrocosm makes way for Murphy, who confronts similar problems, but who decides by the end of the novel to avoid Belacqua's misfortunes with his body by turning to a realm where the physical is no longer relevant: the microcosm.

Beckett's development, therefore, of all the characters from Belacqua to the Unnamable, testifies to his continuing search for a way to cope with human dichotomies, treading a fine line between sanity and insanity. But although the dilemma of relation is a capital issue in the fiction certainly, it is superseded by the dilemma of perception—what to perceive, how to perceive, and how to evaluate what one perceives. This dilemma, confronted by the consciousness, focuses on modes of being. Beckett moves in *Dream* and *More Pricks than Kicks,* then, from an uncertain perception of himself as creator and a confused evaluation of his character, to a position where the confusion becomes the subject, style becomes the expression of the bewildered mind's activity, and final judgments become not only unnecessary, but impossible. The search for the self is synonymous with the creation of a literary work. And since this drama takes place primarily in the microcosm (though the voice may have a body floundering around somewhere up in the light), the voice is neuter for all intents and purposes. In the French fiction, Beckett's personae do not usually face Watt's perceptual difficulty when he sees a figure coming down the road: "But to decide whether it was that of a man, or that of a woman, or that of a priest, or that of a nun, was more than Watt could do, strain as he might his eyes."[32]

Notes

1. Samuel Beckett, *More Pricks than Kicks* (London: Calder and Boyars, 1966), 94. All quotations will hereafter be cited in the text according to page number only.

2. Beckett, *Dream of Fair to Middling Women* (Monkstown, Dublin: Black Cat Press, 1992). Composed primarily during 1932 in Paris, the novel contains two long chapters, prefaced by a terse introduction, divided by a transitional passage, and followed by an epilogue. Beckett labels his five divisions "One," "Two," "Und," "Three," "And." Page numbers of all quotations hereafter cited in the text refer to the Dartmouth typescript.

3. Lawrence E. Harvey, *Samuel Beckett: Poet and Critic* (Princeton: Princeton University Press, 1970). Harvey meticulously studies all of Beckett's poetry (French as well as English). Quotations hereafter cited in the text.

4. See my dissertation, "Fair to Middling Heroes: A Study of Samuel Beckett's Early Fiction" (Columbia University, 1974), for a complete discussion of how *More Pricks than Kicks* is clearly a stylistic and structural advance over the draft novel *Dream*. It is worth noting here that there are several parallels that can be drawn between Beckett's early work and Joyce's *Stephen Hero* and *A Portrait of the Artist*. Beckett often consciously parodies Joyce, and enough critics have mentioned the conclusion of "A Wet Night," where rain is general all over Ireland. There are other even more noteworthy echoes, however, which underline the single most important factor dividing *Dream* and *More Pricks than Kicks,* the distance that the narrator maintains between himself and the hero. Beckett's development, in a sense, is an effort to exorcise the Belacqua in him, to exorcise the artist who is too much in love with words.

5. Belacqua's mystical transfiguration with Ruby in "Love and Lethe" is balked and he winds up "Blaking" her. Even the Belacqua of *Dream* bandied suicide about with the Alba, but their conversation never even neared the planning stage.

6. Beckett, *Murphy* (New York: Grove Press, 1957), 234. Hereafter quotations will be cited in the text according to title and page number.

7. "Astride of a grave and a difficult birth," *Waiting for Godot* (New York, Grove Press, 1954), 58. There is an elaborate series of images concerning Belacqua's "prothanic" nature running through *Dream* and *More Pricks than Kicks*. This theme of arrested development, which connects the womb, birth, and death, appears in the mature work, too.

8. Beckett obviously intends a pun on bog as British slang for toilet—originally "Bog-house. dial. and vulg. 1705. A privy" (OED).

9. There is also a "dauntless nautch girl" in the poem "Sanies I" (from *Echo's Bones and Other Precipitates*) who frustrates the persona. Beckett describes the Alba in almost the same terms in "A Wet Night," where she demonstrates that her forte is inspiring passion, not fulfilling it.

10. *Encyclopedia Judaica* (Jerusalem: Keter Publishing House Ltd., Macmillan, 1971), 14: 1330, cited as *Judaica* in the text. Information about "Shekinah"

is drawn from this source and from *The Interpreter's Dictionary of the Bible: An Illustrated Encyclopedia* (New York, Abingdon Press, 1962).

11. Plato's parable in the *Symposium* comes to mind here. Man, who originally comprised both male and female, divided. Love strives to heal that original breach, to reunite man as a "double being."

12. Belacqua's tripartite mind as a whole (and his third being in particular), as it is described in *Dream,* is a parody of a traditional characterization of God. Jorge Luis Borges, in an essay entitled "Pascal's sphere" from *Other Inquisitions,* traces the history of this formula which describes the Divine Principle as a perfectly proportioned infinitude whose "center" is "everywhere and periphery nowhere, an unsurveyed marsh of sloth" (*Dream,* 107–8). Belacqua, we discover, is Father, Son, and Holy Ghost all wrapped up in one indolent form.

13. It can be argued that later Beckett characters, although they do not have women as actual paramours or even muses, find surrogates that suggest this contradictory relationship between male and female. In *Molloy,* the woman Lousse is identified with wisdom (Sophie Lousse). The only thing she asks of the derelict is that she be allowed to contemplate his body from time to time. Molloy feels that he is being drugged by her (she "mollifies" Molloy) with something that ironically recalls the protective herb Hermes gave to Odysseus to combat Circe's charms. On the other hand, Malone, the creator of Sapo and Macmann, scribbles their adventures with a little green Venus pencil, his instrument of creation.

14. In "Sedendo et Quiesciendo," *transition* 21 (March 1932): 65, Belacqua's addiction to Peeping Tomism is referred to as "livid rapture of the Zurbaran Saint-Onan. . . . Rapturous strange death!" Zurbarán is a seventeenth-century Spanish baroque artist who is particularly noted for his portrayal of the mystic, saint, or monk in contemplation. Belacqua's surname, Shuah, is also connected with his identity as Onan, as the name can refer to the wife of Judah (father of Onan).

15. *Fodor's Ireland: 1971,* ed. Eugene Fodor and Robert C. Fisher (New York: David McKay Co.), explains the legend under the rubric "Columbus and the College": "the Collegiate Church of St. Nicholas of Myra, dated back to 1320. . . . In this church, Christopher Columbus is reputed to have prayed before sailing for the West in the *Santa María.* Earlier (1477), Columbus sailed for some time in one of the Portuguese vessels engaged in the 'Atlantic Corridor trade' . . . he certainly called at Galway. . . . One of the Galway navigators, Rice de Culvey, was among the crew of Columbus's ship on his 1492 voyage of exploration" (405).

16. Beckett also mentions Crusoe in "Yellow." The hero laboring to bring his mind under control (in order to be more comfortable before the operation) listens to an asthmatic choking above his hospital room. After his coughing fit passes, the asthmatic will, Belacqua thinks, be able to doze off: "Meanwhile he coughed, as Crusoe labored to bring his gear ashore, the snugger to be" (p. 173).

17. The "dark care" (of Horace) that accompanies Belacqua is the spirit of Lucy, his dead wife.

18. Frank Charles Laubach, *The People of the Philippines* (New York: George

H. Doran Co., 1925), and James A. Le Roy, *Philippine Life in Town and Country* (New York and London: G. P. Putnam's Sons, 1905). "Babailanes" (primitive soothsayers) or "Mabaleean" are tribal mediums or shamans.

19. Stendhal (Henri Beyle), *Oeuvres Complètes: Correspondance,* tome 2 (Paris: Chez Pierre Larrive, 1954), 24: 290. I am indebted to Professor Michael Wood for calling this use of babilan and Stendhal's letter to my attention.

20. The castration fantasy that follows also supports the fact that Belacqua is not physically impotent. In *Dream* he is raped by the Smeraldina and frequents the red-light district. In *More Pricks than Kicks* he makes love to Ruby, and it is hard to believe that he did not give in to the Smeraldina's ardor. Finally, in "Echo's Bones," an unpublished short story that is a sequel to *More Pricks than Kicks,* Beckett plays a final joke on the dead Belacqua by not only making him a father posthumously, but by first involving him in a posthumous conception.

21. Beckett has specifically exploited the parallel between his hero and Swift earlier in "Fingal," where he links the themes of sex, art, and madness. Belacqua's present affair with Winnie is played out against the back-drop of a mysterious romantic triangle in the past (Swift, Stella, Vanessa), which elucidates his sexual maladjustment.

22. T. H. White, *The Bestiary: A Book of Beasts,* trans. and ed. T. H. White, from a twelfth-century Latin bestiary (New York: G. P. Putnam's Sons, 1960), 29. The moral lesson drawn from the beaver's fate tells the good man how to approach God. "Hence every man who inclines toward the commandment of God and who wants to live chastely, must cut off from himself all vices, all motions of lewdness, and must cast them from him in the Devil's face" (p. 29).

23. Voltaire, *Romans et contes,* ed. René Pomeau (Paris: Garnier-Flammarion, 1966), 201.

24. Belacqua's true consummation will be possible, the poem reveals, only if he is "consumed and fused in the white heat/Of her sad finite essence" (ll. 5–6). This conflagration will then lead to a phoenixlike rebirth: "Conjoined in One and in the Infinite" (l. 14).

25. Belacqua has become embroiled with the racy, pretty Winnie (later reported as "dead to decorum" among Belacqua's departed sweethearts); with the little Alba, "not woman of flesh" (p. 58); with the formerly "appetizing" spinster Ruby; and with the pert, athletic (and suddenly crippled) Lucy. Thelma then appears on the scene.

26. It is worth emphasizing that the order of Belacqua's two primary liaisons in *Dream* is reversed in *More Pricks than Kicks.* His platonic passion for the Alba occurs relatively soon in the stories and is superseded by other precarious amours (Alba Perdue appears once more, but only as a bridesmaid at Belacqua's wedding to Thelma). Finally, however, Belacqua winds up with the Smeraldina. The narrator excuses the hero by indicating that she "was the only sail in sight" (p. 189), all the other ladies having died or disappeared. The poet still, though, "look[s] forward to meeting the girls, Lucy especially, hallowed and transfigured beyond

the veil" (p. 195). One wonders how these fantasies about the afterlife sustain Belacqua joined in wedlock to the Smeraldina, who wrote to him earlier: "Oh! Bel . . . I want your body your soft white body Nagelnackt! My body needs you so terrible, my hands and lips and breasts and everything els [sic] on me" (p. 163).

27. Beckett, "Censorship in the Saorstat," *Disjecta: Miscellaneous Writings and a Dramatic Fragment,* ed. Ruby Cohn (London: John Calder, 1983), 84–88.

28. If Beckett suggests directions rather than solutions in his apprentice fiction, he does nevertheless offer the artist a method of a kind that will keep artistic experimentation from being too haphazard. (Whether this method works is another question.) Like Descartes, Beckett develops a positive way to act that begins with negation. He tells the reader in *Dream* what kind of novel he cannot, in good conscience, write, given his perceptions about human nature and his opinions about what art should be. So, like the traditionalists who define an uncircumscribable God by saying what he is not, Beckett focuses on what kind of novel he will not write, in order to point to what he is trying to do (perhaps even before he is mature enough as a writer to do it).

29. I am not suggesting that we never see women presented or satirized in a familiar way in the later work. Beckett makes use of stereotypes of both male and female behavior. The suffering for the sexes, however, is more nearly equal. In the case of love in particular, Molloy provides instructive examples. Love may have been offered to Molloy by Edith or Ruth; perhaps his paramour was even a man. He would have gladly accepted a goat, to know what true love was. As far as physical threat goes, emotion can be dangerous from any quarter. Lousse threatens Molloy, but so does the old charcoal-burner in the forest, whom Molloy brutally rejects.

30. Beckett uses music in *More Pricks than Kicks* to refer alternately to spiritual and to sexual experience to stress Belacqua's inconsistency. Celia's subsequent relationship with Murphy clarifies Beckett's intention. Murphy comes home looking forward to "nocturne, aubade, etc." with Celia as lover. Beckett puns on her name in more than one way, but as a surrogate St. Cecilia her role in creating musical harmony also refers to the harmony of sexual experience. Murphy does not want to work, but "Celia said that if he did not find work at once she would have to go back to hers. Murphy knew what that meant. No more music. This phrase is chosen with care, lest the filthy censors should lack an occasion to commit their filthy synecdoche" (p. 76).

31. This tower perhaps recalls Joyce's omphalos-shaped Martello tower at Sandymont in *Ulysses.* Stephen associates the sea with his dead mother while he is living in the tower, and suffers from his attempts to reconcile his guilt with her memory in his imagination.

32. Beckett, *Watt* (London: John Calder, Jupiter Books, 1963), 224.

5

Watt: Language as Interdiction
and Consolation

Thomas J. Cousineau

Critics have tended to treat *Watt* as an allegory in which human beings'
rationalistic pretensions are ridiculed.[1] What has generally been ignored
in discussions of this novel is that the portrayal of a rational individual
humiliated by an absurd world is only a special case of a more fundamental concern; the true center of *Watt,* of which the concern with rationality
is merely the visible trace, is the suspicion, apparent in all of Beckett's
fiction, that humans are inhabited by a false consciousness. Their true
subjectivity, the support of their capacity for authentic action, has been
suppressed; in its place we find a surrogate self, distorted and made
unreal by the alienating culture whose mark it bears. This emphasis on
the illusory nature of consciousness and on the loss of an original, unre-
pressed subjectivity points to a profound convergence between Beckett's
fiction and several themes that are central to contemporary philosophy
and psychoanalytical theory. Two concepts in particular seem pertinent
to a study of these motifs as they occur in the fiction: first, Jacques Lacan's
notion of the *stade du miroir,* a model that illuminates the phenomenon of
the alienated self, and, second, the dialectic of destruction and renewal
through which Paul Ricoeur has examined the significance of a postmodern faith. Lacan can help us to understand the impasse in psychic
evolution to which the fiction testifies, while Ricoeur can guide us through
a questioning of what remains after this impasse has been recognized.

Essentially, the *"stade du miroir"* treats three moments in the development of infantile consciousness; in the first the "I" assumes a primordial

form, existing as a pure subjectivity; next, this primitive "I" is transformed by its identification with its objective image (whether the image that is seen in an actual mirror or that which evolves from the child's contact with other humans). At this stage the "I" is transformed into a "me"; pure subjectivity becomes fixed in the alienating image of the self. Finally, the subjectivity that has been lost in this second stage is restored "in the universal" through the acquisition of language.[2]

Beckett's fiction issues from the impasse created by the inability of the alienated self to recapture its subjectivity through language; the movement from the second to the third stage has been obstructed, leaving the "I" frozen in the posture of an object, a prisoner of neurosis in the broad sense given to this term by Lacan: "the enslavement of the subject by the situation."[3] The implication that runs throughout the fiction is that alienation is merely reinforced by the acquisition of language, which allows a corrupt culture to seduce the individual with a distorted conception of self. Lacan has commented on this alienating phenomenon in his discussion of an individual whose culture is based on an "enormous objectification" and which induces the individual to "forget his subjectivity": "He will be able to make an efficacious contribution to the common task in his daily work and will be able to furnish his leisure time with all the pleasures of a profuse culture which, from detective novels to historical memoirs, from educational lectures to the orthopedics of group relations, will give him the wherewithal to forget his own existence and his death, at the same time as that to misconstrue the particular sense of his life in a false communication."[4]

Lacan's vision of an oppressive, pseudoscientific culture that ignores subjectivity represents in exaggerated form a possibility inherent in the circumstances under which consciousness must necessarily evolve. In order to accede to symbolic functions of thinking and acting, the individual must acquire a language; yet language is already codified and impersonal, operating according to preestablished rules. It enjoys an objective status seemingly at variance with the promise of subjectivity that it offers. Yet subjective experience is indeed impossible without the presence of language. As Denis Vasse, a follower of Lacan, has suggested in his study of the *stade du miroir,* the most primitive perception of a visual image, if it is to be an organized perception, demands the mediation of language. Hence, when the child perceives him- or herself in the mirror, the object of the perception is not merely an image (the visible features of the body) but an image that has already been transformed by the name that has been given to him or to her by *others.* The child sees, not the fragmented body of earliest perception, but the unified, socialized self who bears a particular name. "He sees the name which he hears."[5] This original discovery of oneself as a subject (which has, in fact been organized by others) is a stage upon which all later psychic development depends. All of the child's experiences of self and of the world, which will seem direct and immediate because of the anaesthetizing effect of habit, will always rely on the mediating role of language and on the others through whom language is acquired. Acceptance of the names that others have given to the self and to things, and acquiescence in the objectification which this implies ("I admit that the world exists for others") is the debt which must inevitably be assumed in order that the child acquire an identity as well as a place for him- or herself within the symbolic system.

In Beckett's fiction, the acquisition of language is conceived negatively as allowing for entry into a collective myth, in the pejorative sense of a system of illusory beliefs. The purpose of fiction is to reenact the loss of the primordial self, to denounce the apparition of its objectlike surrogates as well as the support given to these false selves by a corrupt language, and to await the restoration of subjectivity through an authentic language. The role that Beckett assigns to fiction is profoundly paradoxical in that it requires that language be used in such a way as to unmask the illusions of which language itself is the principal bearer.

The process of "dis-illusionment" that Beckett attempts with respect to language closely resembles the task of demolishing the "myth" of God undertaken by Nietzsche and Freud. For Nietzsche, the Christian God was primarily a vehicle of interdiction, in whose presence an individual cowered abjectly, crushed by the disparity between his or her own weakness and the Creator's omnipotence. Freud, on the other hand, tended to emphasize elements of consolation in the myth; God represented those perfections to which a human aspired but could not hope to glimpse in this world, and He offered, in the form of an afterlife, a promise which made this life bearable. For Ricoeur, the atheism of Freud and Nietzsche provides a method for unmasking "naive religious feeling," understood as the repository of archaic fears and desires.[6] Nietzsche and Freud, in spite of the differences in their methodologies, are united by their common assumption that the cultural dimension of human life, including ethics and religion, rests on a mystification that can be unraveled only by the mistrustful gaze of suspicion. Ricoeur describes their positive contribution as follows:

Nietzsche and Freud developed, in a parallel way, a type of reductive hermeneutics which is both a kind of philology and a kind of genealogy. It is a philology, a method of exegesis and an interpretation to the degree that the text of our consciousness can be compared to a palimpsest beneath whose surface another text has been written. To decipher this text is the task of this special technique of exegesis. But this hermeneutics is at the same time a genealogy, because the distortion of the text arises from a conflict of forces, of impulses and counter-impulses whose origin must be revealed. Obviously, it is not a genealogy in the chronological sense of the word; even when it resorts to the notion of historical stages, this genesis does not refer to a temporal origin but to a virtual source or, better, to an empty space from which the values of ethics and religion arise. To discover this space as empty is the task of the genealogy.7

Beckett follows in the tradition established by Nietzsche and Freud in the sense that he recognizes that the unmasking of God demands a revaluation of culture: fiction, which has often been guilty of suggesting that the "empty space" was a plenitude, must now reveal the archaic impulses by which it has always been structured. Hence, in *Watt,* language is condemned for having served the twin functions of interdiction, through which human weakness is shown, and consolation, through which an illusory refuge from this weakness is offered. Watt's narrative records his journey through a world constituted by a self and by an Other, whose physical representative is Mr. Knott and who decides ultimately what rules shall prevail in their encounter. Throughout the novel Watt accepts uncritically the real existence of the Other while the novel treats it as an "empty space." His fidelity to the Other leads him to search continuously for the "real meanings" which it has concealed in the visible world; from the point of view of the novel this search for the Truth is merely an "effect of language," in the sense that to speak a language is to assume implicitly the existence of an intelligible world, governed by the Other who founds language, and whose rules correspond to the structure of language. Watt's loyalty to this conception of language leads him to find himself surrounded by objects and events that both invite and resist his power of naming. The resulting parody of thinking is aimed not so much at rationalism as at the illusory Other who, in the scheme of interdiction embraced by Watt, appears to regulate the way in which the visible world shall properly be approached; Watt's weakness, his credulous belief in the authority of a figure who possesses a secret knowledge denied to him is similarly parodied. The revelation of the inadequacy of language to account for phenomena in the visible world, which serves as the explicit philosophical subject of the novel, provides metaphorical expression for a more profound intention: the destruction of the authority of the Other, who expresses his power of interdiction through language.

The uncovering of illusion applies equally to those elements of consolation that appear in the novel. When we are not anguishing with Watt over the intractability of the material world, we are listening to stories that take us far from the dilemmas that Watt is incapable of resolving. The various stories in *Watt* oscillate between moments where they appear to be objectively "true," thus satisfying a desire that had been frustrated in Watt's direct encounter with reality, and moments where they are unmasked and revealed as a purely hypothetical, if not illusory, constructions. While Watt remains fixed within a world determined by the twin illusions of interdiction and consolation, the novel itself, through the many inconsistencies of its formal structure, reveals its indifference to the Other, whose purposes language serves, and to the fears and desires which it arouses.

The functions of interdiction and consolation that characterize the language of *Watt* are represented in the opening scene of the novel: "Mr Hackett turned the corner and saw, in the failing light, at some little distance, his seat. It seemed to be occupied. This seat, the property very likely of the municipality, or of the public, was of course not his, but he thought of it as his. This was Mr Hackett's attitude towards things that pleased him. He knew they were not his, but he thought of them as his. He knew they were not his, because they pleased him."[8] The disparity that this passage establishes, between an external world whose nature can be expressed by reference to a presumably objective code ("property very likely of the municipality") and an internal world of subjective aspirations, whose expressions ("his seat") are negated by the former, reflects the movement of interdiction in the novel. The language of the "real world" operates, in this movement, as a censoring mechanism, a massive, ubiquitous system of repression that thwarts or renders ludicrous the efforts of the subject to achieve an accommodation with it. The narrator's allusion to this disparity in the case of Mr. Hackett points humorously to a conflict that Watt will endure pathetically when he attempts to replace the language he is accustomed to using with one that is "more real." At the same time, language is shown in this opening passage to be capable of offering to the uncritical intelligence a haven from the constraints that it has just imposed; Mr. Hackett uses this power of language to create a fragile imaginary world in which what he thinks is not always subordinated to what he knows.

The element of interdiction is felt in *Watt* principally in those episodes in which Watt attempts to satisfy the desire, created by language, to provide a satisfying description of the visible world. Before entering Mr. Knott's house he is shown to possess a technique for choosing among the alternative explanations of phenomena that might logically present themselves; when, for example, he must decide between two explanations of how a locked door came to be open, "he preferred the latter, as being the more beautiful" (p. 37). Once he has entered Mr. Knott's house, however, he finds it increasingly difficult to decide which of his hypotheses to accept. The scene involving the piano tuners provides the first serious threat to his technique. The event itself is unexceptional, but as it enters Watt's mind it undergoes progressive deterioration until only a meaningless succession of discrete elements remains. In effect, he can no longer connect the visible features of the scene, which are the direct object of his perception, with language about the scene, which can come to him only through the mediation of others. He no longer sees the episode as language, as something heard. The weakening connection between individual perception and cultural interpretation leads to several scenes in which the union between words and things, which begins in the *stade du miroir,* ultimately disappears. First Watt finds himself incapable of naming a pot; later, in a scene that recalls Denis Vasse's example of a child looking into a mirror and "seeing the name which he has heard," Watt realizes that he can no longer persuasively ascribe to himself the name which he had once so casually assumed: "As for himself, though he could no longer call it a man, as he had used to do, with the intuition that he was perhaps not talking nonsense, yet he could not imagine what else to call it, if not a man. But Watt's imagination had never been a lively one. So he continued to think of himself as a man, as his mother had taught him, when she said, There's a good little man, or, There's a bonny little man, or There's a clever little man. But for all the relief that this afforded him, he might just as well have thought of himself as a box, or an urn" (p. 83).

Watt's dilemma represents both a crisis and an invitation; it upsets his habitual ways of organizing his experience yet, at the same time, invites him to dispose of his habits and to enter into an order of experience where the desire to name things, and to preserve the correspondence between the individual and the cultural, is no longer felt. Beckett has commented favorably on the achievement of a state in which one looks indifferently on the loss of relation between regions of experience that had previously been bound together; further, he argues that the artist should not attempt to create new harmonies out of the discordant elements of his or her experience.[9] Hence, Watt's response to the breakdown of his habitual world is contrary to Beckett's suggested ideal and to the position that will be adopted by the narrators of the later novels. He refuses to accept the loss of a world that can be taken at "face value" and tries instead to create a new system of words that will maintain the correspondence between perception and interpretation, between the self and its culture.[10]

Watt's failure to profit from the opportunity presented by the resistance of events and objects in Mr. Knott's house is emphasized later in the novel when Sam describes Watt's manner of speaking, which consists of reordering letters within words and words within sentences. A characteristic result is the following: "Dis yb dis, nem owt. Yad la, tin fo trap. Skin, skin, skin. Od su did ned taw? On. Taw ot klat tonk? On. Tonk ot klat taw? On. Tonk ta kool taw? On. Taw ta kool tonk? Nilb, mun, mud. Tin fo trap, yad la. Nem owt, dis yb dis" (p. 168). Sam assures us that even in its most extreme rearrangements Watt's conversation could, with patience, be understood, and the careful reader will verify this claim. The distortions in Watt's speech indicate that he is trying desperately, by creating an alternative language, to remain within the ordinary human world where the mediating function of language is maintained. Unlike Mr. Knott, who has transcended the human world and who never speaks, Watt chatters interminably, continually adopting new verbal stratagems to prevent himself from being overwhelmed by a world whose language he has failed to master. Each new effort at organizing the visible world through language merely amplifies the fear of interdiction that it was intended to dissipate. Events that occur in this world appear to him in the same way that the park bench had appeared to Mr. Hackett: as tantalizing objects that ultimately frustrate his efforts to possess them through language.

The continual frustration to which Watt's attempts at naming inevitably lead are contrasted in the novel with moments of apparent consolation achieved through the successful elaboration of stories. Individual characters use stories as a way of trying to ignore an apparently invincible reality, while the novel itself, by treating its own stories ironically, uses them to reveal the imaginary nature of this reality. Arthur's story, for example, begins with the ostensible purpose of relieving Mr. Graves of the burden of his impotence yet unfolds in such a way as to suggest that this apparent motive is merely peripheral to his main purpose. Arthur himself senses that his story is guided by intentions less obvious than his desire to be of assistance to Mr. Graves. The real interest of the story lies in Watt's response to it; he is very pleased by Arthur's performance and seems not bothered in the least by the story's inappropriateness to its stated purpose. It appeals to him as an ingenious distraction, a complicated narrative filled with comprehensible details that draw his attention away from the dilemmas that he has encountered at Mr. Knott's. This need for distraction is shared by Watt and Arthur: "Watt learned later, from Arthur, that the telling of this story, while it lasted, before Arthur grew tired, had transported Arthur far from Mr. Knott's premises, of which, of the mysteries of which, of the fixity of which, Arthur had sometimes more, than he could bear" (p. 198).

Arthur's remark points to Beckett's conception of stories as merely furtive, temporizing instruments for dealing with a situation that is at once unbearable and inescapable; they provide an imaginary form of consolation. The difficulty that Beckett faces, partially in *Watt* and more extensively in the French novels, is how to use stories in such a way as to avoid the spurious consoling function that they tend to assume. Watt's story about the Lynch family contains some examples of the way in which the difficulty is confronted in this novel. The story originates with Watt's contemplation of the arrangement whereby the food that Mr. Knott does not eat at his mealtime is disposed of. He is instructed to leave the leftovers for a dog; but, as there is no dog living in the house, Watt begins an elaborate series of speculations designed to reveal the system that has been created to ensure that the leftovers are always eaten. He finally concludes that the task of providing a dog is assured by a family named Lynch who maintains a whole kennel of dogs.

The most significant aspect of the assumptions on which this story is based is that they become less and less subjective. Thus, the existence of the Lynch family, which is merely hypothetical, is presented as an incontrovertible fact, as when the narrator adopts a tone of objectivity when describing them: "The name of this fortunate family was Lynch, and at the moment of Watt's entering Mr Knott's service, this family of Lynch was made up as follows" (p. 100). The authority that this story appears to possess is unmasked, however, when the narrator introduces Sam Lynch's daughter Kate, "aged twenty-one years, a fine girl but a bleeder" (p. 102), and then, as if to answer the obvious objection, tells us in a footnote "Haemophilia is, like enlargement of the prostate, an exclusively male disorder. But not in this work" (p. 102). This device of encouraging the reader to believe in the validity of his story and then exposing it as an illusion occurs again when the narrator attempts to explain Erskine's behavior in terms of a metaphor: "Or perhaps Erskine, finding the first floor trying, is obliged to run upstairs every now and then for a breath of the second floor, and then every now and then downstairs for a breath of the ground floor, or even garden, just as in certain waters certain fish, in order to support the middle depths, are now forced to rise and fall, now to the surface of the waves, and now to the ocean bed. But do such fish exist? Yes, such fish exist, now" (p. 120). Throughout the entire novel, in fact, the illusion of verisimilitude is continually deflated, not only by such intrusions as these but also by the narrator's own uncertain position within the novel. *Watt* begins omnisciently; yet, when the narrator describes Watt's experiences at Mr. Knott's, he suggests that he is not an omniscient narrator but merely Watt's biographer.[11] That this admission is itself untenable becomes clear when we recall that the novel records several episodes that Watt could not have observed and that could not, therefore, have been known to Sam.

This unresolvable contradiction in the narrative structure of *Watt* reveals the narrator's indifference to the consolation which his stories are intended to afford. He presents Watt as wanting desperately to restore a lost harmony, yet he leaves the discordant elements of his own stories untouched. While Watt remains trapped by the cycle of fear and desire, struggling to know what a thing is and to describe it "correctly," the narrator ignores all rules and, by so doing, dissipates the power of the illusory Other who lies behind them.

The unmasking of the authority of language that Beckett offers in *Watt* was compared earlier with the denunciation of theism associated with Nietzsche and Freud. He shares with these "masters of suspicion" the view that language serves the discredited supernatural function of accusing humans of weakness and of providing refuge from this accusation. What, then, remains after the origin of this function in archaic human fears and desires has been deciphered? For Paul Ricoeur, who has meditated with remarkable insight on the meaning of modern suspicion, the answer lies essentially in the separation of the concept of the Other, ultimately of God, from the anthropocentricity implied by its association with the fear of interdiction and the desire for consolation. He regards atheism, and its denunciation of false idols, as a moment in the transition from religion, which has been condemned as a cultural edifice erected by archaic impulses, to faith, which involves the acceptance of risk and the belief in a God "who does not protect but who yields us to the dangers of a life worthy of being called human."[12] The vision of a postmodern faith that Ricoeur describes cannot be reduced to a formula (he often comments himself on the dangers of a "new dogmatism"), but the spirit of his vision may be clarified by noting that he takes as his model the "tragic faith" of Job which he juxtaposes with the attachment to "the archaic law of retribution professed by his pious friends."[13] For Ricoeur the essential quality of the God who appears in *Job* is that he exceeds any human standard of measurement. His existence cannot be explained by reference to narcissistic human desires; he exists apart from any human interests that he might be imagined as serving:

> It is this unfolding of being, in the absence of personal concerns and by means of the fullness of the word, which was already at work in the revelation with which *Job* culminates: "Then from the heart of the tempest Yahweh gave Job his answer. He said . . . ." But what does he say? Nothing which can be construed as a response to the problem of suffering and death; nothing which can be used as a justification of God within theodicy; on the contrary, he speaks of an order foreign to man, of a measure which has no human proportion: "Where were you when I laid the Earth's foundations? Tell me, since you are so well informed!" The way of theodicy is closed; even the vision of Behemoth and Leviathan, with which the revelation culminates, has no relation with Job's personal problem; no theology emerges from the tempest, no intelligible relation between the physical and the ethical orders; what remains is the unfolding of all in the fullness of the word, the possibility of an acceptance which would be the first stage of a consolation which was beyond the desire for protection.[14]

The higher form of consolation that Ricoeur discovers in Job has been freed from all infantile fears of punishment and reward; it invites what he calls an "obedience to being," by which he means a silent attentiveness to a word that *is,* which opens the possibility of a dialogue with "being" without reducing itself to the plane of purely human concerns. The relation between God and Job offers a model for this word because in *Job* God speaks to Job but not *about* Job.

The disgust that Beckett expresses throughout *Watt* for a language that is inescapably about human beings and whose dependence on archaic fears and desires renders it undeserving of faith, introduces a period of waiting for a renewed language. The adventure of the self begins in the *stade du miroir* with the discovery of an objectified and alienating image; it reaches an impasse with the acquisition of a language that confirms the subject's captivity within this image. The possibility of an eventual triumph over this narcissistic destiny depends on the capacity for identifying with a word that cannot be confined to its tangible representation: "Thus to say that man is conceived in the image of God means nothing else than this: man cannot conceive of himself according to his own conception, according to his own image. If he does, he dies, like Narcissus. To conceive of oneself in the image of God is to conceive of oneself in the image of nothing which can be seen. It is to conceive of oneself paradoxically in the image of a word which says that it is and who is, a word which affirms being."[15]

Beginning with *Murphy* Beckett has continuously explored in his fiction the predicament of a subject attempting to free itself from its representations and to identify with "being." In that novel, the hero struggles to transcend his conscious, tangible experience and to achieve a level of being in which "he was not free, but a mote in the dark of absolute freedom."[16] In his late short pieces, the same desire to free the subject from the constraints of its alienating images results in the splitting between an "I" that corresponds to Lacan's "primordial form" and a "he" that represents the objectified image into which the subject risks falling:

> I gave up before birth, it is not possible otherwise, but birth there had to be, it was he, I was inside, that's how I see it, it was he who wailed, he who saw the light, I didn't wail, I didn't see the light, it's impossible I should have a voice, impossible I should have thoughts, and I speak and think, I do the impossible, it is not possible otherwise, it was he who had a life, I didn't have a life, a life not worth having, because of me, he'll do himself to death, because of me, I'll tell the tale, the tale of his death, the end of his life and his death, his death alone would not be enough, not enough for me, if he rattles it's he who will rattle, I won't rattle, he who will die, perhaps they will bury him, if they find him, I'll be inside. . . .[17]

The "I" who speaks in this passage recalls Vasse's comment about the fate of Narcissus. He is a subject who exists apart from his reflected image and who in his affirmation that he will not die, claims for himself a destiny reserved for "nothing which can be seen." The precise nature of his survival could probably not be articulated without falling into the pattern of discredited religious sentiment; it can only be approached negatively, as the renewal that follows upon the destruction of archaic desires and their representations, as the unimaginable plenitude that arises out of "lessness."[18] Beckett's fiction resembles contemporary philosophy in its determination to unmask illusions, yet neither the fiction nor the philosophy can pretend to say what lies beyond. The achievement and the limits of both have been admirably suggested by Lacan in a remark on the role of psychoanalysis: "In the recourse which we maintain to a relation of subject to subject, psychoanalysis can accompany the patient as far as the ecstatic limit of the *'You are that'* which reveals to him the cipher of his mortal destiny, but it is not in our power as practitioners to lead him to the moment where his true journey begins."[19]

Notes

1. The first critic to stress the inadequacy of rational thinking as a key to reading *Watt* is Jacqueline Hoefer in "*Watt*," *Perspective* 11, 3 (Autumn 1959): 166–82. The continuing influence of this emphasis may be seen in this recent judgment by Frederick N. Smith: "To read *Watt* as an anti-logic for today's students is to read it as a polemic against our cock-sure belief in our own rationality. It just ain't true, says Beckett"; "Beckett and the *Port Royal Logic*," *Journal of Modern Literature* 5, 1 (February 1976): 108.

2. "L'assomption jubilatoire de son image spéculaire par l'être encore plongé dans l'impuissance motrice et la dépendance du nourissage qu'est le petit homme à ce stade *infans* nous paraîtra dès lors manifester en une situation exemplaire la matrice symbolique où *je* se précipite en une forme primordiale, avant qu'il ne s'objective dans la dialectique de l'identification à l'autre et que le langage ne lui restitue dans l'universel sa fonction de sujet." Jacques Lacan, "Le stade du miroir comme formateur de la fonction du Je," in *Écrits* (Paris: Éditions du Seuil, 1966), 90. Lacan's notion of the universal derives from Hegel; it indicates that the object expressed by language is not "the thing itself" but an abstract essence that language has conferred by negating the thing.

3. "Ainsi se comprend cette inertie propre aux formations du *je* où l'on peut voir la définition la plus extensive de la névrose: comme la captation du sujet par la situation donne la formule la plus générale de la folie, de celle qui gît entre les murs de asiles, comme de celle qui assourdit la terre de son bruit et de sa fureur." Ibid., 96.

4. "Il collaborera efficacement à l'oeuvre commune dans son travail quotidien et meublera ses loisirs de tous les agréments d'une culture profuse qui, du roman policier aux mémoires historiques, des conférences éducatives à l'orthopédie des relations de groupe, lui donnera matière à oublier son existence et sa mort, en même temps qu'à méconnaitre dans une fausse communication le sens particulier de sa vie." "Fonction et champ de la parole et du langage en psychanalyse." Ibid., 162. Translated as "The Function of Language in Psychoanalysis," in *The Language of the Self*, ed. Anthony Wilden (Baltimore: The Johns Hopkins Press, 1968), 45.

5. "Le *nom* est le lieu symbolique, le lieu du sujet où s'opèrent la rupture et le retournement. La structure, ainsi mise en évidence, opère le déplacement constitutif de la reconnaissance: l'enfant ne voit plus l'image de son corps, l'agrégat de ses membres, il voit 'Pierre' ou 'Anne': *il voit le nom qu'il entend*." Denis Vasse, "La loi," in *L'ombilic et la voix* (Paris: Éditions du Seuil, 1974), 120.

6. "En outre, c'est la même figure du dieu qui menace et qui réconforte. Je prends donc la religion comme une structure archaïque de la vie qui doit toujours être surmontée par la foi et qui repose sur la crainte de la punition et le désir de la protection." Paul Ricoeur, "Religion, athéisme, foi," in *Le conflit des interprétations: Essais d'herméneutique* (Paris: Éditions du Seuil, 1969), 432. This essay is probably Ricoeur's most concise statement of a topic, modern suspicion as a source of destruction and renewal, which is recurrent in his work.

7. "Nietzsche et Freud, d'une manière parallèle, ont développé une sorte d'herméneutique réductrice qui est en même temps une sorte de philologie et une sorte de généalogie. C'est une philologie, une exégèse, une interprétation dans la mesure où le texte de notre conscience peut être comparé à un palimpseste sous la surface duquel un autre texte est écrit. Déchiffrer ce texte est la tâche de cette exégèse spéciale. Mais cette herméneutique est en même temps une généalogie, parce que la distorsion du texte procède d'un conflit de forces, de pulsions et de contre-pulsions, dont l'origine doit être désoccultée. Évidemment, ce n'est pas une généalogie au sens chronologique de ce mot; même quand elle recourt à des stades historiques, cette genèse ne ramène pas à une origine temporelle, mais plutôt à un foyer virtuel ou mieux à une place vide, d'où les valeurs de l'éthique et de la religion procèdent. Découvrir cette place comme vide, telle est la tâche de la généalogie." Ibid., 433; my translation.

8. Samuel Beckett, *Watt* (New York: Grove Press, 1959), 7. Further page references will appear within parentheses in the text.

9. Beckett, "Three Dialogues," *Transition Forty-Nine* 5 (December 1949): 97–103; reprinted in Martin Esslin, ed., *Samuel Beckett: A Collection of Critical Essays* (Englewood Cliffs, NJ: Prentice Hall, 1965).

10. Molloy expresses a more resigned, and a more lucid attitude than Watt when he comments on the inevitability of division: "And even my sense of identity was wrapped in a namelessness often hard to penetrate, as we have just seen I think. And so on for all the other things which made merry with my senses. Yes, even then, when already all was fading, waves and particles, there could be no things but nameless things, no names but thingless names." *Molloy* (New York: Grove Press, 1955), 41.

11. "For there we have to do with events that resisted all Watt's efforts to saddle them with meaning, and a formula, so that he could neither think of them, nor speak of them, but only suffer them, when they recurred, though it seems probable that they recurred no more, at the period of Watt's revelation, to me, but were as though they had never been" (p. 79).

12. "Ce serait une foi qui s'avancerait dans les ténèbres, dans une nouvelle 'nuit de l'entendement'—pour prendre le langage des mystiques—, devant un Dieu qui n'aurait pas les attributs 'de la providence,' d'un Dieu qui ne me protégerait pas mais qui me livrerait au dangers d'une vie digne d'être appelée humaine." Ricoeur, "Religion, athéisme, foi," 450.

13. Ibid., 445.

14. "C'est ce déploiement de l'être, en l'absence du souci personnel et par le moyen de la plenitude de la parole, qui était déjà en jeu dans la révélation sur laquelle s'achève le *Livre de Job*: 'Yahvé répondit à Job du sein de la tempête et dit . . .'; mais que dit-il? rien qui puisse être considéré comme une réponse au problème de la souffrance et de la mort; rien qui puisse être utilisé comme une justification de Dieu dans une théodicée; au contraire, il est parlé d'un ordre étranger à l'homme, de mesures qui n'ont pas de proportion à l'homme: 'Où étais-tu quand je fondai la terre? Parle, si ton savoir est éclairé!' La voie de la théodicée est fermée; même la vision du Béhémoth et du Léviathan, dans laquelle culmine la révélation, n'a aucun rapport au problème personnel de Job; nulle théologie n'émerge de la tempête, nulle connexion intelligible entre un ordre physique et un ordre éthique; reste !e déploiement du tout dans la plenitude de la parole; reste seulement la possibilité d'une acceptation qui serait le premier degré de la consolation, par-delà le désir de protection." Ibid., 451; my translation.

15. "Ainsi, dire que l'homme est conçu à l'image de Dieu ne signifie rien d'autre que ceci: l'homme ne peut se concevoir selon sa propre conception, selon sa propre image. S'il le fait, il meurt, tel Narcisse. Se concevoir à l'image de Dieu, c'est bien se concevoir à l'image de *rien* de ce qui se voit. C'est se concevoir paradoxalement à l'image d'une parole, selon une parole qui dit qu'elle est et qui est, qui dit l'être." Vasse, "La loi," 116; my translation.

16. *Murphy* (New York: Grove Press, 1957), 112.

17. *Fizzles* (New York: Grove Press, 1976), 31-32.

18. In an anecdote concerning their attempt to find a French equivalent for "lessness," a word which Beckett had coined as the title of one of his short prose works, E. M. Cioran suggests the elusive, paradoxical significance of this word: "Together we had considered all possible forms suggested by *sans* and *moindre*. None of them seemed to us to come near the notion of the inexhaustible lessness, a combination of loss and infinitude, an emptiness linked with apotheosis." "Encounters with Beckett," translated from the French by Raymond Federman and Jean M. Sommermeyer, *Partisan Review* 43, 2 (1976): 282.

19. "Dans le recours que nous preservons du sujet au sujet, la psychanalyse peut accompagner le patient jusqu'à la limite extatique du *'Tu es cela,'* où se révèle à lui le chiffre de sa destinée mortelle, mais il n'est pas en notre seul pouvoir de practicien de l'amener à ce moment où commence le véritable voyage." Lacan, "Le stade du miroir," 97; my translation.

6

Murphy's Metaphysics

▬

James Acheson

By convention, the omniscient author knows everything about the characters he or she creates, and is in this sense an analogue to God. Normally the author does not suggest that this omniscience extends beyond the world of his or her novel; but in *Murphy,* Beckett gives us to understand that he knows everything about the world at large. "The sun shone, having no alternative, on the nothing new," *Murphy* begins. "Murphy sat out of it, as though he were free . . ." (*Murphy,* p. 5).[1] The tone is comic, the material philosophical: in the novel's opening sentences, Beckett comments boldly and authoritatively on the question of freedom.

But although Beckett possesses ostensible God-like omniscience, in places he ostentatiously limits the amount of information he is prepared to disclose to the reader. An important example is his description of Murphy's mind in chapter 6, where he stresses that he is presenting us not with Murphy's mind "as it really was . . . but solely with what it felt and pictured itself to be" (*Murphy,* p. 76). Though omniscient—though capable of picturing Murphy's mind accurately and objectively—Beckett prefers to describe his character's obviously subjective image of it. His immediate purpose is to suggest that Murphy's image of his mind is a distortion of the reality. Yet he has also a larger purpose—hitherto unrecognized by critics—in describing Murphy's mind in this way. His larger purpose is to demonstrate satirically that it is impossible to draw absolutely certain conclusions about metaphysical issues.

This becomes clear when we examine chapter 6 in detail. Here it is revealed that, in forming his image of his mind, Murphy has drawn heavily on his knowledge of traditional metaphysics. The influence of Leibniz,

Geulincx, and Schopenhauer is especially important; being ostensibly omniscient, Beckett knows their works infinitely better than Murphy does, and is able to turn them against him satirically.

Leibniz is the source of Murphy's belief that his mind is a hollow sphere containing in microcosm the entire universe as it is, was and is to be.[2] "Nothing," Murphy believes, "ever had been, was or would be in the universe outside [his mind] but was already present as virtual, or actual, or virtual rising into actual, or actual falling into virtual, in the universe inside it" (*Murphy,* p. 76). Whether Murphy's mind is really a microcosm is something Beckett never reveals. But in the course of the novel he makes satiric capital of Murphy's interest in Leibniz by stressing that Murphy's *image* of his mind mirrors the world inadequately.

Murphy differs from Leibniz in distinguishing between the actual and virtual of his mind "not as between form and the formless yearning for form, but as between that of which he had both mental and physical experience and that of which he had mental experience only" (*Murphy,* p. 76). But he agrees with Leibniz that "[imagination] imitates, in its own province and in the little world [of the mind], . . . what God [did] in the great world."[3] The three zones of his mind, Murphy believes, are zones of imagination, in which he can create images based on his "actual" and "virtual" experiences with the complete autonomy of God.

Murphy's first zone is a zone of light, in which he subjects to imaginary reprisal people of whom he has had "actual," unpleasant experience. "Here the chandlers were available for slow depilation, Miss Carridge for rape by Ticklepenny, and so on" (*Murphy,* pp. 78–79). His second zone, in contrast, is one of half-light, in which he imagines himself in worlds of which he has only "virtual" (*Murphy,* p. 76) experience: in zone two he pictures himself in Antepurgatory, for example, occupying the position of Belacqua, Dante's archetype of sloth. Zone three, finally, is in darkness: it consists of virtual rising into actual and actual falling into virtual in "a perpetual coming together and falling asunder of forms" (*Murphy,* p. 79) reminiscent of St. Augustine's Chaos.[4] Transposing himself in imagination into this last zone, Murphy has the sensation not of being free, but of being caught up in the actual/virtual flux as a "mote in the dark of absolute freedom" (*Murphy,* p. 79).

To demonstrate that Murphy is mistaken in thinking his image of his mind is an accurate image of the world at large, and more generally, that there are no definitive answers to metaphysical questions, Beckett creates in *Murphy* a fictional world embodying important counterparts to the three zones. Murphy's third zone is for satiric purposes the most important, and has two counterparts in the novel. The first of these is the "big blooming buzzing confusion" Neary speaks of in his farewell speech to Murphy:

> Their farewell was memorable. Neary came out of one of his dead sleeps and said:
> "Murphy, all life is figure and ground."
> "But a wandering to find home," said Murphy.
> "The face," said Neary, "or system of faces, against the big blooming buzzing confusion. I think of Miss Dwyer." (*Murphy,* p. 7)

Neary's contribution to this odd exchange is based on the work of two famous psychologists, Edgar Rubin and William James. In *The Principles of Psychology,* James describes the welter of sense-data with which we are daily assailed as a "great blooming, buzzing confusion,"[5] while Rubin holds that we make sense of sense-data by distinguishing perceptually between "the figure, the substantial appearance of objects, and the ground, the . . . environment in which the [objects are] placed."[6] What Neary is saying is that all our knowledge derives from sense-data, ordered according to figure-ground principles. His comments are comic because it is clear that the only figures of interest to him are female; yet the above passage has a larger significance to the novel as a whole.

Experiments performed by some of Rubin's contemporaries show that the figure-ground distinction is invariably a simplification of what is perceived. "[Experienced] perceptual wholes," they found, "tend toward the greatest regularity, simplicity, and clarity possible under the given conditions."[7] The world as we know it through perception is merely an approximation (because it is a series of approximations of sense-data in different situations) of the world as it really is. But because our perceptual faculties are the only tools we have for making sense of the world around us, we will never be able to gain more than a partial idea of its true nature. Derived from perception, the "actual" and "virtual" experiences of Murphy's mind necessarily mirror the world inadequately.

Beckett makes use of Schopenhauer, another of the philosophers Murphy has studied, to extend his satiric attack. Schopenhauer holds that our senses furnish knowledge "only of relations between individual phenomena and by no means knowledge of the essential nature of things and the universal totality."[8] Perception is limited by human self-centeredness: according to Schopenhauer, the individual's every experience of sense-data is colored by personal predilections and prejudices.[9] Whatever conclusions we reach about metaphysical issues like the mind's relationship to the world at large or the question of freedom are therefore nothing more than self-centered simplifications: this Beckett stresses satirically in reference to Murphy and the other characters.

As an ironic comment on the characters' tendency to simplify, Beckett's account of what happens in *Murphy* is itself a deliberate simplification. Ostensibly *Murphy* relates what happened to a group of "real" people who lived in London, Cork, and Dublin between February and October 1935. Having assumed God-like omniscience, Beckett knows everything these people "did" in the period concerned; yet his narrative is a selection of events. In itself this is not remarkable: every author who tells a story about "real" people must decide what is relevant, and what irrelevant, to his or her purposes. But in *Murphy* Beckett lays special emphasis on the idea that a selection of events has been made, by suggesting that the novel consists of a number of "filmed" and "edited" scenes. *Murphy* abounds in self-conscious flash-backs, close-ups, and long-shots; at one point, Tickle-penny appears "as though thrown on the silent screen by Griffith in mid-shot soft-focus" (*Murphy*, p. 132).[10] The fact that three speeches are described as "expurgated, accelerated, improved and reduced" (*Murphy*, pp. 12, 37, 84) conveys that the characters concerned have had their lines dubbed in, in a compressed and stylistically improved form, by Beckett in the role of "film-editor."

Like Beckett's description of the events in *Murphy,* his descriptions of the characters are self-conscious simplifications. Little more is said of Miss Carridge, for example, than that she has an offensive body odor; of Miss Dew, than that her thighs are misshapen; or of Murphy, than that his clothing is ridiculously outmoded. Beckett pointedly withholds other information about the characters as a means of satirizing their simplified metaphysical opinions, his satire being a counterpart to Murphy's activities in the first zone of his mind. In zone one—the zone of his "actual" experiences—Murphy takes God-like revenge in imagination on the people he knows and dislikes. Similarly, in return for their self-centered tendency to simplify, Beckett vengefully transforms *Murphy's* "real" people into comic caricatures, while ensuring that the story of their activities is set against the largely undistorted background of London, Cork, and Dublin.

Beckett emphasizes that the background is realistic by specifying place names so meticulously as to make it possible for us to follow the characters' peregrinations on street maps of the three cities.[11] Yet it is clear from a passage in chapter 2 that his careful attention to detail is a means of implicating the reader in his satire: "[Celia] entered the saloon bar of a

Chef and Brewer and had a sandwich of prawn and tomato and a dock glass of white port off the zinc. She then made her way rapidly on foot, followed by four football pool collectors at four shillings in the pound commission, to the apartment in Tyburnia of her paternal grandfather, Mr. Willoughby Kelly" (*Murphy,* pp. 11–12).

Some of the details in this passage are acceptably realistic: the "Chef and Brewer" is an actual chain of English pubs, and the description of Celia's lunch and the football pool collectors is well observed and convincing. On the other hand, there is no such district in London as "Tyburnia": the name is a portmanteau of "Tyburn" and "Hibernia" intended partly as a joke about Mr. Kelly.[12] More importantly, though, "Tyburnia" undermines the sense we might have had that *Murphy* has a straightforwardly realistic background—just as the ludicrous surfeit of detail in the above passage contradicts our impression that *Murphy* is a carefully edited film from which irrelevancies have been excised. If we accept too readily the illusion of reality Beckett is offering us, we are guilty of simplifying the data available for critical interpretation. At fault is our complacent tendency to overlook details that do not conform to our preconceptions about realistic fiction.

The picture of London, Cork, and Dublin that *Murphy* presents is a counterpart not just to zone one of Murphy's mind but to zone two as well. The second zone is represented partly by fictitious places such as Tyburnia and the Magdalen Mental Mercyseat, and also by the character Cooper. In contrast to the novel's other characters, who, though comic grotesques, are still recognizably real people, Cooper is a purely imagined creation. He is not simply a caricature: with his unheard-of infirmity—the inability to sit down or take off his hat—he belongs to a fictional world like that of *The Divine Comedy,* where the usual physical laws are overturned. Because Murphy never meets him, Cooper is not a part of his "actual" experience; because he never imagines him, or even a character like him, Cooper is not a part of his "virtual" experience either. Through Cooper, Beckett reaffirms both that Murphy's experience is too narrow for the "actual" and "virtual" of his mind to mirror the world accurately, and that our impression that *Murphy* is a straightforwardly realistic novel is a complacent oversimplification.

Murphy's tendency to simplify his experience is evident not only in his belief that his mind is a microcosm of the world at large, but in his approach to the question of freedom. Partly on the basis of his reading in psychology, Murphy holds that human behavior is deterministically regulated. Thus it is no surprise to find him seeking to confirm one of the findings of the Külpe school of experimental psychology in the act of ordering a cup of tea.

A colleague of Külpe's, Ach, performed experiments to show that in certain conditions people behave deterministically.[13] He presented subjects with a series of cards, each with four different letters, and asked them to mention a particular letter, say "S," whenever it appeared. As each card bearing an "S" was removed from view, the subjects were asked to name the other letters appearing with it. It was found that they had perceived the "S" alone, and had disregarded the other letters. Ach believed their response to the cards had been determined by the experimenter's assigned task. He distinguished four main phases in the task's performance;[14] Murphy remembers three of them as he gives the waitress his order:

> "Bring me," [he said], in the voice of an usher resolved to order the chef's special selection for a school outing. He paused after this preparatory signal to let the fore-period develop, that first of the three moments of reaction in which, according to the Külpe school, the major torments of response are undergone. Then he applied the stimulus proper.
>
> "A cup of tea and a packet of assorted biscuits."
>
> . . . As though suddenly aware of the great magical ability, or it might have been the surgical quality, the waitress murmured, before the eddies of the main period drifted her away: "Vera to you, dear." This was not a caress.
>
> Murphy had some faith in the Külpe school. Marbe and Bühler might be deceived, even Watt was only human, but how could Ach be wrong? (*Murphy,* p. 58)[15]

Vera's response to the stimulus is not a caress (that is, a pleasing mental experience) because it fails to demonstrate that his order has determined her behavior. Instead of attending strictly to the task presented to her, she has responded to the stimulus of the experimenter—the stimulus, perhaps, of Murphy's sex appeal (his notorious "surgical quality"), or perhaps of his magical gaze, mentioned in his horoscope. Surprised, Murphy asks himself how Ach could be wrong. What he forgets is that Ach performed his experiments in controlled conditions in which the stimulus of the experimenter played no part. Under such conditions, people may behave deterministically; but throughout *Murphy,* Beckett avoids omnisciently endorsing conclusions about metaphysical issues, and to emphasize that people may also behave freely, ends the scene as follows: "Vera concluded . . . her performance in much better style than she had begun.

. . . She actually made out the bill there and then *on her own initiative*" (*Murphy*, p. 58; my italics). Murphy, we have been shown, is wrong to assume that human behavior is at all times determined. He has behaved egotistically in treating Vera as the subject of a private experiment rather than as a complex human being worthy of a polite request for biscuits and tea. Characteristically, he is unmoved by the experiment's failure, preferring to ignore evidence that does not accord with his preconceived ideas.

Murphy's enthusiasm for the idea that a human being behaves deterministically is influenced not only by his interest in experimental psychology, but by his interest in philosophy as well. He is especially attracted to the work of Arnold Geulincx, who holds that our every bodily action is "occasioned" by God's intervention between mind and body. The efficacy of our acts of volition is confined to our mental states: we lack the power to initiate bodily actions, but are free to imagine whatever we please.[16]

As Richard Coe has observed, Murphy believes that mental-physical interaction is occasioned not by God, but by another source of "supernatural determination" (*Murphy*, p. 77)—the stars.[17] The novel opens, as we have seen, with the sun having no alternative but to shine, and Murphy imagining that, having withdrawn into his mind, he is free from astrological influence. But by comparing him to a personified heavenly body that is itself deterministically regulated, Beckett implies that Murphy is mistaken: his attempt to achieve freedom through meditation is presented as futile.

Equally mistaken, though, is the reader who concludes from this that Beckett believes in astrological determinism. At the start of the novel it suits Beckett's purposes to imply that human activity is astrologically regulated; but elsewhere he suggests that the world is (in Schopenhauer's phrase) a "kingdom of chance and error" (*WWI*, 1: 417). Celia meets Murphy for the first time when, "chancing to glance to her right she saw . . . a man. Murphy" (*Murphy*, p. 13). Murphy's job at the Magdalen Mental Mercyseat is obtained through a chance meeting with Ticklepenny; he dies when a flow of gas is released into his room by someone accidentally pulling the gas chain rather than the lavatory chain. The reader who fails to notice the ambivalence of Beckett's attitude to astrological determinism is as much an object of satire as Murphy, for such a reader is just as guilty of simplifying his or her experience.

Murphy's sessions in his rocking chair represent an attempt to achieve not only the temporary freedom afforded by imagination, but ultimately, the permanent freedom he believes to follow from the complete transcendence of worldly desire. Though it has become a critical commonplace to note that his faith in the rewards of self-transcendence derives partly from Geulincx, the way in which Beckett draws Spinoza and Schopenhauer, too, into his satire has not been discussed.[18] Geulincx and Spinoza agree that complete self-transcendence is a supreme good; for once an individual has renounced the world, they argue, that individual is able to discover the will and thought of God and make his or her volitions conform to divine reason. What the individual achieves, in Geulincx's terms, is "the unique love of right reason," the equivalent, as S. V. Keeling tells us, of Spinoza's "intellectual love of God."[19] In both Spinoza and Geulincx love of God is clearly distinguished from self-love, which is held to be the root of all moral evil. Murphy, however, is either unaware of this, or has dismissed it from mind on the basis that God does not exist. For, as Beckett's parody of Spinoza in the epigraph to chapter 6 indicates, Murphy's behavior is based not on the intellectual love of God, but on the love of himself.[20]

The self he loves is in Schopenhauerian terms his will-less self: Murphy believes that by loving it, he can attain to complete freedom from deterministic influence. As we have already seen, Schopenhauer believes we are all subject to an inner striving force, "the will to live," which drives us unceasingly toward the gratification of physical and psychological needs. The pleasures that accrue from the satisfactions of will are ephemeral: the satisfaction of our desire for food, for example, is inevitably followed by renewed hunger, our desire for power by a yearning for more power, and so on. As will-motivated (or "willing") subjects we consistently treat people as the means to our own well-being. We are all basically selfish.

Yet it is open to us to deny our selfishness. In search of a better life, Schopenhauer notes, the mystic (of whatever persuasion) traditionally dedicates himself to voluntary chastity, renounces all worldly goods, and learns to welcome every "injury, ignominy and insult" (*WWI*, 1: 493) the world has to offer. As a result of his deliberate denial of the will to live, the mystic's willing self languishes, and his latent will-less self—the part of himself that is free from desire—comes to the fore. Paradoxically, the mystic's asceticism is motivated by self-love; it is, however, love of his will-less, rather than of his willing self, that underlies his behavior.[21] The extreme ascetic undergoes transformation into a "*pure*, will-less . . . timeless *subject of knowledge*" (*WWI*, 1: 231). As such, he is completely free from selfish desire, and totally indifferent to the world at large— which for him fades into "[N]othing" (*WWI*, 1: 532).

Murphy eventually experiences "Nothing." But in a careful selection of "filmic" scenes, Beckett demonstrates first, that the path he follows in pursuit of freedom is one of imperfect asceticism; and second, that his assumption that freedom *from* will is equivalent to freedom *of* will is mistaken. Early in the novel, Murphy is revealed as too weak to undertake voluntary chastity: though his will-less self wants to deny Celia, his willing self craves for her, and it is in answer to this craving that he agrees to abandon his search for freedom temporarily in order to find work. His failure to cultivate indifference to worldly objects is clear from his attempt to defraud a tea shop by paying for one cup of tea, but consuming "1.83 cups approximately" (*Murphy,* p. 60). His inability to welcome insult and suffering is revealed in his meeting with Miss Dew: when her dog eats his biscuits—a circumstance a more dedicated ascetic would regard with indifference—Murphy protests loudly and rudely. He is oblivious to Miss Dew's attempts to palliate her loneliness by establishing contact with a stranger.

The episode with Miss Dew parallels Murphy's efforts to befriend Mr. Endon, whose indifference to the world at large he admires. Murphy believes that Mr. Endon's ostensible invitations to chess represent a desire to admit him to the fellowship of those who are wholly immured in mind; but on the night of their last game, he realizes for the first time that Mr. Endon is interested only in the disposition of the players on the board, and is indifferent to his opponent. The result for Murphy is an unprecedented "torment of mind" (*Murphy,* p. 168), followed by an involuntary trance in which he experiences "Nothing." "His . . . senses . . . found themselves at peace, an unexpected pleasure. Not the numb peace of their own suspension, but the positive peace that comes when the somethings give way, or perhaps simply add up, to . . . Nothing . . ." (*Murphy,* p. 168). In Schopenhauer, this sense of peace is well nigh permanent. But Murphy has reached it by the wrong route, and is thrown into a state of high agitation. After leaving Mr. Endon he finds himself subject to an obscure inner compulsion to remove his clothes and lie naked in the hospital grounds. He tries to call to mind people he has known: Celia, his mother, his father. At best, however, he is only able to picture fragmentary cinematic images: "[s]craps of bodies, of landscapes, hands, eyes, lines and colours evoking nothing, rose . . . as though reeled upward off a spool level with his throat" (*Murphy,* p. 172).

"Seeing" with the mind's eye—the eye of imagination—can be subject, Beckett reveals, to forces beyond one's control, even after one has attained "Nothing." Earlier in the novel, Beckett has noted that "[in] the days when Murphy was concerned with seeing Miss Counihan, he had had to close his eyes to do so. And even now when he closed them there was no guarantee that Miss Counihan would not appear. That was Murphy's really yellow spot" (*Murphy,* pp. 64–65). Murphy's "yellow" (i.e., weak) spot is his refusal to accept that there can be anything but freedom in the mind.[22] He is aware that his imagination is not entirely within his control, just as he is aware that in the third zone of his mind, he is not free, but a mote in the actual/virtual flux. But in his enthusiasm for the idea that freedom is to be gained via self-transcendence, he has chosen to ignore experience that fails to conform to his private amalgam of the theories of Geulincx, Spinoza, and Schopenhauer.

While in the hospital grounds, though, he manages to stop the illusory fragments from appearing, and returns to his garret to meditate. En route (introspectively) to his third zone, to the spurious freedom of inner chaos, he becomes unaware of his surroundings, of the gas pouring into his room. Earlier, Murphy had linked "gas" etymologically to "chaos": ironically, it is "excellent gas, superfine chaos" (*Murphy,* p. 173)—the novel's second counterpart to zone three—that causes his death.

Like Murphy, the novel's minor characters come under satiric attack for failing to transcend their drive to satisfy various needs. Cooper and Miss Carridge are satirized for making no attempt to overcome their need for drink and money, respectively; other characters are mocked for their intense and incessant need for either love or friendship. Neary, for example, is tormented initially by unrequited love for Miss Dwyer and then for Miss Counihan; and later, by a desire for Murphy's friendship. When Murphy is not to be found, Neary suffers an anguish of yearning, and is heavily satirized:

> He writhed on his back in the bed, yearning for Murphy as though he had never yearned for anything or anyone before. He turned over and buried his face in the pillow. . . . [Keeping] his head resolutely buried and enveloped, he groaned: "*Le pou est mort. Vive le pou!*" And a little later, being by then almost stifled: "Is there no flea that found at last dies without issue? No keyflea?"
>
> It was from just this consideration that Murphy, while still less than a child, had set out to capture himself, not with anger but with love. This was a stroke of genius that Neary, a Newtonian, could never have dealt himself nor suffered another to deal him. There seems really very little hope for Neary, he seems doomed to hope unending. . . . The fire will not depart from his eye, nor the water from his mouth, as he scratches himself out of one itch into the next, until he shed his mortal mange, supposing that to be permitted. (*Murphy,* pp. 137–38)

Here need is compared to a flea bite: the sufferer scratches the bite to alleviate the itching, but the flea meanwhile has given birth to another flea, which by biting creates another itch, and so on. Just as there is no end to the fleas' continuing torment, so in Neary's view, there is no end to need. Neary's concept of need derives from Wylie, who uses Proverb 30.15 as a basis for arguing that we are all creatures of need, and that it is our lot no sooner to satisfy one need than to have another take its place. Wylie's theory is self-centered, since it views other people as means rather than ends. Moreover, it is a simplification in that it does not explain, for example, why Celia is allowed to "rest from need" (*Murphy*, p. 175) after Murphy's death; or why Neary's need for Miss Counihan gives way to a need for Murphy, even though Miss Counihan fails to requite Murphy's love. In accordance with Schopenhauer, Beckett implies in the above passage that the cycle of need can be transcended by loving one's will-less self. Neary not only lacks the wit to see this, but is too self-centered to benefit from its being demonstrated to him. He is a "Newtonian" in the sense that he believes, by analogy with Newton's Third Law, that the satisfaction of one need invariably gives rise to the demands of another.

What the transcendence of need presupposes, however, is that humans are free—as Beckett acknowledges at the end of the passage. It may be that man is not permitted to "shed his mortal mange": it may be, in other words, that we are the deterministic slaves of need, and that willed self-transcendence is impossible. If we are free, and some people choose to behave selfishly rather than to deny themselves, the satirist is justified in mocking them. But if we pursue the satisfactions of need deterministically, we cannot be held responsible for our selfishness, and satire is inappropriate. With this consideration in mind, Beckett satirizes some of *Murphy's* characters while arbitrarily sparing others. Thus Neary is attacked for his failure to transcend need, while Wylie, author of the theory to which Neary subscribes, is spared. He is spared in spite of the fact that he is just as selfish as Neary, and as disinclined to asceticism.

Beckett also deliberately alternates between mocking some characters and expressing sympathy for them. He presents Miss Dew, for example, not only as a lonely woman undeserving of Murphy's rudeness, but as a comic grotesque with a charlatan medium's talent for making "the dead softsoap the quick" (*Murphy*, p. 73). Celia, too, is treated ambivalently: Beckett introduces her to us as a comic antithesis to Murphy—as a body, rather than as a mind—but she is ultimately the least satirized character in the novel. According to Ruby Cohn, the reason for this is that Celia's "need of Murphy is less egotistical than that of the others."[23] Celia, says

Cohn, experiences a "catharsis" following the death of the Old Boy;[24] assuming this to be a mystical catharsis, one could argue that she is ultimately saintly. Yet there is evidence in the novel that Celia's need for Murphy drives her to behave just as selfishly as any of the other characters: though Beckett tries to conceal it, she lies to Murphy about Miss Carridge's unwillingness to cheat Mr. Quigley, in order to force Murphy to look for work.[25] In addition, she inconsiderately neglects the lonely Mr. Kelly after moving in with Murphy, and even appears to contemplate killing herself without thought for her grandfather's feelings.

Beckett's hints that Celia is thinking of suicide are important in relation to what Cohn describes as her "catharsis." The first hint appears in chapter 2, when, like the prostitute Martha in *David Copperfield,* the Dickens character she is partly modeled on, she goes down to the banks of the Thames: "Celia's course was clear: the water. The temptation to enter it was strong, but she set it aside. There would be time for that" (*Murphy,* p. 14).[26] Another clue to Celia's intentions is the passage where she tells Miss Carridge that she has been busy: "my swan crossword you know Miss Carridge, seeking the rime, the panting syllable to rime with breath" (*Murphy,* p. 156). The syllable she seeks, of course, is "death."

Clearly, what Beckett is trying to do in these passages is to mislead the "gentle skimmer" (*Murphy,* p. 60)—just as he also tries to mislead us in suggesting that the first twelve chapters of *Murphy* correspond to the twelve houses of the zodiac, and that the events of the novel are astrologically determined.[27] "[All] things hobble together for the only possible" (*Murphy,* p. 155) says Beckett at one point, implying that *Murphy* could not have worked out differently. The only possible end to Murphy's career of self-love, he suggests, is death. Equally, Celia's love for Murphy could end in no other way but her suicide.

But if we have allowed ourselves to be seduced by Beckett's rhetoric—if we do believe at the end of chapter 12 that this is the only possible end for Celia—chapter 13 comes as a surprise. Here we find that Celia has not killed herself, but has returned to the streets, and to visiting Mr. Kelly, instead. The twelfth chapter was to have portended "the only possible," but there are at least two explanations for what actually happens. It may be that Celia's behavior has been deterministically regulated, though by self-interest rather than by the stars: in Wylie's terms we could say that her need for Murphy has been replaced by a need for Mr. Kelly, and that she has shrunk from suicide through a behavioristic horror of pain. Alternatively, she may have achieved, by way of self-transcendent meditation, what Murphy and Neary both fail to: it may be that she has experienced a mystical "catharsis" enabling her to "rest from need" (*Murphy*, p. 175) and freely choose to comfort Mr. Kelly in his declining years. Further explanations are possible, based on different assumptions about need and freedom: to accept any one to the exclusion of the rest is to simplify our experience of the novel.

Another surprise in chapter 13 is Beckett's change of tone. Miss Dew appears in the chapter for the last time, though in a more sympathetic light than earlier. Beckett still scorns her interest in the occult, but in mentioning that her patron, Lord Gall, has threatened to find a new control if she continues to produce unsatisfactory results, presents her more clearly than before as a lonely, pathetic figure. Mr. Kelly, too, is treated more sympathetically. At the start of the chapter, he appears, as earlier in the novel, as a caricatured egotist, with hat too big and coat too small. But when the wind rises suddenly, and his kite blows away, he becomes in pursuit of it a "ghastly, lamentable figure" (*Murphy*, p. 191) Beckett would have us pity.

Whether Mr. Kelly and Miss Dew enjoy freedom of will is not at issue in the chapter; yet it is clear that they both lack the power to control their environment in a way that would ensure happiness. Miss Dew cannot command the spirits to Lord Gall's satisfaction; Mr. Kelly is powerless to control the wind. Soon the latter will die, unable to prevent the imminent failure of his now "tired heart" (*Murphy*, p. 192), and Celia will be left alone. If she had married Murphy and been permitted to leave her sordid profession, she might have found comfort in a child—a child, perhaps, who enjoyed flying kites. But like the other characters, she has been unable to control the course of events, and Beckett's description of her wheeling Mr. Kelly out of the park at closing time, at the command of the attendants, emphasizes how little life has in store for her now. "Celia toiled along the narrow path into the teeth of the wind, then faced north up the wide hill. There was no shorter way home. The yellow hair fell across her face. . . . She closed her eyes. *All out*" (*Murphy*, p. 192). Celia's case is especially pathetic, because she can do nothing to prevent the death of her grandfather, and lacks the financial and educational resources to start a new life for herself in any but a futureless job. It is this fact, rather than Beckett's satiric arbitrariness, or (as Ruby Cohn has suggested) Celia's relative selflessness, that accounts for her being treated with special sympathy throughout the novel.

Beckett's extension of that sympathy in the last chapter to Miss Dew and Mr. Kelly is in fact an expression of sympathy for humankind as a whole. For the command *"All out"* applies not only to Celia, but to humanity generally: whether free or not, none of us can control all the forces that limit our enjoyment of life, or defy nature's command to depart from it. In its earlier chapters *Murphy* is a sardonically omniscient author's demonstration of the impossibility of answering metaphysical questions. But in the final chapter, Beckett allows his satiric mask to drop, and ends the novel as a lament—a personal and sincere, rather than omnisciently ironic lament—for human beings' inability to determine their own happiness and their impotence in the face of death.

Notes

1. All quotations from *Murphy* are from the Calder and Boyars edition (London, 1970). Page numbers are given in the text, preceded by *Murphy*.

2. See "An Elucidation Concerning the Monads" (1714; reprinted in *The Monadology of Leibniz*, trans. H. W. Carr [London: Favil Press, 1930]), 151, where Leibniz writes that each mind is a "living mirror" of the universe. See also "The Principles of Nature and of Grace, Founded on Reason" (1714; reprinted in *The Monadology and Other Philosophical Writings*, ed. Robert Latta [London: Oxford University Press, 1898]), 420–21, where Leibniz observes that, of God, "[it] has been very well said that as a centre, He is everywhere, but His circumference is nowhere." Various philosophers before Leibniz also held the mind to be a microcosm, or monad; but Beckett emphasizes Murphy's special interest in Leibniz in his French translation of the novel. (See *Murphy* [Paris: Minuit, 1947], 119.)

3. "The Principles of Nature," 421.

4. See St. Augustine, *The Confessions*, trans. R. S. Pine-Coffin (Harmondsworth: Penguin, 1970), Book XII.

5. *The Principles of Psychology* (London: Macmillan, 1902), 1: 488. In *The Development of Samuel Beckett's Fiction* (Urbana/Chicago: University of Illinois Press, 1984), 99 n. 32, Rubin Rabinovitz observes that James also speaks of the "great blooming buzzing confusion" in "The World We Live In," an essay included in *The Philosophy of William James* (New York: Modern Library, 1953), 76. "The phrase did not really originate with James," Rabinovitz comments. "[H]e says it was first used by another, unnamed person."

6. Robert I. Watson, *The Great Philosophers from Aristotle to Freud* (Philadelphia: J. B. Lippincott, 1968), 439.

7. Solomon E. Asch, "Gestalt Theory," in *The International Encyclopedia of the Social Sciences*, ed. David Sills (London: Macmillan and the Free Press, 1968), 6: 168.

8. "On the Antithesis of the Thing in Itself and Appearance," in *Essays and Aphorisms*, trans. R. J. Hollingdale (Harmondsworth: Penguin, 1970), 58.

9. See Arthur Schopenhauer, *The World as Will and Idea*, trans. R. B. Haldane and J. Kemp (London: Kegan Paul, Trench, Trübner and Co., 1909), 2: 336.

Hereafter, all quotations will be from this edition; page and volume numbers will be given in the text, preceded by *WWI*.

10. The "Griffith" in this passage is of course D. W. Griffith, whose early silent films are described by Ernest Lindgren in *The Art of Film* (London: George Allen and Unwin, 1963), 72–75. In *Samuel Beckett: a Biography* (London: Jonathan Cape, 1978), 204–5, Deirdre Bair reveals that Beckett's interest in silent film was such that he wrote to Eisenstein and Pudovkin in 1936 to see if he could work with them. Neither producer replied to his letters.

11. See Malcolm Stuart, "Notes on Place and Place Names in *Murphy*," *RANAM* 14 (1981): 227–35. See also J. C. C. Mays, "Mythologized Presences: *Murphy* in its Time," in *Myth and Reality in Irish Literature,* ed. Joseph Ronsley (Waterloo, Canada: Wilfrid Laurier University Press, 1977), 197–218. Mays suggests that some of *Murphy*'s characters are based on real-life citizens of Dublin whom Beckett knew.

12. Tyburn is, of course, the place in London where criminals were publicly hanged; "Hibernia" is another name for Ireland. Beckett is hinting not only that Tyburnia is Mr. Kelly's bit of Ireland in England, but that life for him is not, as for John Gay (see his couplet, "My Own Epitaph"), a jest, but a choke. In the beginning was the pun!

13. See George Humphrey's *Thinking: An Introduction to its Experimental Psychology* (London: Methuen, 1951), 68–83.

14. Ibid., 68.

15. The reference here is not to the character Watt of Beckett's next novel, but to the psychologist H. J. Watt, whose work is discussed in Humphrey.

16. See S. V. Keeling, *Descartes* (London: Oxford University Press, 1968), 234.

17. See Richard Coe, *Beckett* (London/Edinburgh: Oliver and Boyd, 1964), 30.

18. Hugh Kenner was the first critic to discuss at length the part played by Geulincx in *Murphy*. See *Samuel Beckett: A Critical Study* (London: Calder, 1962), 83–84. Most subsequent discussions of the novel make some mention of this philosopher, but do not comment as I do on the role played by Spinoza and Schopenhauer in Beckett's satire.

19. Keeling, *Descartes,* 234.

20. The epigraph is a parody of Spinoza's well-known proposition, "Deus se ipsum amore intellectuali infinito amat," Book V, Prop. 35, of "Ethica Ordine Geometrico Demonstrata."

21. In *WWI*, 1: 504, Schopenhauer describes the will-less self as "our better self." Significantly, Beckett tells us in chapter 5 that "[the] only thing Murphy was seeking was what he had not ceased to seek from the moment of his being strangled into a state of respiration—the best of himself" (*Murphy*, 52). The implication is that Murphy has found in Schopenhauer, as an adult, both purpose and justification for his childhood tendency to asceticism.

22. This is, of course, a variation on the idea that all is yellow to the jaundiced eye.

23. *Samuel Beckett: The Comic Gamut* (New Brunswick, NJ: Rutgers University Press, 1962), 47.

24. Ibid.

25. At the start of chapter 5, Beckett describes Miss Carridge as being "a woman of such astute rectitude that she not only refused to cook the bill for Mr. Quigley, but threatened to inform that poor gentleman of how she had been tempted" (*Murphy*, 47). Since it is Beckett who conveys this information to us, rather than Celia, we accept it as true. But later, when Celia is negotiating with Miss Carridge to rent the Old Boy's room, it emerges that Celia and Miss Carridge have been swindling Mr. Quigley all along, without Murphy's being aware of it (see *Murphy*, 102). Clearly, the earlier description of Miss Carridge as a woman of principle was Celia's rather than Beckett's. Beckett has tried to protect her from the reader's disapproval via a narrative sleight-of-hand.

26. See *David Copperfield* (1849–50; reprint, Harmondsworth: Penguin, 1969), 749. Celia is not the only character to owe something to this novel. Like David, Murphy is born with a caul on his head; Miss Dew resembles Miss Mowcher; and as Victor Sage has pointed out in "Dickens and Beckett: Two Uses of Materialism," *Journal of Beckett Studies* 2 (Summer 1977): 19, Mr. Kelly is based on Mr. Dick.

27. In *Samuel Beckett's* Murphy: *A Critical Excursion* (Athens, GA: University of Georgia Press, 1968), 76, Robert Harrison argues convincingly that the first twelve chapters of *Murphy* "occupy, in sequence, each of the twelve houses of the zodiac, beginning with the House of the Native. . . ."

7

Embers: An Interpretation

███████

Paul Lawley

The critic of *Embers* might be forgiven for feeling that when Hugh Kenner called it "Beckett's most difficult work"[1] he unwittingly sanctioned its neglect. Which would be strange indeed, for one expects the "most difficult work" to attract an appropriately large mass of explication and interpretation. Yet it would not be going too far to say that *Embers* is neglected. To suggest that critics have failed to deal fully with the play because it is difficult would of course be ingenuous (to say the least). On the other hand, it is impossible to tell for sure to what extent the neglect of the play is due to a belief that its difficulties are the result of fundamental flaws— of its being an imperfectly achieved work. Kenner maintains that the piece "coheres to perfection,"[2] but John Pilling disagrees, remarking that *Embers* "is the first of Beckett's dramatic works that seems to lack a real centre";[3] and Richard N. Coe considers the play "not only minor, but one of [Beckett's] very few failures."[4] When I say that this play has been neglected, I mean that it has not been recognized for the achievement it is. In what follows, I shall try to locate its "real centre" and to show how and in what it succeeds. In doing so, it must be noted, I shall be disagreeing with the author's own brief estimate: "It's not very satisfactory, but I think just worth doing. . . . I think it just gets by for radio."[5]

Beckett himself has made the most important point about *Embers*: "*Cendres*," he remarked in an interview with P. L. Mignon, "repose sur une ambiguité: le personnage a-t-il une hallucination ou est-il en présence de la réalité?"[6] The question has an obvious bearing on certain details in the play: Ada moves along and sits down on the shingle noiselessly where Henry makes the expected sound; the episodes concerning Addie certainly do not occur in a realistic way; the hooves Henry hears are the "traditional" BBC coconut shells, butt of so many jokes; and Henry himself finds the "sea" worthy of mention: "That sound you hear is the sea. (*Pause. Louder.*) I say that sound you hear is the sea, we are sitting on the strand. (*Pause.*) I mention it because the sound is so strange, so unlike the sound of the sea, that if you didn't see what it was you wouldn't know what it was."[7] Such details exemplify the nonrealistic, perhaps even antirealistic style we should expect in a radio play by the author of *All That Fall.* They are not, however, any more than in the earlier play, merely the quirky manifestations of an habitual self-consciousness. As Beckett's comment suggests, they serve to open up the large pervasive concerns of the play.

The Addie episodes are more obviously hallucinatory than anything else in the play, yet they are rather more complex than the word "hallucination" might suggest. When Ada asks him "What do you suppose is keeping her?," Henry (but not Ada) hears a "smart blow of cylindrical ruler on piano case" from Addie's music master; Addie herself plays some scales and then a Chopin waltz, number 5 in A Flat Major. "In first chord of bass, bar 5, she plays E instead of F. Resounding blow of ruler on piano case. ADDIE stops playing" (p. 29):

MUSIC MASTER: (*violently*). Fa!

ADDIE: (*tearfully*). What?

MUSIC MASTER: (*violently*). Eff! Eff!

ADDIE: (*tearfully*). Where?

MUSIC MASTER: (*violently*). Qua! (*He thumps note.*) Fa! (*Pause. ADDIE begins again, MUSIC MASTER beating time lightly with ruler. When she comes to bar 5 she makes same mistake. Tremendous blow of ruler on piano case. ADDIE stops playing, begins to wail.*)

MUSIC MASTER: (*frenziedly*). Eff! Eff! (*He hammers note.*) Eff! (*He hammers note.*) Eff! (*Hammered note, 'Eff!' and ADDIE's wail amplified to paroxysm, then suddenly cut off. Pause.*)

ADA: You are silent today.

HENRY: It was not enough to drag her into the world, now she must play the piano.

ADA: She must learn. She shall learn. That—and riding. (*Hooves walking.*)

RIDING MASTER: Now Miss! Elbows in Miss! Hands down Miss! (*Hooves trotting.*) Now Miss! Back straight Miss! Knees in Miss! (*Hooves cantering.*) Now Miss! Tummy in Miss! Chin up Miss!

(*Hooves galloping.*) Now Miss! Eyes front Miss! (*ADDIE begins to wail.*) Now Miss! Now Miss! *Galloping hooves, 'Now Miss!' and ADDIE's wail amplified to paroxysm, then suddenly cut off. Pause.*
ADA: What are you thinking of? (*Pause.*) I was never taught, until it was too late. All my life I regretted it. (pp. 30–31)

The two episodes are aural images of coercion, "domestic" situations which turn into nightmares. The gulf between the domestic and the nightmarish—and yet their strange forced coexistence—is caught in the typically Beckettian bathos of Henry's reaction: "It was not enough to drag her into the world, now she must play the piano"; and Ada's chilling rejoinder: "She must learn. She shall learn. That—and riding." Or of Ada's comment on riding: "I was never taught, until it was too late. All my life I regretted it." The reactions seem out of joint; they lack, one might say, adequate objective correlatives. Consequently there is an eerie gap between piano playing and riding on the one hand and the violence, frenzy, and "paroxysm" of Henry's imaginative realization of them on the other. Of course it is precisely this creative gap that the images are about. Addie's inability to play the right note and ride according to instructions mirrors Henry's inability to find an objective correlative for what is essentially his own creative predicament. The Addie "hallucinations" are images created by Henry of his own situation: like Addie he cannot "eff the ineffable" (a favorite Beckett joke here "amplified to paroxysm"); he can only recruit memories or scenes which are available to him and press them into service by modifying and shaping them into images of the self in creation. (The idea of the coerced artist becomes especially prominent—though it is implicitly present throughout Beckett's work—in the radio plays of the early 1960s: *Words and Music, Cascando,* and *Rough for Radio II.*) But the images of inadequacy are themselves inadequate—they too miss ("Now Miss! Now Miss!") their target—and this creative failure is powerfully suggested in Henry's oddly fractured reaction, "It was not enough to drag her into the world, now she must play the piano." The significance of the line consists not in what piano playing (or riding) means, but in what Henry has made it mean.

The Addie episodes are not realistic, but does it necessarily follow that they are to be seen as totally hallucinatory, merely happenings within Henry's mind, exclusive of anything external? It is important to note that what we hear *is* Addie's voice (and her music / riding master's) and not just Henry's version of it. The distinction is important enough for Beckett to have made it some moments earlier:

HENRY: . . . horrid little creature, wish to God we'd never had her, I use to walk with her in the fields, Jesus that was awful, she wouldn't let go my hand and I mad to talk. "Run along now, Addie, and look at the lambs." (*Imitating* ADDIE'S *voice.*) "No papa." "Go on now, go on." (*Plaintive.*) "No papa." (*Violent.*) "Go on with you when you're told and look at the lambs!" (ADDIE'S *loud wail.* . .). (p. 26)

The moment of Addie's "loud wail" is one of the most haunting in a play full of haunting moments. The difference between imitation and real imagining is a crucial one for Henry, since he needs to believe that others—not just his own invented characters—are with him. We have seen that the Addie episodes are essentially Henry's own unsuccessful images of himself (though they might be based on memories), but he needs to believe that they do concern someone other than himself. Part of the impact of his curious reaction to the piano-playing paroxysm is, I think, the compassion it shows for the child. It cannot be reduced to self-pity. Indeed it is partly because Addie is still, to Henry, another person, that the image is unsuccessful in its own terms. Although he dare not, for purposes of survival, admit his own failing creativity, Henry can imagine and even sympathize with the predicaments of others: it is the lack of impersonality in his imaginings that betrays him and his own failing creativity.

Several details in *Embers* suggest its protagonist's creative decline. Henry repeats a strange line in his story: "Vega in the Lyre very green" (p. 23). Vega is the brightest star in the constellation Lyra, here fading and sickening: the name comes from the Arabic for "the falling (vulture)";[8] and of course the lyre itself is a traditional emblem of artistic creation. Ada contrasts the sea as it was when she and Henry made love by it with what it is now: "It was rough, the spray came flying over us. (*Pause.*) Strange it should have been rough then. (*Pause.*) And calm now" (p. 29). They remember the hollow where they "did it at last for the first time":

ADA: The place has not changed.
HENRY: Oh yes it has, I can see it. (*Confidentially.*) There is a levelling going on! (p. 34)

The hooves which Henry invokes function as, among other things, an index of his power to invoke, his imagination. He can call them up before the conversation with Ada, but not after. And during the conversation:

HENRY: Hooves! (*Pause. Louder.*) Hooves! (*Sound of hooves walking on hard road. They die rapidly away.*) Again! (*Hooves as before. Pause.*)

ADA: Did you hear them?

HENRY: Not well.

ADA: Galloping?

HENRY: No. (pp. 27–28)

But the most complex and important image and index of Henry's creative decline is of course the one involving the embers of the play's title: the story of Bolton and Holloway. "This I fancy," says the thirty-nine-year-old Krapp, "is what I have chiefly to record this evening, against the day when my work will be done and perhaps no place left in my memory, warm or cold, for the miracle that . . . (*hesitates*) . . . for the fire that set it alight" (pp. 15–16). The miracle-fire is a creative fire, the writer's energy, and the next-to-last sentence we hear in the play, as we look at the Krapp who "crawled out once or twice, before the summer was cold," to sit "shivering in the park," is: "Not with the fire in me now" (pp. 18, 20). *Embers* takes up the image and modifies it. The association of fire and warmth with artistic creation is commonplace. For an example—which is itself an allusion—we need go no further than Joyce's Stephen Dedalus: "when the esthetic image is first conceived in [the artist's] imagination . . . [t]he mind in that mysterious instant Shelley likened beautifully to a fading coal."[9] Or Kafka—as might be expected, the inventor of the Bucket-rider is even closer in spirit to Beckett than is Joyce:

> 6 December. From a letter: "During this dreary winter I warm myself by it." Metaphors are one among many things which make me despair of writing. Writing's lack of independence of the world, its dependence on the maid who tends the fire, on the cat warming itself by the stove; it is even dependent on the poor old human being warming himself by the stove. All these are independent activities ruled by their own laws; only writing is helpless, cannot live in itself, is a joke and a despair.[10]

In enacting the "law" (that writing is always dependent on something other than itself) by building up a symbolic image of domestic interdependence, this passage from Kafka's diaries anticipates *Embers,* and indeed much else in Beckett, in a quite remarkable way. It not only brings forth an image which might fairly be taken by anyone as typical of Beckett (compare the first of the poems in *Words and Music*); more importantly, it gives us a succinct and accurate description of the basic structure of all Beckett's plays, a structure generated by the central consciousness (Hamm, Krapp, Henry, Winnie, Mouth, May) in the process of its response to the creative-ontological predicament which we must now attempt to define.

Henry's "unfinished" narrative about Bolton and Holloway ("I never finished it, I never finished any of them, I never finished anything, everything always went on for ever," pp. 22–23) contains the chief symbolic image of *Embers*. He makes three attempts at the story during the play (two before and one after the conversation with Ada), the last ending in an impasse which we can only presume is familiar to him. He starts off (but where is his real beginning?) with the invocation of "an old fellow called Bolton" (p. 22) "standing there on the hearthrug in the dark before the fire with his arms on the chimney-piece and his head on his arms, standing there waiting in the dark before the fire in his old red dressing-gown and no sound in the house of any kind, only the sound of the fire," and "no light, only the light of the fire, . . . an old man in great trouble" (like Kafka's "poor old human being"). "Ring then at the door and over he goes to the window and looks out between the hangings, fine old chap, very big and strong, bright winter's night, snow everywhere, bitter cold, white world, cedar boughs bending under load, and then as the arm goes up to ring again recognizes . . . Holloway . . . (*long pause*) . . . yes, Holloway, recognizes Holloway, goes down and opens" (p. 23).

Holloway is brisk, terse, businesslike, vulgar even: he stands "on the hearthrug trying to toast his arse, . . . fine old chap, six foot, burly, legs apart, hands behind his back holding up the tails of his old macfarlane" (p. 24). But Bolton continues to gaze out through the hangings at the "white world" outside. Henry's cadence is slow but vertiginous: "great trouble, not a sound, only the embers, sound of dying, dying glow, Holloway, Bolton, Bolton, Holloway, old men, great trouble, white world, not a sound" (p. 24). He breaks off the story momentarily, but resolves to "try again." Holloway starts to complain about being called out by his "old friend, in the cold and dark, . . . urgent need, bring the bag, then not a word, no explanation, no heat, no light." Bolton does not explain: the only word he can summon is "Please! PLEASE!" Ignoring him, Holloway complains even more, but his judgment of Bolton's hospitality ("no refreshment, no welcome") merges with Henry's judgment of his own narrative ability: "white beam from window, ghastly scene, wishes to God he hadn't come, no good, fire out, bitter cold, great trouble, white world, not a sound, no good. (*Pause.*) No good. (*Pause.*) Can't do it" (p. 25). Thus the second attempt at the story peters out.

The third and last attempt comes near the end of the play, when Ada has left Henry and the fragments of narrative "rubbish" she had provided for him have been exhausted. It seems he has reached a crisis of imaginative energy, for he can no longer call up even the "sound of hooves walking on hard road" (pp. 21–22) that served to assure him of his creative strength at the beginning of the play. The continuation of the story is strange and, as Henry himself admits, "difficult to describe." Nevertheless it is vital to the understanding of the play and therefore demands to be quoted in toto:

Christ! (*Pause.*) "My dear Bolton. . . ." (*Pause.*) "If it's an injection you want, Bolton, let down your trousers and I'll give you one, I have a panhysterectomy at nine," meaning of course the anaesthetic. (*Pause.*) Fire out, bitter cold, white world, great trouble, not a sound. (*Pause.*) Bolton starts playing with the curtain, no, hanging, difficult to describe, draws it back, no, kind of gathers it towards him and the moon comes flooding in, then lets it fall back, heavy velvet affair, and pitch black in the room, then towards him again, white, black, white, black, Holloway: "Stop that for the love of God, Bolton, do you want to finish me?" (*Pause.*) Black, white, black, white, maddening thing. (*Pause.*) Then he suddenly strikes a match, Bolton does, lights a candle, catches it up above his head, walks over and looks Holloway full in the eye. (*Pause.*) Not a word, just the look, the old blue eye, very glassy, lids worn thin, lashes gone, whole thing swimming, and the candle shaking over his head. (*Pause.*) Tears? (*Pause. Long laugh.*) Good God no! (*Pause.*) Not a word, just the look, the old blue eye, Holloway: "If you want a shot say so and let me get to hell out of here." (*Pause.*) "We've had this before, Bolton, don't ask me to go through it again." (*Pause.*) Bolton: "Please!" (*Pause.*) "Please!" (*Pause.*) "Please, Holloway!" (*Pause.*) Candle shaking and guttering all over the place, lower now, old arm tired, takes it in the other hand and holds it high again, that's it, that was always it, night, and the embers cold, and the glim shaking in your old fist, saying, Please! Please! (*Pause.*) Begging. (*Pause.*) Of the poor. (*Pause.*) Ada! (*Pause.*) Father! (*Pause.*) Christ! (*Pause.*) Holds it high again, naughty world, fixes Holloway, eyes drowned, won't ask again, just the look, Holloway covers his face, not a sound, white world, bitter cold, ghastly scene, old men, great trouble, no good. (*Pause.*) No good. (*Pause.*) Christ! (pp. 38–39)

Hersh Zeifman, for whom *Embers* "dramatizes a quest for salvation, a quest which, as always, ultimately proves fruitless,"[11] sees this scene as "a paradigm of human suffering and divine rejection":

> Bolton's desperate plea to Holloway for help mirrors the confrontation between Henry and his father. Bolton is thus a surrogate for Henry—implicitly identified with Christ as sufferer. Both his name (*Bolt*on) and the fact that he wears a red dressing gown (the color is repeated three times in the text) link him with the Crucifixion (before Christ was *nailed* to the cross, he was dressed in a *scarlet* robe). And Holloway, the recipient of Bolton's supplication, is a surrogate for Henry's father—implicitly identified with Christ as savior. Like Christ, Holloway is a physician, a potential healer of men's souls. But the identification is an ironic one. The Physician of the Gospels exclaimed, "I am the way, the truth, and the life: no man cometh unto the Father, but by me" (*John* 14:6); the physician of *Embers* is a *hollowway*, a way leading nowhere. And whereas Christ's death on the cross at "the ninth hour" represents birth into a new life and the promise of salvation, Holloway's actions, likewise at the ninth hour, result in the death of new life, a universal *denial* of salvation: "If it's an injection you want, Bolton, let down your trousers and I'll give you one, I have a *panhysterectomy* at *nine*." (emphasis added [by Zeifman])[12]

The point is well made: Henry's story introduces a religious dimension into *Embers* by means of an emblematic structure. Zeifman's exegesis concentrates on emblems: the red dressing gown, the encoding names of the characters (Henry/I.N.R.I.), the Physician-figure and the mention of the "ninth hour." This approach fits in well with the creating character's reflexivity in composition—Henry is no doubt meant to be seen to be using emblems. Thus the religious-emblematic reading is illuminating as far as it goes; yet it leaves out rather too much in the way of detail. For example: why does Bolton play with the hanging in the way he does? (Or rather, why does Henry take such trouble to describe what he thinks of as being merely "playing"?) What is the significance of the candle? Of Bolton's eyes? Why does Holloway react as he does? These questions need to be answered if the full significance of the scene is to be drawn out.

Bolton's embers are dead ("Fire out, bitter cold"), and whereas before there had been "no light, only the light of the fire" (p. 23), he now has to create his own light for the interview with Holloway. Thus he starts "playing with the curtain, no, hanging, difficult to describe, draws it back, no, kind of gathers it towards him. . . ." The "difficulty" here, for both

Henry and Beckett, concerns suggestion: "hanging" has a wider application than "curtain," though still specific; the alteration from "draws it
back" to "kind of gathers it towards him" (which also involves a movement toward vagueness) has a similar effect. The alternate "white, black,
white, black" when Bolton plays with the hanging enacts the effect of an
eye blinking, and I think it is to gain this suggestion that Henry's alterations are made: the hanging is a kind of eyelid—a very tired one, and thus
is "kind of gathered" rather than drawn. The implication of this detail is
that, as with the stage-picture of *Endgame,* Henry's story presents an
image of a skullroom in the midst of a wasteland. The wasteland of this
story is a landscape of snow, a "white world"—perhaps this is a Christ-
mas story like Hamm's "chronicle." The inner fire being dead, Bolton is
"playing with" the eyelid/hanging in order to let in the light of the outer
world. The candle he then lights is the last resort, the last creative deed in
a literally "naught(y) world." Holloway is willing to give Bolton an anaesthetic to remove his creativity altogether, thus setting the seal on his predicament. In fact the ambiguity in Henry's narration at this point suggests
that the anaesthetic and the "panhysterectomy" are the same thing: "'If
it's an injection you want, Bolton, let down your trousers and I'll give you
one, I have a panhysterectomy at nine,' meaning of course the anaesthetic." "Anaesthetic" refers back to "injection," but Henry's delay in
saying so has the effect of eliding this idea with that of the "panhysterectomy," as though that concerned Bolton as well. Indeed in an important
sense it does, for anaesthetic is a pun, where an- is a negative prefix: anaesthetic. Both the panhysterectomy Holloway mentions and the anaesthetic he offers Bolton are ways of negating and finally destroying creativity.

It seems that Bolton's plea is not for the an-aesthetic (or the anaesthetic).
We might assume that he is pleading for exactly the opposite: a creative
fire, a warmth and light that Holloway cannot give. And yet we are never
told that: Henry's narrative does not give us the information which is
necessary for an understanding of it. It is as though Henry had again
failed to find an adequate objective correlative for those inner needs
which he is apparently obliged to express. Hence one feels that something
important is being hidden behind the puzzlingly intense reaction of Holloway to Bolton when the latter looks him "full in the eye": "Stop that for
the love of God, Bolton, do you want to finish me? . . . We've had this
before, Bolton, don't ask me to go through it again." Finally, "Holloway
covers his face." We remember Henry's admission: "I never finished any
of them, I never finished anything." So why should Holloway feel that a
look from the "eyes drowned" would "finish" *him*?

I would suggest that the existence of these questions itself indicates their solutions. They exist because Henry's creativity is breaking down and he can no longer maintain his narrative impersonality (but how desperately important to him is that process to which one can only attach a critical tag). The story is coming apart, but at the same time it is managing to produce an image which counterpoints its own failure. Henry is losing his creative impersonality and is consequently moving inexorably into identity with his fictional creation, Bolton. And this process is exactly what is being represented by the story: what Holloway fears—the thing which will quite literally "finish" his identity *as* Holloway—is a merging of identity with Bolton. The narrative image can be said to counterpoint Henry's own creative predicament rather than merely mirror it because it contains an extra element—that of Bolton's pleading. Nevertheless, Henry makes his identity with Bolton more or less explicit: "that's it, that was always it, night, and the embers cold, and the glim shaking in your old fist, saying, Please! Please! (*Pause.*) Begging. (*Pause.*) Of the poor. (*Pause.*) Ada! (*Pause.*) Father! (*Pause.*) Christ!" Henry's own fiction has revealed his begging (the "Please!" is now Henry's) for what it is and always was. Ada's "prophecy" (which Henry seems to ignore) is fulfilled: "The time comes when one cannot speak to you any more. (*Pause.*) The time will come when no one will speak to you at all, not even complete strangers. (*Pause.*) You will be quite alone with your voice, there will be no other voice in the world but yours" (p. 35).

Ada's and Addie's voices have disappeared long since; now Henry cannot even manage impersonations of his fictional characters. All his fictions, from whatever direction, end up merging with him. Ada and Addie seem real enough—particularly the former—as *other* presences, but they are revealed as being essentially projections of his own mind, based on reality though they might be (but what is the Beckettian "reality"?). And his story ("a great one") from which he seems at first so detached, reveals itself in the end to have been all about him. Perhaps it was not so detached from him after all: Ada advising him about his talking, tells him to "see Holloway" (p. 34). One of his inventions commends him to another; "a-t-il une hallucination ou est-il en présence de la réalité?"

Bolt(on) and Hollow(way) are complementary, made for each other. The imagery which portends and attends their merging and Henry's consequent creative collapse relates importantly to, and takes its place within, the symbolic structure of the play. From the skullroom with its window-eyes (and hanging-lids) the narrative focus abruptly contracts, when Bolton "lights a candle, catches it up above his head, walks over and looks

Holloway full in the eye," concentrating on Bolton's own skull, with its "old blue eye, very glassy, lids worn thin, lashes gone, whole thing swimming. . . ." The eye becomes a kind of sea, for, despite Henry's dismissal of tears with a "long laugh," the "whole thing" is "swimming" until "eyes drowned" and "Holloway covers his face." It is as though Holloway himself were drowning in Bolton's eye. Earlier it is when, because of Bolton's playing with the hanging, "the moon [controller of the seas] comes flooding in," that Holloway declares, "Stop that for the love of God, Bolton, do you want to finish me?" In the context of what we have already noted about the merging of the identities of Bolton and Holloway, the pun on "eye" is clear (this is after all an aural and not a visual text): Holloway is indeed drowning in Bolton's "I"—hence the ambiguous "eyes drowned," which could apply to either character but which of course applies to them both: "I's drowned." One might say that the symbolic structure of *Embers* (which is also Henry's own imaginative structure) rests on the punning relation of eye-I to see-sea.

Holloway's terror of drowning in Bolton's eye is Henry's created image of his own terror of drowning in or being drowned by (the distinction is important) the sea. The sound of the sea is the reason why Henry has to keep talking: "Today it's calm, but I often hear it above in the house and walking the roads and start talking, oh just loud enough to drown it, nobody notices" (p. 22). The real sea (but then what is the *real* sea in the play?) colludes with the one in his head: "I'd be talking now no matter where I was, I once went to Switzerland to get away from the cursed thing and never stopped all the time I was there" (p. 22). Indeed what Henry hears—and the listener with him—seems at once like the sea but not the sea. "Listen to it!" he cries at a moment when words seem to fail him, "Close your eyes and listen to it, what would you think it was?" (p. 24). The command comes several times, for as the creator of Dan Rooney is always aware, our eyes too are, in effect, closed. When, at the beginning of the play, Henry addresses the Rooney-ish "old man, blind and foolish" whom he declares to be his father "back from the dead, to be with me . . . in this strange place," he is also addressing the radio listener:[13] "I say that sound you hear is the sea, we are sitting on the strand. (*Pause.*) I mention it because the sound is so strange, so unlike the sound of the sea, that if you didn't see what it was you wouldn't know what it was" (p. 21).

Even as we take up Henry's invitation to construct a visual scene, we are suspicious of a description of "this strange place" which seems so anxious to familiarize it. "Sea" states Beckett's direction baldly, but what we hear in the original BBC production (by Donald McWhinnie) is indeed very "unlike the sound of the sea." "Listen to it!" orders Henry again, "What is it like?" (p. 29). "Like my Hoover," wrote a BBC Third Programme panel member.[14] As we shall see, he or she was not far from the truth. What then does the sea sound mean? Or what does it suggest? Obviously the real sea "means" nothing, but the sea in Henry's head has a palpable significance for him, elusive though that may be.

The salient facts can be pieced together from Henry's monologue. His self-questioning hints at them: "And I live on the brink of it! Why? Professional obligations? (*Brief laugh.*) Reasons of health? (*Brief laugh.*) Family ties? (*Brief laugh.*) A woman? (*Laugh in which* [ADA] *joins.*) Some old grave I cannot tear myself away from? (*Pause.*)" (pp. 28–29). The absence of a laugh confirms the accuracy of the last question, though it is always difficult for Henry to admit this possibility. He favors indirection, describing his father's drowning in the sea as "that evening bathe you took once too often" (p. 22). The evasive irony draws attention to another of the play's significant ambiguities: was Henry's father washed out to sea while taking his evening bathe, or did he commit suicide? Or again, did he allow himself to be washed out while bathing? This death bears a deeply ambiguous relation to suicide, and suicide casts its shadow over the whole play, for it is one of Henry's alternatives—in the end, perhaps, the only action which remains for him.

At this juncture I think some interesting parallels between *Embers* and Tennyson's *Maud* are worth dwelling upon, since they point us in a necessary direction. The propriety of the comparison is first of all formal, for the hero of *Maud*, as Christopher Ricks notes, "is so near madness—and does indeed go mad" ["There's something wrong with your brain," Ada tells Henry (p. 33)]—that it is possible, apt, and compelling for 'successive phases of passion in one person [to] take the place of successive persons.' The dislocations of self in the hero can be turned—with creative appositeness—to something that is lamentably like the company of successive persons."[15] In a footnote Ricks invokes *Krapp's Last Tape,* but *Embers* would have done as well (Tennyson subtitles *Maud* "a monodrama," an apt description of either Beckett piece), and indeed this play provides further remarkable parallels with *Maud.*[16] To begin with, Tennyson's own father's death (of drink) stands in much the same relation to suicide as that of the fictional Henry's father. "Suicide: the word about his father was out before Tennyson was born, and the nature of his father's death was later to haunt him. How much was there of metaphor when people saw his father's drinking as suicidal?"[17] The opening lines of *Maud* are hysterically affirmative: "I hate the dreadful hollow behind the little wood,/ Its lips in the field above are dabbled with blood-red heath,/ The red-ribbed ledges drip with a silent horror of blood,/ And Echo there, whatever is asked her, answers 'Death.'"[18]

The hollow is the place into which his father "dashed" himself down in his madness. "He does not hate a person, but a place," observes Ricks, "—but then the place has a surrealistic lunacy which suggests a bleeding woman."[19] We have already noted the hollow ("There is a levelling going on") and the Holloway in *Embers*. There is also a drip: "Listen to it! (*Pause.*) Close your eyes and listen to it, what would you think it was? (*Pause. Vehement.*) A drip! A drip! (*Sound of drip, rapidly amplified, suddenly cut off.*) Again! (*Drip again. Amplification begins.*) No! (*Drip cut off. Pause.*) Father!" (p. 24).

The question is, what does Henry think it is? We assume the drip is water, but compare Hamm in *Endgame*: "Something dripping in my head, ever since the fontanelles . . . Splash, splash, always on the same spot. . . . Perhaps it's a little vein. . . . A little artery."[20] The *Embers*-sea also has lips—and not only lips: "Listen to it! (*Pause.*) Lips and claws! (*Pause.*) Get away from it! Where it couldn't get at me! The Pampas! What?" (p. 28). Henry's later description of the sea-sound as "this . . . sucking" (p. 33; "Like my Hoover"?) compounds the suggestiveness. His intensely physical revulsion from a place or thing, as if it were some sexually devouring female (vagina dentata?) presents a parallel to the lines in Tennyson—"I hate the dreadful hollow. . . ." The sea does not wait passively to receive him but seems physically to pursue him and to insinuate itself into his mind.

Despite Henry's obsession with his father's death, the relationship between the two of them appears to have been far from harmonious:

> Father! (*Pause.*) You wouldn't know me now, you'd be sorry you ever had me, but you were that already, a washout, that's the last I heard from you, a washout. (*Pause. Imitating father's voice.*) "Are you coming for a dip?!" "Come on, come on." "No." Glare, stump to door, turn, glare. "A washout, that's all you are, a washout!" (*Violent slam of door. Pause.*) Again! (*Slam. Pause.*) Slam life shut like that! (*Pause.*) Washout. (*Pause.*) Wish to Christ she had. (p. 25)

The father is not blamed for his harshness; in fact by imagining the reproof (which parallels, at least verbally, Henry's outburst at his own child, "remembered" a few moments later) Henry acquiesces in it: though "an old man, blind and foolish," the father still holds sway (like the Freudian superego) in the son's mind. Henry's need for his father makes him at times even servile. On the other hand, there are traces of a grudge borne against his mother. He wishes to Christ she had slammed life shut on him by "washing him out" (aborting him: a violent joke in the context of his father's last "evening bathe" and his own sea-haunted mind). There is an interesting pun concerning her (noticed by the *TLS* reviewer on the play's first appearance in print[21]): "Father! (*Pause.*) Tired of talking to you. (*Pause.*) That was always the way, walk all over the mountains with you talking and talking and then suddenly mum and home in misery and not a word to a soul for weeks" (p. 26).

"Mum" is the termination of talking. Is she also the termina*tor* of talking, formerly his father's and now Henry's own? Henry's only other reference to his mother is similarly indeterminate and suggestive: "We never found your body, you know, that held up probate an unconscionable time, they said there was nothing to prove you hadn't run away from us all and alive and well under a false name in the Argentine for example, that grieved mother greatly" (p. 22). What "grieved mother greatly"? Was it the suggestion of the father's abandonment of the family? Or the fact that the body was never found? If the latter, was her grief because "that held up probate an unconscionable time"? Henry tells us that he got the money, and presumably his mother knew he would: her grief would in that case bespeak her concern for him. But does he hold against her something unspecified concerning his father?

The "psychologizing" of characters is almost always a wrong move in the discussion of Beckett's plays, but this particular line of speculation does point toward a very relevant (and not specifically psychological) question about the significance of the sea in *Embers*. In Buck Mulligan's words: "Isn't the sea what Algy calls it: a great sweet mother?"[22] Or rather, for Henry, a great devouring mother? Perhaps we have here another version of that obsessive Beckett image, the imperfect birth,[23] with Henry striving to free himself completely from the womb of the mother-sea which is at once devouring and seductive. At this point it will help to consider how the *Embers*-sea contrasts with the "oceanic" feeling discussed by Freud:

> . . . originally the ego includes everything, later it separates off an external world from itself. Our present ego-feeling is, therefore, only a shrunken residue of a much more inclusive—indeed, an all-embracing—feeling which corresponded to a more intimate bond between the ego and the world about it. If we may assume that there are many people in whose mental life this primary ego-feeling has persisted to a greater or less degree, it would exist in them side by side with the

narrower and more sharply demarcated ego-feeling of maturity, like a
kind of counterpart to it. In that case, the ideational contents appropriate to it would be precisely those of limitlessness and of a bond
with the universe—the same ideas with which my friend elucidated
the "oceanic" feeling.[24]

In their vastly different media, Beckett and Freud (after Romain Rolland,
who is the friend he mentions) both use the sea as a covering metaphor for
the external world as perceived by the abnormal or extraordinary (using
those words in the most literal sense possible) mind. It represents the
"non-self" that may at any moment engulf the self. The crucial diver-
gence, of course, is in the attitudes toward that prospective engulfment.
For Freud, insofar as he follows Rolland's lead, it is nothing to be feared;
indeed, the promised sensations of "limitlessness and of a bond with the
universe," immediately recognizable as the great aims of one strand of
European romanticism, seem nothing if not positive—although Freud
himself is skeptical.[25] Both romantic abandon and Freudian sobriety
stand in stark contrast to the horror of Beckett's Henry: "Listen to it! . . .
Lips and claws! . . . Get away from it! Where it couldn't get at me!"
   The contrast has not prevented David J. Alpaugh from attempting a
Freudian critical analysis of *Embers*. This approach introduces a moral-
istic note that is alien not only to this play but to all Beckett's drama.[26]
But if *Embers* resists a Freudian reading, the relation of Henry's sea in the
play to the "oceanic" feeling is nonetheless worth consideration. Anton
Ehrenzweig accords the latter concept an important place in his theory of
artistic creation, thus bringing it within the orbit of our concern:

Freud spoke of an "oceanic" feeling characteristic of religious experience; the mystic feels at one with the universe, his individual existence
lost like a drop in the ocean. He may re-experience a primitive state of
mind when the child was not yet aware of his separate individuality,
but felt at one with his mother. Fantasies of returning to the womb
may have this mystic oceanic quality. It is now widely realised that
any—not only religious—creative experience can produce an oceanic
state. In my view this state need not be due to a "regression," to an
infantile state, but could be the product of the extreme dedifferentiation in lower levels of the ego which occurs during creative work.
Dedifferentiation suspends many kinds of boundaries and distinctions; at an extreme limit it may remove the boundaries of individual
existence and so produce a mystic oceanic feeling. . . .[27]

Some fine exegesis by Hersh Zeifman indicates that ideas of this sort are not altogether foreign to *Embers*. The last lines of the play are very puzzling:

Little book. (*Pause.*) This evening. . . . (*Pause.*) Nothing this evening. (*Pause.*) Tomorrow . . . tomorrow . . . plumber at nine, then nothing. (*Pause. Puzzled.*) Plumber at nine? (*Pause.*) Ah yes, the waste. (*Pause.*) Words. (*Pause.*) Saturday . . . nothing. Sunday . . . Sunday . . . nothing all day. (*Pause.*) Nothing, all day nothing. (*Pause.*) All day all night nothing. (*Pause.*) Not a sound. (*Sea.*) (p. 39)

Zeifman notes that in the poem "Calvary by Night," included in the short story "A Wet Night" (*More Pricks than Kicks*), Beckett speaks of the death of Christ as being a "re-enwombing" in "the water/the waste of water,"[28] a plumbing of the depths, in other words: "Keeping in mind the image of Christ's death as a descent into water, the 'plumber' [at the end of *Embers*] is thus seen to refer to Jesus, who was crucified on Friday at the ninth hour. Christ therefore 'plumbs' the waste ('the waste/the waste of water'). But 'waste' also refers to the significance of his death. For on Saturday, the day of waiting, there is nothing; but there is likewise nothing on Sunday, the day of resurrection, the day on which Christ should rise from the dead and regain paradise for man."[29] (The "waste" is of course also the word Henry uses and has used.) After this "re-enwombing" there is no rebirth.

Ehrenzweig also connects the "oceanic" feeling with a reenwombment ("fantasies of returning to the womb . . ."), and he goes on to assert that the "creative experience can produce an oceanic state." He discards the notion (adopted by Alpaugh) that such experience is "infantile" and goes on to claim that the oceanic state "could be the product of the extreme dedifferentiation in lower levels of the ego that occurs during creative work." The idea of "dedifferentiation," which "suspends many kinds of boundaries and distinctions," and "at an extreme limit . . . may remove the boundaries of individual existence and so produce" the oceanic feeling, is recognizable as a neo-Freudian reformulation of one of the major preoccupations of romanticism (which we noted earlier in connection with Freud's own account).[30] It is interesting to note that the radical formal and stylistic responses of several modernist writers to epistemological and ontological problems closely related to the romantic ones were described by one great modern poet in terms strikingly similar to those used by Ehrenzweig in his theory. W. B. Yeats (editor of Blake and admirer of Shelley) wrote in 1936 of modern artistic attitudes toward the external world and its relation to the perceiving subject: "Change has come suddenly, the despair of my friends in the 'nineties part of its preparation. Nature, steel-bound or stone-built in the nineteenth century, became a flux where man drowned or swam; the moment had come for some poet to cry 'the flux is in my own mind.'"[31] He had written earlier, in 1932:

> Certain typical books—*Ulysses,* Virginia Woolf's *The Waves,* Mr.
> Ezra Pound's *Draft of XXX Cantos*—suggest a philosophy like that of
> the Samkara school of ancient India, mental and physical objects alike
> material, a deluge of experience breaking over us and within us,
> melting limits whether of line or tint; man no hard bright mirror
> dawdling by the dry sticks of a hedge, but a swimmer, or rather the
> waves themselves. In this new literature . . . as in that which it super-
> seded, man himself is nothing.[32]

"The flux is in my own mind"; man is "a swimmer, or rather the waves themselves . . . man himself is nothing." Compare Beckett on Bram van Velde in *Three Dialogues*: "But if the occasion appears as an unstable term of relation, the artist, who is the other term, is hardly less so."[33] (Where Yeats's artist is a swimmer, Beckett's is a "fodient rodent," with his "warren of modes and attitudes."[34]) Against the identityless mind-flux of the swimmer-become-waves must be set Yeats's evocation of his own creative state: "I have been cast up out of the whale's belly though I still remember the sound and sway that came from beyond its ribs, and, like the Queen in Paul Fort's ballad, I smell of the fish of the sea."[35] Yeats's depths, as the context of this passage makes clear, are mythical and national-cultural ones, but the shared metaphor is the point of interest. In the process of creation Yeats retains his own identity, Jonah-like, in the whale's belly, before being cast up to perfect it in prophecy. He is aware, with a creative awareness, both of the sea and of the solid mass that prevents its invasion, "from beyond [the] ribs," of his identity. In a sense the whale's ribs, in this state of immersion, are the new boundaries, during the creative state, of that identity—hard, basic, regular, and reassuring.

Returning to *Embers,* we can now consider, in the light of Yeats's images, Henry's strange yet urgent need for hard, regular sounds, seemingly to offset the undifferentiated "sucking" roar of the "lips and claws" of the sea: the "violent slam of door" he imagines twice as his father calls him (its antithesis) a "washout"; Addie's music master "beating time lightly with ruler as she plays" (p. 29; and his "tremendous blow of ruler on piano case"); Ada's strong point at school, "geometry, I suppose, plane and solid. . . . First plane, then solid" (p. 31); their lovemaking ("Years we kept hammering away at it," p. 34); Henry's desire to go for a row (p. 34); his childish response to Ada's question, "Did you put on your jaegers, Henry?": "What happened was this, I put them on and then I took them off again and then I put them on again and then I took them off again and then I put them on again and then I—" (p. 27); the remorseless drip that he invokes; Bolton's playing with the hanging ("Black, white, black, white"); the scrunching sound of the shingle as Henry walks. Most obvious of all is the sound of hooves that Henry invokes repeatedly, "hooves walking on hard road." We hear them in Addie's nightmare riding lesson ("amplified to paroxysm")—again imagined by Henry. They are the index of his imaginative power—at the end of the play he cannot hear them. They must be rhythmically regular; his strangest fancies are about hooves marking time: "Train it to mark time! Shoe it with steel and tie it up in the yard, have it stamp all day! (*Pause.*) A ten-ton mammoth back from the dead, shoe it with steel and have it tramp the world down! (*Pause.*) Listen to it!" (p. 22).

And later, having called up the hooves again:

HENRY: Could a horse mark time? (*Pause.*)
ADA: I'm not sure that I know what you mean.
HENRY: (*irritably*). Could a horse be trained to stand still and mark time with its four legs?
ADA: Oh. (*Pause.*) The ones I used to fancy all did. (*She laughs. Pause.*) Laugh, Henry, it's not every day I crack a joke. (p. 28)

Ada reduces Henry's frantic obsession to a joke. Indeed it is she who tries to seduce him into abandoning himself to the sea in an insinuatingly powerful passage that makes explicit the antithesis of the dedifferentiated "sucking" ocean and the rhythmic solidity of individual identity:

ADA: It's silly to say it keeps you from hearing it, it doesn't keep you from hearing it and even if it does you shouldn't be hearing it, there must be something wrong with your brain. (*Pause.*)
HENRY: That! I shouldn't be hearing that!
ADA: I don't think you are hearing it. And if you are what's wrong with it, it's a lovely peaceful gentle soothing sound, why do you hate

it? (*Pause.*) And if you hate it why don't you keep away from it?
Why are you always coming down here? (*Pause.*) There's something
wrong with your brain, you ought to see Holloway, he's alive still,
isn't he? (*Pause.*)

HENRY: (*wildly*). Thuds, I want thuds! Like this! (*He fumbles in the
shingle, catches up two big stones and starts dashing them together.*)
Stone! (*Clash.*) Stone! (*Clash. "Stone!" and clash amplified, cut off.
Pause. He throws one stone away. Sound of its fall.*) That's life! (*He
throws the other stone away. Sound of its fall.*) Not this . . .
(*Pause.*) . . . sucking!

ADA: And why life? (*Pause.*) Why life, Henry? (pp. 32–33)

Ada's arguments are designed to deprive Henry of arguments, and her
questions to deprive him of answers. To her last, quiet, terrible question
there *is* no answer, for his "life" is only to be found in the thuds he wants.
Ada's voice is "low" and "remote" (p. 26) throughout, like the sound of the
sea. In a sense she *is* the sound of the sea, its siren-voice. Her invitations to
Henry are almost sexual—and yet something else too. Her voice carries
the promise of inevitable oblivion:

ADA: Underneath all is as quiet as the grave. Not a sound. All day, all
night, not a sound. *(Pause.)*
HENRY: Now I walk about with the gramophone. But I forgot it today.
ADA: There is no sense in that. (*Pause.*) There is no sense in trying to
drown it. (p. 34)

She even makes jokes:

ADA: Who were you with just now? (*Pause.*) Before you spoke to me.
HENRY: I was trying to be with my father.
ADA: Oh. (*Pause.*) No difficulty about that. (p. 35)

It is against such insinuations that Henry sets the thudding stones of the
real, solid identity he aspires to. His aspiration is heroic in its pertinacity,
as well as occasionally absurd, for everything and everyone, even his
"wife," seems intent on luring him into the "lips and claws." This is the
central dynamic of the play: the struggle between Henry's constant desire
for a "hard" differentiation of identity and the insidious but seductive pull
(or sucking) of "oceanic" dedifferentiation that finds its low remote voice
in Ada.

We have been considering the *Embers*-sea by the side of passages in which two other modern writers use in metaphoric form the ancient idea of the sea as creative element or agent of rebirth—Ehrenzweig in his psychoanalytic theory of artistic creation and Yeats in his impressionistic critical view of modernism (with his account of his own creative state). The Beckettian sea seems to be in complete contrast: although, as Hersh Zeifman's explication of the end of the play suggests, Beckett is well aware of the traditional connection of the sea with creativity, his sea in *Embers* is felt to be almost actively hostile to the creative endeavor of the central consciousness. It is, in fact, anticreative. Yet it is for this very reason that it can be regarded as a major element in the creative process. For without the sea Henry would presumably have no need to create. In the dialectical sense, it is the prime mover of his invention and the *sine qua non* of the play's dynamic. It is, we might say, the reason why Henry is "obliged to express."[36] Indeed it *is* the obligation.

We have reached what I think must be considered the core of the play. it is not easy to grasp because it is realized almost entirely by means of the image. What Beckett said of Denis Devlin's poetry in 1938 can be applied to *Embers*: "It is naturally in the image that this profound and abstruse self-consciousness first emerges with the least loss of integrity. To cavil at Mr. Devlin's form as over-imaged (the obvious polite cavil) is to cavil at the probity with which the creative act has carried itself out . . . and indeed to suggest that the creative act should burke its own conditions for the sake of clarity."[37]

The polarization of "probity" and "clarity" ("art has nothing to do with clarity, does not dabble in the clear and does not make clear . . ."[38]) is prompted by a nagging awareness of the "obvious polite cavil." However, in affirming the "probity with which the creative act has carried itself out" (not, notice, "has been carried out") in *Embers,* in emphasizing its dogged adherence to the image as the least inadequate approach to the ineffable, we need not apologize for any absence of clarity. The "real centre" of the play is defined by its symbolic organization, the logic of its images.

Is *Embers* then essentially an example of "play as dramatic poem"? Surely not, for any attempt to locate and define its "real centre" must take into account the radical ambiguity that we made the starting point of our investigation. This ambiguity manifests itself in the metatheatrical current that ultimately *de*-centers the play's symbolic structure. Let us return for a moment to the religious theme pointed out by Zeifman. As we saw, this operates on an emblematic rather than a symbolic level, and in doing so reminds us that the symbolic structure of *Embers* is to be seen as

Henry's as well as Beckett's; its reflexivity suggests an invention of the protagonist rather than a "secret meaning" of the playwright's. Thus the religious dimension of Henry's story points again to the pivotal ambiguity of the whole play: how much of what the audience hears is really Henry's invention? Our examination has still not indicated the full extent of this ambiguity.

Consider the opening of the play:

> *Sea scarcely audible.* HENRY'S *boots on shingle. He halts. Sea a little louder.*
> HENRY: On. (*Sea. Voice louder.*) On! (*He moves on. Boots on shingle. As he goes.*) Stop. (*Boots on shingle. As he goes, louder.*) Stop! (*He halts. Sea a little louder.*) Down. (*Sea. Voice louder.*) Down! (*Slither of shingle as he sits . . .*). (p. 21)

The sea sound is given (becoming progressively louder) and the sound of the "boots on shingle" is introduced against it: is this perhaps just another of the "hard" sounds Henry needs to set against the sucking sea sound? Is not the shingle another of his inventions? His instructions, "On! . . . Stop! . . . Down!," which we automatically assume to be exhortations to his body, might after all be exhortations to his imagination. They resemble, we might feel, the orders of a director to his special-effects department. We become aware of our role: the listener hears the aural effect and instantly constructs the obvious cause. Shingle sound: footsteps; footsteps: body. The cause/effect process itself moves in steps. Its workings are underlined by the very absence of sound at the arrival of Ada. The directorial character of Henry's instructions is confirmed by their coming in pairs; the pattern recurs throughout the play—the hooves, the drip, the slamming door, Bolton's pleas, Bolton himself, Holloway, Ada, Christ, all are invoked twice. Finally, if, as the recurring pattern hints, the shingle is Henry's invention, what of the sea itself? We recall the note of anxious (self-) assurance in "I say that sound you hear is the sea, we are sitting on the strand." Is the sea perhaps the desperate fictional definition Henry seizes upon for his obligation, the definition in which the nature and characteristics of his "strange place" originate and from which they follow? We must entertain the possibility that the whole geography of the play, strand, bay, and sea is a fiction of the central consciousness rather than merely an evocative setting for the action. Indeed the play's "action" might properly be said to be the process of fictionalization and its gradual, inevitable failure.

What, in the light (or half-light) of these instabilities, are we to make of the story of family disruption that underlies Henry's predicament, the train of events that led to the disappearance and probable suicide of his father? Is this really what happened to his father? "We never found your body, you know," remarks Henry, "that held up probate an unconscionable time, they said there was nothing to prove you hadn't run away from us all and alive and well under a false name in the Argentine for example, that grieved mother greatly." The "for example" introduces a note of selfconsciousness which might go unnoticed were it not for Henry's later plans to escape the sea sound: "Get away from it! Where it couldn't get at me! The Pampas! What?" Henry's father may be "in the Argentine *for example,*" and Henry himself thinks about escaping to the Pampas.[39] To suggest an implicit identification here of Henry with his father might be fanciful were it not for another, more telling detail. Henry addresses his "silent" father: "You would never live this side of the bay, you wanted the sun on the water for that evening bathe you took once too often. But when I got your money I moved across, as perhaps you may know" (p. 22). Toward the end of the play Ada recalls Henry's father "sitting on a rock looking out to sea" (p. 36), but Henry finds a geographical anomaly when he takes up the story: "Left soon afterwards, passed you on the road, didn't see her, looking out to. . . . (*Pause.*) Can't have been looking out to *sea. (Pause.)* Unless you had gone round the other side. (*Pause.*) Had you gone round the cliff side? (*Pause.*) Father! (*Pause.*) Must have I suppose" (p. 37). Ada's tactic has been to contest Henry's fiction: by sending his father round the cliff side in her account, she identifies him with Henry, who (perhaps as a gesture of independence) is now apparently living on that side of the bay. She seems to be trying to induce in Henry his father's resignation just before the suicide, a resignation that combines in its physical manifestation the solidity Henry craves with the impending loss of consciousness he fears: "Perhaps just the stillness, as if he had been *turned to stone*" (p. 36; my emphasis). And later: "Perhaps, as I said, just the great stillness of the whole body, as if all the breath had left it" (p. 37).

By the end of the play the identification of Henry and the fictional father is almost complete. Ada has described the sea (ending with a phrase familiar from Henry's story): "Underneath all is as quiet as the grave. Not a sound. All day, all night, not a sound" (p. 34); Henry's last words echo her: "Nothing, all day nothing. (*Pause.*) All day all night nothing. (*Pause.*) Not a sound." Finally we hear "sea," nothing else.

What is the implication of the identification of Henry with his father? *Embers* opens with Henry trying to be with his father, "an old man, blind and foolish . . . simply back from the dead, to be with me, in this strange place. . . . Just be with me" (p. 21). It is as though Henry needs the presence of the father-audience as a guarantor of his own existence. As their names hint, Ada and Addie may not be wife and daughter at all, not even imagined wife and daughter, only father-surrogates: Ada is an "inside-out" anagram of Dad and Addie a rhyme for Daddy. And Henry himself? Is he perhaps just another of the fictions? Ruby Cohn notes that "Henry is a name derived from German *Heimrih,* meaning head of the family":[40] he too is a father or father-surrogate—his own. The head of the family is its creator—a patriarchal perspective in which Henry acquiesces. Thus it is creation that is Henry's obligation, or, to put it more precisely, the obligation of the imperfect consciousness whose creator-surrogate "Henry" is. For "Henry" is, in Alain Robbe-Grillet's phrase, a "provisional being,"[41] the "existence by proxy"[42] of the creator who is obliged continually to create himself.

Yet to conclude in such a way would be to lose sight of the ambiguity upon which, as Beckett himself pointed out, *Embers* rests. I have emphasized the metatheatrical elements because these lead us more readily to the core of the play—its concern with the creative-ontological obligation—but the complementary emphasis needs to be made on the elements of realism. The realism of *Embers* is important for the critic because it is necessary to Henry. His ability to maintain the realistic otherness of Ada, and indeed of the silent father who is his imagined audience for part of the play, serves as an index of his creative power. When these "other" presences desert him and he is finally left alone with his own voice, unable even to call up the coconut-shell hooves, he knows that the end is approaching. It is the *Not I* situation in embryonic form. Not I but He or She or They. The aim of Henry the artist in multiplying the voices is indeed exactly this: realism. His need is to objectify himself and those others, to make himself and his creations *real.* They are his *company,* social and theatrical.

We took as our starting point Beckett's own observation about *Embers.* Zilliacus also notes it, but contends that "the ambiguity of *Embers* . . . can hardly be central to the work, as its author claims," because "some of Ada's lines . . . must make most listeners assume that she is present in Henry's mind rather than 'on the strand.'"[43] Yet her voice, though very different in intonation, inescapably exists within the same aural dimension as Henry's (and ought to in any production). This being so, why should his voice really be any more substantial a proof of "existence" than hers? And are their sounding voices any more potent than the silent presence of the father "in this strange place" in the opening minutes of the play? (This is one of the work's weirdest effects.) "Le personnage a-t-il une hallucination ou est-il en présence de la réalité?" As we have seen, even "le personnage" himself can be regarded as a kind of "hallucination." We recall Yeats's description of modernist nature as "a flux where man drowned or swam" and where the poet, swimmer-become-wave, cries "the flux is in my own mind." If the object has dissolved, how can the subject remain solid? In Beckett's own words, "if the occasion appears as an unstable term of relation, the artist, who is the other term, is hardly less so." Presenting as it does the tenacious but futile struggle, through fictions of the self, for survival and identity amid both outer and inner flux, *Embers* embodies the central Beckettian preoccupation.

Notes

1. *Samuel Beckett: A Critical Study* (London: John Calder, 1962), 174.

2. *Critical Study,* 174.

3. *Samuel Beckett* (London: Routledge and Kegan Paul, 1976), 98.

4. *Beckett* (London: Oliver & Boyd, 1964), 102.

5. Quoted in Clas Zilliacus, *Beckett and Broadcasting: A Study of the Works of Samuel Beckett for and in Radio and Television* (Abo, Finland: Abo Akademi, 1976), 76.

6. Quoted in *Beckett and Broadcasting,* 83.

7. *Krapp's Last Tape and Embers* (London: Faber and Faber, 1965), 21. All references, cited parenthetically in text, are to this edition.

8. OED etymology. Compare "The Vulture" in *Echo's Bones* (1935): "dragging his hunger through the sky / of my skull shell of sky and earth" (*Collected Poems in English and French* [London: John Calder, 1977], 9). Himself a scavenger of narrative "rubbish," Henry too imagines a "skull shell" (see below). Birds of prey are a recurring motif in Beckett's work. Their qualities are those to which the terminal artist must aspire. Here, for example, is Malone on Sapo: "But he loved the flight of the hawk and could distinguish it from all others. He would stand rapt, gazing at the long pernings, the quivering poise, the wings lifted for the plummet drop, the wild reascent, fascinated by such extremes of need, of pride, of patience and solitude" (*Molloy, Malone Dies, The Unnamable* [London: Calder and Boyars, 1959], 191); hereafter, *Trilogy.*

9. *A Portrait of the Artist as a Young Man* (1916) (Harmondsworth: Penguin, 1960), 213.

10. *The Diaries of Franz Kafka, 1910-23,* ed. Max Brod, trans. Joseph Kresh and Martin Greenberg (Harmondsworth: Penguin, 1964), 397-98.

11. "Religious Imagery in the Plays of Samuel Beckett," in *Samuel Beckett: A Collection of Criticism,* ed. Ruby Cohn (New York: McGraw-Hill, 1975), 90.

12. "Religious Imagery," 92.

13. For "you" the French version (by Beckett and Robert Pinget) has "on." *La dernière bande suivi de Cendres* (Paris: Éditions de Minuit, 1959), 38.

14. Quoted in Zilliacus, "Samuel Beckett's *Embers:* A Matter of Fundamental Sounds," *Modern Drama* 13 (1970): 221.

15. *Tennyson* (London: Macmillan, 1972), 249.

16. There is also an interesting coincidence of fact concerning the two works: *Embers* was written in 1959, twenty-six years after Beckett's own father's death; *Maud* was written in 1854–55, twenty-three years after Tennyson's father's death. (In *Krapp* the son plays back the taped account of his mother's death thirty years after the event.) It is intriguing to note that "within a week after his father's death [Tennyson] slept in the dead man's bed, earnestly desiring to see his ghost, but no ghost came. 'You see,' he said, 'ghosts do not come to imaginative people'" (Hallam Lord Tennyson, "Materials for a Life of Alfred Tennyson," draft version, quoted by Ricks in *Tennyson,* 28).

17. *Tennyson,* 2.

18. *Tennyson: A Selected Edition,* ed. Christopher Ricks (London: Longman, 1989), 516–17.

19. *Tennyson,* 253. See also Jonathan Wordsworth, "'What is it, that has been done?': The Central Problem of *Maud,*" *Essays in Criticism* 24 (1974): 356–62.

20. *Endgame* (London: Faber and Faber, 1964), 35.

21. Anon., "The Dying of the Light," *Times Literary Supplement,* January 8, 1960, 20.

22. James Joyce, *Ulysses: The Corrected Text,* ed. Hans Walter Gabler (London: Bodley Head, 1986), 4.

23. Maddy Rooney remembers "one of these new mind doctors" lecturing on a little girl patient: "The trouble with her was she had never been really born!" (*All that Fall* [London: Faber and Faber, 1965], 36–37); and Malone feels he is "far already from the world that parts at last its labia and lets me go." "Yes," he affirms, "an old foetus, that's what I am now, hoar and impotent, mother is done for, I've rotted her, she'll drop me with the help of gangrene, perhaps papa is at the party too, I'll land head-foremost mewling in the charnel-house, not that I'll mewl, not worth it." "The feet are clear already, of the great cunt of existence" (*Trilogy,* 190, 226, 285). The phrase "never been properly born" is buried in the "Addenda" of *Watt* (1953 [London: Calder and Boyars, 1963]), 248; and the idea is surely present in the climactic image of *Godot:* "Astride of a grave and a difficult birth" (*Waiting for Godot* [London: Faber and Faber, 1965], 90). Beckett spoke to Lawrence E. Harvey of "a presence, embryonic, undeveloped, of a self that might have been but *never* got born, an *être manqué*" (*Samuel Beckett: Poet and Critic* [Princeton, NJ: Princeton University Press, 1970], 249); and he explained to Hildegard Schmahl, the first German May in *Footfalls* (*Tritte*), with reference to the "new mind doctor" C. G. Jung and the lecture he had made Mrs. Rooney speak of, that "this girl wasn't *living*. She existed but didn't actually live." (See Walter D. Asmus, "Practical Aspects of Theatre, Radio and Television: Rehearsal Notes for the

German Première of Beckett's *That Time* and *Footfalls* at the Schiller Theater Werkstatt, Berlin," trans. Helen Watanabe, *Journal of Beckett Studies* 2 [Summer 1977]: 83–84, reprinted in *On Beckett: Essays and Criticism,* ed. S. E. Gontarski [New York: Grove Press, 1986], 335–49.)

24. *Civilization and its Discontents,* trans. Joan Riviere, ed. James Strachey (London: Hogarth Press, 1963), 5.

25. "I may remark that to me this seems something rather in the nature of an intellectual perception, which is not, it is true, without an accompanying feeling-tone, but only such as would be present with any other act of thought of equal range. From my own experience I could not convince myself of the primary nature of such a feeling" (*Civilization and its Discontents,* 2).

26. For example, Alpaugh finds that Henry's consciousness is "infantile," "his sense of a private self . . . hypertrophied and over-defined, the boundaries of his ego having been too tightly drawn through a revulsion to the omnipresent sea of anti-self" ("*Embers* and the Sea: Beckettian Intimations of Mortality," *Modern Drama* 16 [1973]: 320). The *Embers*-sea seems to attract psychoanalytical interpretations. There is also John Fletcher's oedipal approach in "Interpreting *Molloy,*" in *Samuel Beckett Now,* ed. Melvin J. Friedman (London: Chicago University Press, 1970), 163.

27. *The Hidden Order of Art: A Study in the Psychology of Artistic Imagination* (St. Albans, England: Paladin, 1970), 304.

28. The narrator of the story refers to it, with a strong dose of irony, as "this strong composition." *More Pricks than Kicks* (1934; reprint, London: Calder and Boyars, 1970), 65.

29. "Religious Imagery," 93.

30. René Wellek wrote of "the great endeavor to overcome the split between subject and object, the self and the world, the conscious and the unconscious. This is the central creed of the great Romantic poets in England, Germany and France" (*Concepts of Criticism,* ed. Stephen G. Nichols Jr. [London: Yale University Press, 1963], 220).

31. Introduction to *The Oxford Book of Modern Verse 1892–1935,* chosen by W. B. Yeats (Oxford: Clarendon Press, 1936), xxviii; reprinted in *W. B. Yeats, Selected Criticism* (London: Pan, 1976), 228.

32. "Introduction to *Fighting the Waves,*" in *Explorations* (London: Macmillan, 1962), 373.

33. *Proust and Three Dialogues with Georges Duthuit* (London: John Calder, 1965), 124.

34. *Three Dialogues,* 124. The "fodient rodent" is from *Rough for Radio II* in *Collected Shorter Plays* (London: Faber and Faber, 1984), 122. Here a creature called Fox (Vox?) speaks of tunneling for his goal, "age upon age, up again, down again, little lichens of my own span, living dead in the stones" (p. 119). The artist as excavator or burrower is another Beckettian leitmotif. In *Proust* he speaks of "the labours of poetical excavation" (p. 29) and states that "the only fertile research is excavatory, immersive, a contraction of the spirit, a descent" (p. 65). He

spoke to Harvey "of the attempt to find [the] lost self in images of getting down, getting below the surface, concentrating, listening, getting your ear down so you can hear the infinitesimal murmur. There is a gray struggle, a groping in the dark for a shadow" (*Poet and Critic,* 247). The decisive comment comes in *The Unnamable:* "Are there other pits, deeper down? To which one accedes by mine [a pun?]? Stupid obsession with depth" (*Trilogy,* 295).

35. "A General Introduction for My Work," in *Essays and Introductions* (London: Macmillan, 1961), 524. Yeats is describing his state of being when speaking blank verse—especially that of his own earlier plays ("For Deirdre and Cuchulain and all the other figures of Irish legend are still in the whale's belly," p. 525). But that his image applies also to the creative state itself is, I think, clear. Later in the same essay he says that Mallarmé "had topped a previous wave" and that the young English poets of the 1930s "attempt to kill the whale" by ignoring "what the Upanishads call 'that ancient Self'" (pp. 525–26).

36. In *Three Dialogues* B[eckett] speaks of "[t]he expression that there is nothing to express, nothing with which to express, nothing from which to express, no power to express, no desire to express, together with the obligation to express" (p. 103).

37. "Denis Devlin," *transition* 27 (1938): 293; reprinted in *Disjecta: Miscellaneous Writings and a Dramatic Fragment,* ed. Ruby Cohn (London: John Calder, 1983), 94).

38. "Denis Devlin," 293.

39. The BBC broadcast script, which preceded the text published by Faber, had "Venezuela" for "the Argentine" and "Tibet" for "The Pampas." Of the latter change, Zilliacus notes that Elmar Tophoven informed him "that the change was made because SB wanted to avoid undue topical associations with the Dalai Lama" (*Beckett and Broadcasting,* 89). Although this accounts for one of the alterations, it does not indicate why he specifically chose "the Argentine" and the Pampas" (where Henry would hear hooves and more hooves). The significant factor is presumably the geographical relation between the places: having changed "Tibet" to "The Pampas," why then change "Venezuela" to "the Argentine"? I would contend that the geographical tie-up, like most of Beckett's internal correspondences, is more than just a mechanical device. In any case, if one thing emerges from the study of Beckett's composition-processes, it is that his second thoughts are invariably better—more refined and more careful—than his first.

40. *Samuel Beckett: The Comic Gamut* (New Brunswick, NJ: Rutgers University Press, 1962), 250.

41. "Samuel Beckett, or 'Presence' in the Theatre," in *Samuel Beckett: A Collection of Critical Essays,* ed. Martin Esslin (Englewood Cliffs, NJ: Prentice-Hall, 1965), 115.

42. The phrase is Beckett's own. Harvey reports his using it "repeatedly" in conversation (*Poet and Critic,* 247).

43. *Beckett and Broadcasting,* 83.

8

The Orphic Mouth in *Not I*

Katherine Kelly

Hung eight feet above the stage, fixed by a spotlight, the mouth in Samuel Beckett's *Not I* is like the ghost of a diminished Orpheus drastically reduced from his ancient fame and glory. In Ovid's version of the myth, Orpheus triumphs over his suffering through the power of his poetry that continues, even from his dead tongue, to charm "the multitude of beasts, stones and trees." The story of the mythic poet has three parts. In the first, Orpheus is described as singing to the accompaniment of his lyre, the beauty and power of which attracts and charms the wild and insensible elements in nature. In the middle section, he descends to the underworld in pursuit of his lost wife, Eurydice, where, although his song succeeds in moving the king and queen of darkness to release her, he is unable to keep the conditions for her return, and finally leaves Hades without her. The third movement begins with his dismemberment by the Maenads after which it is written that his head floated downstream singing, while all of nature mourned him. He descends to Hades for the last time, making his way to Elysium where he is reunited for eternity with his beloved wife.

Mouth undergoes the first part of the third movement of the myth, that of dismemberment and descent into an underworld, but she makes her journey in solitude, unmourned by nature, society, or, for that matter, by the reader / spectator who finds her image and her music painfully comic. "We laugh," Bergson has said, "every time a person gives us the impression of being a thing." Mouth is somewhere between person and thing, eliciting neither a wholly detached nor an entirely sympathetic reaction to her plight. We want to laugh at the isolated object on stage, but its painful history eclipses our amusement. She has only one companion in her misery—the Auditor—a tall, standing figure shrouded in the folds of a full-length *djellaba*. The action of the play consists of Mouth's rapid, staccato uttering of short phrases and Auditor's raising of his arms at those moments when, as the stage directions indicate, Mouth most vehemently refuses to speak in first person: "What! . . . Who? . . . No! . . . She!"

Her isolation is complete in spite of her compulsive speech since that, too, is inaccessible to her audience and even to herself. She pours it out with "half the vowels wrong," the audience staring at her "uncomprehending." Like Orpheus, she is at once the instrument and the song played upon it, but her instrument is fractured, and her song is, by her own account, doomed to fail. It fails to reunite her with the world outside of her, just as it fails to make whole the fragments in her skull.

In his portrayal of the Orphic figure, Beckett has varied in a significant way the structure of Ovid's myth by discounting all but the torment of its third movement. Orpheus's heroic relation to the life around him is replaced by Mouth's utter isolation from nature and society. Far from charming the gods of her underworld, she suspects that they manipulate her reality as "part of the same wish to . . . torment." As for Elysium—it is inconceivable in this work. Beckett's disfigurement of Ovid's heroic story is his own grimly comic myth of Orpheus in which the poet's voice, while obliged to express, has not even a command of coherent speech, let alone story and thought as vehicles of expression.

These remarks, focusing on the written text of the play as the reader experiences it, will make only an occasional reference to its stage spectacle which has already received critical attention.[1] While it is true that Beckett intended the words to be spoken so quickly as to be nearly incomprehensible to a stage audience, a careful reading of them gives the reader not more, but a different quality of comprehension by concentrating on the narrative remains of what was once (apparently) a human history. Although any work for the theater is essentially three-dimensional, a one-dimensional study of the language in *Not I* is a study of its most active element. What really moves in this play is not bodies or stage props, but words.

As critics have noted,[2] Mouth, though not the first of Beckett's autobiographers, bears an unusual resemblance to the protagonist of her own story. Although Krapp, the constipated hero of *Krapp's Last Tape,* makes no attempt to disguise the fact that he has put himself on tape in order to relive in solitude all the old miseries of his older selves, Hamm, more typically, tells in *Endgame* a story that metaphorically conceals the anguish of his own life. It takes the form of an ongoing chronicle of a father and son who sought shelter in Hamm's room. As long as he exists, Hamm can never complete his chronicle because it represents his wish to prevent the regeneration of life that is, by extension, his desire to terminate his own existence. Maddy, the obese heroine of the radio drama *All that Fall,* tells the story of her fictional child Minnie whose death is a metaphor for the terminal hopelessness of Maddy's grotesque preoccupation with fertility and reproduction. Winnie of *Happy Days* also has a make-believe child, Mildred, who has a doll. While playing with her doll, a mouse runs up Mildred's thigh in what appears to be (if it is meant to be anything at all), an allegory of sexual violation, disguising trauma behind the same kind of happy, innocuous mask that conceals Winnie's suffering. In contrast to these earlier fictionalizers, Mouth's storytelling is not metaphorical. The elements of her story, from her premature birth to something very like death, constitute the actual shape of her life in her consciousness.

The autobiographical history that Mouth attempts to attribute to a fictional "She" is made up of a number of incidents that, when taken together, sum up what she calls a "typical" life, sharing with the comic world of Leopold Bloom an unremarkable mundanity foregrounded by the mythic frame that surrounds it. It begins, predictably enough, with her birth, which was premature and was followed by her childhood in an orphanage where she and the other waifs were taught to believe in a merciful God. Except for rare wintertime babbling, she drifts around in silence, surviving miraculously, even in supermarkets. At one point, she stood trial and, when asked to enter a plea, simply waited to be led away. Except for the time when she was supposed to be enjoying herself but in fact was not (a mysterious, possibly sexual occurrence), the rest of her memories are of Croker's Acres, the scene of her descent. She was there at dusk, watching her tears dry on her upturned palms, and on an April morning gathering cowslips—or was she hurrying toward a distant bell? Then she found herself face down in the grass, with all the light gone out. Mouth's story of her ineffectual search for love and comfort in a lifetime clouded by guilt epitomizes the history of the suffering voice on stage and all of Beckett's characters for whom life must not only be lived, but talked about as well.

In spite of her efforts to insist that she is not telling her own story, the identity of Mouth with "She" comes slowly into focus in the first part of the monologue. It is first hinted at quite early in the piece by means of a physical correspondence between her story and the spectacle on stage. Drifting around in a field, "suddenly, gradually" all the light went out.

The ray of light that Mouth began to perceive after all natural light was extinguished shines from the spotlight trained on the mouth; likewise, her inability to sense her physical position corresponds to the audience's inability to see anything of the speaker at all except her mouth. Mouth fails in her attempt to fictionalize herself by revealing, perhaps unwittingly, that her heroine's predicament is identical to her own as the audience perceives it. Her narrative becomes a more explicit description of her stage appearance, "whole body like gone . . . just the mouth [. . .] stream of words."[3] Mouth has "no idea . . . what she was saying" until, finally, it tells the story of itself, "she began trying to . . . delude herself . . . it was not hers at all . . ." (p. 81). Yet Mouth persists in telling what appears to be a stubborn lie: that she is not speaking of herself, but of someone else. Curiously, the fictionalizing impulse survives the ontological instability that threatens to blow the remains of the heroine's "self" into pieces. Stories, like habit, die hard, especially if one is a writer and stories are one's habit. Whatever delusions and confusions Mouth may be suffering, she persists in her refusal to relinquish third person, perhaps because she must refuse, being habitually addicted to storytelling, or perhaps because she chooses to refuse, recognizing in storytelling the means of gaining a distance from the chaos of memory and experience that her brain generates.

One of the effects of Mouth's transparent denial of her fragmented self is to attach to that denial the aspect of suffering; to give her, even in this eccentric and austere work, the status of a feeling being. The first person pronoun, in itself unimportant, is associated with a series of hurts and disappointments; specifically, with the absence of love and the exception that "tender mercies" will alleviate the pain of existing. The particular kind of hell inhabited by Beckett's heroines is created by their eternally thwarted desire for love, mercy, and renewal, yearned for in the form of children, spring and morning. Winnie, Maddy, and Mouth, are all Earth mothers of sorts. Maddy never tires of contemplating the reproductive habits of barnyard animals. Terrestrial Winnie, rooted in a mound of scorched grass, shares Maddy's fascination with animal life.

Mouth's metaphorical descent into the underworld occurs on or near a mound of grass in Croker's Acres while she is looking for cowslips. She has been "sucked under" more completely than Winnie, leaving behind nature and a three-dimensional sense of her existence in space. Avoiding "I" could be Mouth's linguistic strategy for avoiding pain. She is, after all, Maddy's old wish come true, for Maddy wanted to be released from her "dirty old pelt" through a violent fragmentation of her being: "oh to be in atoms . . . ATOMS!" Disguised autobiography, something that would, in spite of Mouth's resistance, tell "how it was," appeals to her as it appealed to Hamm and Winnie, both of whom are lonely like "the solitary child who turns himself into children, two, three, so as to be together, and whisper together in the dark." Storytelling is resorted to as a self-protective device, but it is finally ineffective as a pain killer; the head still buzzes and roars; the beam still ferrets; the brain strains; even memory occurs in disorienting flashes.

Mouth's denial of "I" paradoxically heightens the reader's sense that she has a feeling self, that she is, in fact, human and not inhuman; but Beckett's pronominal preoccupation began long before he wrote this play. Critics[4] have traced Beckett's wrestling with the "cursed first person" from his 1932 contribution to *transition* magazine through the trilogy of novels in which the Unnamable, after threatening to desert "I," returns to it in despair, and finally to *Film,* a cinematic equivalent of the self-splitting Mouth, in which the protagonist is "sundered into object (O) and eye (E)."

The nine co-authors of the 1932 manifesto in *transition* magazine entitled "Poetry Is Vertical" proposed to use a revolutionary, even a hermetic language as a diving instrument in their desire to evade the influence exerted by the self in the creative act. But as hard as he tries to escape it, the protagonist of *The Unnamable* returns to first person, always with the awareness that what he means by "I" is finally inscrutable. He puts off speaking of "I" because he knows nothing of his self. Fictions are all lies invented in order to "put off the hour when I must speak of me." Like Mouth, the narrator speaks with his "own" voice which he concludes must be his own because he speaks it in solitude. However, he is also like Mouth in sensing that while he is telling the stories of his "dying generations" another voice speaks to him, barely perceptible, telling him what to do to escape from the need to go on talking. In her inaudible dialogue within her monologue, Mouth appears to be hearing this outside voice that directs, edits, and deletes from her store of utterances, though it does not purify her stories or render them true. The Unnamable appears to be eager, but is finally unable to say "I" with any confidence. Mouth, feeling her dilemma more keenly, insists on remaining separate from "I," reiterating her hope that, should it continue long enough, her narrative will eventually gain her release from suffering.

Beckett recasts his struggle with the "I" in *Film,* in which a simultaneous search for the self and flight from the self finds its expression in the splitting of a single figure into object (O) and eye (E); the former in flight from perception and the latter in pursuit. Raymond Federman has noted[5] that the perceiving eye is identified with the eye of the camera in pursuit of the object, and the eye of the object in pursuit of itself. In this Beckettian conception of Berkeley's maxim *Esse est percipi* (To be is to be perceived), the subject and object of perception are one and the same, an identification that is not clarified until the end of the piece.[6] Upon realizing that the eye of the camera is the eye of the object perceiving itself, the viewer experiences a double focus in which it seems to be both looking at and out of the subject simultaneously. This same illusion is achieved in *Not I* when it becomes clear to the spectator (if it does at all) that Mouth is describing from her side of the stage the image the audience sees before itself. All the while that Mouth squirms under the intensity of the spotlight, she is fixed by the uncomprehending stare of the audience that, unknowingly implicated in her suffering, worsens it by preventing her from dissolving into nonbeing. Seeking a way out of existence, Mouth recalls from the word that it meant to symbolize a sound, ontological core: the I.

Audience reaction to the piece is embodied by its onstage surrogate, the Auditor who is, according to Ruby Cohn, the play's "seed image."[7] Paired with the pulsing Mouth, the shrouded figure completes the spectacle by providing it with an interior audience, rendering its hermetic isolation complete. Mouth and Auditor inhabit this underworld together, but it is uncertain whether they speak to or hear one another. It is even possible that they are the sundered parts of a single being.

They are distinguished by a series of contrasts that, in addition to adding to the visual complexity of the spectacle, isolate and embody the realm of possibility that exists in their world: silence and logorrhea, activity or receptivity, exposure and concealment. Undoubtedly each of these "possibilities" is as imprisoning as the other, and the two of them may be inextricably intertwined as the functions of Beckett's couples so often are. In the mythic context in which this play may be said to take place, Auditor stands in for the stones, trees, and gods of the underworld who suffered in tune with Orpheus's suffering. But the exact nature of the relation between these two shades is a mystery. It seems to closely parallel that of the speaker and auditor in the poetic form of the dramatic monologue in which the speaker's intense search for meaning totally absorbs him or her in what is said and accounts for the failure to connect with the auditor.[8] Mouth, like Eliot's Prufrock and Browning's Andrea del Sarto, is finally a voice directing talk about itself to itself; however, unlike these poetic speakers, Mouth is prohibited from understanding what her own voice is saying. Yet Mouth does function (or some part of her functions) as critic, narrowing her range of possible subjects: "nothing she could tell? . . . all right . . . nothing she could tell [. . .] nothing she could think? . . . all right . . . nothing she could tell . . . nothing she could think" (p. 85). She finds herself mouthing the artist's position outlined by Beckett in his record of a dialogue with Georges Duthuit, "The expression that there is nothing to express, nothing with which to express, nothing from which to express, no power to express, no desire to express, together with the obligation to express."[9]

In his study of the Orphic theme in twentieth-century literature, Walter A. Strauss defines the Orphic voice as one that "presupposes the possibility of song and the relevance of poetry to the life of the individual soul and the community."[10] This voice not only believes song to be possible, but powerful. Elizabeth Sewell's work on the Orphic tradition reveals its roots to lie in the equation between poetry and power.[11] It is precisely the absence of this equation that characterizes the work of Beckett, Kafka, and others, whose comic Orphic heroes make an ironic descent into Hades convinced of the impossibility of art and the inevitability of silence. Beckett's Orphic mouthpiece in the underworld demonstrates by her compulsive inchoate babble the heroism of the artist who *must* fail in his or her expressive vocation.

For Mouth, as for Prufrock, the artistic occasion is the assertion of one's being in an outburst of song; the lyrical expression of the sum of the speaker's life up to the present moment—what Robert Langbaum has called the lyric impulse as an expression of pure will. But it is expressly will, existence, and lyricism from which Mouth is in flight. Prufrock's song functions as a heuristic device, showing him the shape that his life has taken up to the moment of his singing. By contrast, how little Mouth gains from her utterance! How disinterested her song is; how far it leaves her from a comprehension of her past or an apprehension of her future. The failure of the lyric intelligibly and melodically to sum up the singer's life is the equivalent of the failure of the Orphic power in this piece. The will being expressed in Mouth's monologue is at best the deluded hope that self-expression can expiate guilt; that, by continuing to speak, the need for fictions will be revealed and satisfied. However, by the end, nothing is revealed to the heroine of this drama who, running short of memories, begins to retell how it was that day in Croker's Acres when all the light went out. Nothing changes. Mouth does not journey to Elysium to be reunited with her "self." She is simultaneously condemned to inhabit her hell of babble and to keep its fires burning: "try something else," she insists, "think of something else."

Burdened with her story, the function of expression has, for her, lost its ancient connection with prayer and power as well as its romantic association with truth and beauty. This Orphic Mouth wishes to exhaust the substance of her being through language, but her language is the product of an unhinged mind, out of touch with itself. Even with both feet in the grave, Mouth continues the search for silence through language, for nothingness through memory and feeling, turning Orpheus's skill against himself, settling down for a long stay in Hades in the company of troops of Beckettian lunatics.

Notes

1. For a description of the Lincoln Center production, see Enoch Brater's "The 'Absurd' Actor in the Theatre of Samuel Beckett," *Educational Theatre Journal* (May 1975): 197–207.

2. H. Porter Abbott, "A Poetics of Radical Displacement: Samuel Beckett Coming up to Seventy," *Texas Studies in Language and Literature* 17 (Spring 1975): 232.

3. Quotations from Samuel Beckett, *First Love and Other Stories* (New York: Grove Press, 1974), 82. Subsequent page references are in text.

4. Vincent J. Murphy, "Being and Preception: Beckett's *Film*," *Modern Drama* 18 (March 1975): 44.

5. "Samuel Beckett's *Film* and the Agony of Perceivedness," *Film Quarterly* 20, 2 (1966): 46–51.

6. *Murphy* (New York: Grove Press, 1957): 44.

7. Ruby Cohn, *Back to Beckett* (Princeton, NJ: Princeton University Press, 1973), 213.

8. Robert Langbaum, *The Poetry of Experience* (London: Chatto and Windus, 1957).

9. "Three Dialogues by Samuel Beckett and Georges Duthuit," *Samuel Beckett: A Collection of Critical Essays,* ed. Martin Esslin (Englewood Cliffs, NJ: Prentice-Hall, 1965), 17.

10. *Descent and Return* (Cambridge: Harvard University Press, 1971), 249.

11. *The Orphic Voice: Poetry and Natural History* (New Haven: Yale University Press, 1960).

9

Jung and the "Molloy" Narrative

J. D. O'Hara

Molloy is Beckett's fictional masterwork. Its major characters, Molloy and Moran, are developed and individualized more extensively than any other of his characters. The structure is also praiseworthy. In our century many major novels have presented multiple interpretations of life by way of multiple major characters: *Doctor Faustus, Pale Fire, Ulysses,* and *To the Lighthouse* are obvious examples. *Molloy*'s two narratives (we will call them "Molloy" and "Moran") present yet another variety of these doublings and triplings contrived elsewhere.

It may be asserted that in all the texts named above, the sense of existence associated with each character is generally valid, though different from other such senses. Yet in each case the sense of existence is developed psychologically: the individual character's psyche shapes his world, however valid that world may be philosophically. Molloy and Moran create such generally valid senses of existence, and they do so with the aid of Jungian and Freudian psychologies.

The present essay condenses drastically an analysis of Beckett's use of psychological authorities in his fiction and early dramas. Here one can only assert that this use occurred and that its most remarkable example is *Molloy*. In *Molloy*, Molloy is Jungian, Moran Freudian. "Molloy" acts out a plot that is thoroughly and tightly Jungian, as "Moran" acts out a similar Freudian plot. A basic justification of the pairing of these stories is the recognition that the two characters and their two plots form a whole. But into this essay is crammed only the report on "Molloy" as a deliberately Jungian work.

Some hasty remarks about Carl Gustav Jung (1875–1961), briefly heir-apparent to Freud's depth psychology, may save Jung from his followers for this study at least. Jung accepted Freud's split of the psyche into a conscious ego and an unconscious. In the unconscious he found a personal unconscious and a racial or collective unconscious. In the latter are the archetypal beings and stories that are evoked and reenacted in all generations and cultures and that shape every individual's psychic development.

Jung's primary interest in the psyche is teleological. Where Freud sought to undo the traumas of childhood and youth, Jung emphasized the individualizing of the self, largely a matter of completing its potential development. The self has a dominant and an inferior side, sexually determined. The masculine self therefore has a feminine side that is largely neglected or repressed during the first half of one's life. Access to the neglected half and development of it are subjects that Jung usually describes in stories about the encounters of the masculine side, the animus, with its feminine side, the anima. Especially in cases of neurosis, these encounters are likely to be hostile or fearful ones. (Already one may be reminded of "Molloy.") Therapy is then required to aid the conscious ego to accept its inferior half and to achieve the necessary integration and control that will complete the individualization of the self.

The animus and the anima are archetypes, but they divide and multiply like amoebas. What's more, each has "a positive and a negative aspect" (*Archetypes,* p. 37). For our purposes the anima as an Earth Mother, Wise Old Woman, and seductress are especially important. The ominous Shadow of the animus will also appear, in various guises.

These archetypes cannot be perceived directly; they are like platonic Ideas. They are embodied in significant images, usually in humans who play dominant roles in any individual's psychic drama. The drama's events enact "archetypes of transformation": "typical situations, places, ways and means, that symbolize the kind of transformation in question" (*Archetypes,* p. 37f.). This transformation of the psyche is therefore a symbolic process:

> The symbolic process is an experience *in images and of images.* Its
> development usually shows an enantiodromian structure . . . , and so
> presents a rhythm of negative and positive, loss and gain, dark and
> light. Its beginning is almost inevitably characterized by one's getting
> stuck in a blind alley or in some impossible situation; and its goal is,
> broadly speaking, illumination or higher consciousness, by means
> of which the initial situation is overcome on a higher level. . . . As

regards the time factor, the process may be compressed into a single dream or into a short moment of experience, or it may extend over months and years. . . . (*Archetypes*, p. 38f.)

The relevance of these assertions to "Molloy" may already be obvious. Molloy's movements toward and away from his mother's apartment act out an enantiodromian structure. He has much to mutter about light and dark, speech and silence; after leaving Lousse he is stuck in a blind alley, and recurrently he spends time in a ditch; he is somehow taken from a ditch at the story's end. But "a higher level"? Molloy begins on a mountainside and ends in that ditch, or flat out on his mother's bed. "Molloy" is not a success story.

Jung says that, unlike Freud, "I attribute to the personal mother only a limited aetiological significance. . . . All those influences which the [Freudian] literature describes as being exerted on the children do not come from the mother herself, but rather from the archetype projected upon her, which gives her a mythological background and invests her with authority and numinosity" (*Archetypes*, p. 83). This projection is important for Jungian psychology; "so far as a neurosis is really only a private affair, having its roots exclusively in personal causes, archetypes play no role at all" (*Archetypes*, p. 47).

Molloy's problems are archetypal, not only a private affair. His basic problem is to find his mother—not his "personal mother" but the mother within him, as a primary variant of his anima. But proliferation necessarily results. "In a man, the mother-complex is never 'pure,' it is always mixed with the anima archetype, and . . . a man's statements about the mother are always emotionally prejudiced in the sense of showing 'animosity'" (*Archetypes*, p. 94). A mother also is threefold: "There are three essential aspects of the mother: her cherishing and nourishing goodness, her orgiastic emotionality, and her Stygian depths" (*Archetypes*, p. 82).

That trinity may appear at once relevant and obviously absurd: one recalls Molloy's mother and Lousse and Ruth/Edith. But they are absurdly inadequate to the descriptions above, while Molloy's search for his mother is deadly serious. That term is not casual; here comes Jung again:

"The search for one's mother": this phrase has almost obligatorily touching overtones, and it implies such phrases as "the lost child" and "the maternal bosom." . . . This is the mother-love which is . . . the mysterious root of all growth and change; the love that means homecoming, shelter, and the long silence from which everything begins and in which everything ends. Intimately known and yet strange like

Nature, lovingly tender and yet cruel like fate, joyous and untiring giver of life—mater dolorosa and mute implacable portal that closes upon the dead. (*Archetypes,* p. 92)

Relevance and absurdity once more. Molloy is not a lost child but a hairy, dirty, ill-clad, antisocial old man. He describes his mother as "happy to smell me" (*Three Novels,* p. 17), but that joyous and untiring giver of life (and money) also "did all she could not to have me, except of course the one thing" (p. 18). Beckett's entire report of that mother and child reunion is indelicate and, yes, absurd. Comic.

Jung as well as Beckett warns us against sentimentality. Because of "this massive weight of meaning" that ties the child to the mother and her to the child, "to the physical and mental detriment of both, . . . mankind has always instinctively added the pre-existent divine pair to the personal parents—the 'god'-father and 'god'-mother of the newborn child—so that . . . he should never forget himself so far as to invest his own parents with divinity" (*Archetypes,* p. 92f.). But time presses; we must stop quoting Jung.

Mag is presented not as a credible human but as a comic image of the Earth Mother. Jung exalts this idea with high-minded references to Demeter, Kore, and Cybele (*Archetypes,* p. 81). Beckett brings it down to earth. Like Mother Nature, Mag is dirty, incontinent, and smelly; her affections are vague and general (she can't tell Molloy from her husband); she can't understand messages, nor can she speak intelligibly. Obviously she is not a complete image of the Mother. She requires to be supplemented by an image of the "god"-mother, the Wise Old Woman, to which term Jung adds the Mother of God, the Virgin, and Sophia (*Archetypes,* p. 81).

This supplementing is acted out in "Molloy." We might usefully turn away from characterization for a while to consider that acting out, the plot of "Molloy." The closeness and rigor of Beckett's presentation can only be hinted at in this short survey.

As if in a dream, Molloy undergoes a sequence of experiences that reaches a climax. It is a Jungian dream. Time and space are imaginary; the sequence is important. This notion must be simplistically overstated: in the psyche everything happens at the present moment. So if one experiences an act, imagines a future consequence, recalls a memory, imagines an alternative act, and fears a discovery, the psychic sequence of experienced act : imagined consequence : remembered act : imagined act : discovery constitutes the plot, the actual experience of the psyche. Whether memory or experience or imagination or emotion generates the event does not substantially matter. One example might suffice: by remembering Mag, shortly after deciding to seek her out, Molloy reaches her. If Mag were Molloy's personal mother and Molloy's problems were personal, the story would have proceeded very differently from that point. But Molloy's incentive is described and presented mythically: "I speak in the present tense, when speaking of the past. It is the mythological present, don't mind it," Molloy says (p. 26). Turning from his imaginings of A and C, he adds: "But talking of the craving for a fellow let me observe that having waked between eleven o'clock and midday (I heard the angelus, recalling the incarnation, shortly after) I resolved to go and see my mother" (p. 15).

Much is embedded here. Molloy speaks mythologically because he is reporting the events of a Jungian myth, the search for the mother. The reference to the angelus becomes a motive for Molloy's search and anticipates its continuation past any personal mother. The craving for a fellow states an even more general motive: Molloy cannot find a fellow ("frère" in the original) in his present psychic state, which has caused him to withdraw from life and brood like Sordello or Belacqua in isolation. To find a fellow would be to "be myself less lonely" (p. 11). His withdrawal from social life is caused by his hostility to his mother. He must come to terms with her before he is psychologically healthy enough to find a fellow.

"Come to terms with her" is vague. Molloy's own phrasings are similarly so and justifiably so; one cannot ask a patient in therapy to state clearly and explicitly the diagnosis of his or her case. But awareness will increase as the patient learns from the experiences.

His earliest formulation interrupts his account of Mag: "If ever I'm reduced to looking for a meaning to my life, you never can tell, it's in that old mess I'll stick my nose to begin with, the mess of that poor old uniparous whore and myself the last of my foul brood, neither man nor beast" (p. 19). "Neither man nor beast" reminds us that he has no fellow; he is not part of the human brotherhood.

Much later, his journey nearly at an end, he acknowledges that his "imperatives" have been insisting on his going to his mother for most of his life. (He clarifies the term with a reference to Kant; they are "hypothetical imperatives" [p. 87].) He describes them with reference to Jung's ideas and his light image: "they nearly all bore on the same question, that of my relations with my mother, and on the importance of bringing as soon as possible some light to bear on these and even on the kind of light that should be brought to bear and the most effective means of doing so" (p. 86). One can hear an echo of a real patient's reference to his psychiatrist's urgings. One may also recall Jung's goal, cited above, of "illumination or higher consciousness" (*Archetypes,* p. 38).

"It's in that old mess I'll stick my nose to begin with." Yes, indeed; and Molloy rubs our nose in it too with his long description of Mag and of his relation to her. But that's only the beginning. The enantiodromic quality of Molloy's search for his maternal anima is acted out as a recurrent vacillation. That vacillation leads him to move toward his mother, then away, then toward again, then away . . . far away, and then back toward the town where she lives (he will never bring himself to speak of it as his own home town).

But he cannot move away from his mother into a vacuum (although he will find some approximation of one), nor can he move toward her through a vacuum. His "unreal journey" (p. 8) takes him through a real psyche, populated with Jungian characters large and small. Since, as his hostility to Mag demonstrates, Molloy is unwilling to raise his anima to the light of consciousness, his psyche must try to change his mind (le mot juste; Jung understands the psyche as oriented toward health; its dreams, for instance, attempt to alert the ego consciousness to psychic problems). So Molloy's psyche will warn him by showing him the qualities and the ominous implications of his masculine animus.

Predictably, for the Jungian, the images of Molloy's animus are dualistic. Those that one probably recalls soonest are the bearded old man on the barge outside of Bally and the shepherd with his dog and flock (to be echoed, like so much of "Molloy," in "Moran"). We can only glance at them. At a glance they appear positive: the wise old man and the leader shepherding his flock. But our glance includes the offstage sounds of "angry cries and dull blows" as the barge approaches (p. 26), the boatman's hidden eyes (set against "my eyes caught a donkey's eyes"), and the boatman's spitting in the water ("even spits still pain me," Molloy announced earlier, p. 22). Similarly the ticks covering the shepherd's dog and the slaughterhouse awaiting his flock darken these images of protection. The boatman's cargo of nails and timber may suggest not only future buildings but also crosses for crucifixions. And of course Molloy's arrest for resting and his stay at the police station emphasize (or would, if we had time) the rules of the masculine social world in which Molloy's "prompters" have never taught him to "act" properly.

The police and then the boatman and shepherd bracket Molloy's first approach to and retreat from his mother. (They also suggest that the masculine world is to be found in both city and country.) His second retreat, to the seashore, is complex and best saved for shrunken discussion later.

Molloy is crippled. We may tentatively assert that Beckett's cripples act out a psychic crippling. Molloy on his mountainside is almost immobile. But when he responds to the angelus's imperative and sets out to find his mother, a bicycle appears and as is common in dreams is easily accommodated: "I found my bicycle (I didn't know I had one) in the same place I must have left it" (p. 16). His motivating force is given an image. When he weakens in his resolve, the predictable occurs: the bicycle goes out of control—it is already on the sidewalk rather than the street—and Molloy falls literally into Lousse's world.

His leaving the mountainside constituted his first substantial transformation (Jung's term); this is his second. He had been rationalizing his lethargic search for his mother (he can't even be sure that he's in the right town) by deciding that no transformation was possible: "the most you can hope is to be a little less, in the end, the creature you were in the beginning, and the middle" (p. 32). At this point the anima makes a vigorous effort; Lousse takes him in; and in an echo of *A la recherche du temps perdu* Molloy awakens the next morning quite changed: "You don't remember immediately who you are, when you wake" (p. 38).

His psyche's new world takes its characteristic qualities from his hostess. Molloy's inability to accept anima figures is reflected in his uncertainty about her name: it is Sophie Loy or Lousse, and he settles for the unintimate latter. But Beckett has signaled her importance. "Loy" suggests the French word for "law." "Lousse" implies "light." "Sophie" is "Sophia," which means "wisdom," "knowledge." Mag is now supplemented by an image of the "god"-mother, the Wise Old Woman, "the feminine and motherly Sophia" (*Archetypes*, p. 64).

Jung attaches other characters to his central archetypal figures. (His term is "syzygy.") "As mythology shows," he reports, "one of the peculiarities of the Great Mother is that she frequently appears paired with her male counterpart." The ordinary male psyche repeats this pairing: "Accordingly the man identifies with the son-lover on whom the grace of Sophia has descended, with a puer aeternus or a filius sapientiae" (*Archetypes*, p. 106). Jung also links Sophia with the Virgin Mother, and Molloy reports that Lousse denies any physical desire for him (p. 47). He will also connect her with the idea of his own crucifixion.

"Molloy" is divided into three approximately equal sections. Taking a cue from *How It Is,* we might describe them as Before Sophie, With Sophie, and After Sophie. Sophia is the dominant form of the anima in Molloy's psychic life, and her section of the narrative has a unity that the others do not have. But the unity is not static. Although the uninstructed reader may experience only a jumble of events, Molloy moves quite systematically through his surrender to Lousse and his slow and difficult recovery from that surrender. Little of this material can be presented briefly.

When Molloy awakens in Lousse's mansion, he finds himself shaved and powdered and dressed in a gown. When he manages to find a servant and throw a tantrum, he is able to get most of his clothes back. (He also claims to have lost a knife, hoping to be given one.) He spends the rest of his time chez Lousse in her extensive gardens. There he sleeps and watches the gardeners and occasionally (despite his crutches) leaps about. He eats and drinks erratically, sometimes going without food and drink and sometimes consuming large quantities of both. He is occasionally aware of Lousse's watching him from the house, and once, early on, she comes to him as he is lying on the grass and tells him extensively of her interest in him and her desire to care for him.

Molloy scatters most of these facts through his narrative so that few readers are likely to put them together. Put together, they suggest that Molloy is in his second childhood. He is. That is, he is acting out the part of Sophia's partner in syzygy, the puer aeternus or filius sapientiae.

The large house and the extensive grounds (real estate recycled from Knott's holdings in *Watt*) extend Molloy's experience of life far beyond Mag's dark and dank room. Lousse's parrot, her gardeners, and Molloy's insistence on his role as a replacement for her dead dog Teddy may suggest that she is a Circe figure. (One servant reminds Molloy of a chamois.) The gate that seems to hold Molloy within the estate but is never locked will recur at Macmann's sanatorium. Beckett is always willing to provide layers of implication. But primarily Lousse's estate is a form of the timeless Earthly Paradise (presided over by women at the summit of the Mount of Purgatory in Dante's *Purgatorio*).

Sophia is linked also with the complementary Wise Old Man. Her feminine wisdom is earthly and wordless. It is embodied in a garden preserved as much as possible from change, Molloy notes. It is associated with food and drink and sleep and the manicured natural world. It detains Molloy for a long time, and the tired and troubled reader might wonder why Molloy would wish to leave it.

The tired and troubled reader of the present article might have a more serious occasion for wonder. It has been asserted that Molloy's psyche, especially that part of it allied to his anima, has nudged him off his mountainside isolation and sent him to find his mother, implying that finding her is a necessary preliminary to his finding a fellow or frère. It has also been asserted that the mother in question is not his merely personal mother but the archetypal mother who is for him the dominant form of his anima. Now he has found the dominant form of that dominant form: he has reached the feminine wisdom he had previously rejected. He has become a filius sapientiae. Why is this transformation not treated as the success it ought to be?

That's a good question, as teachers say when a student asks a tough one. The answer requires that we go back to Jung and his reports on the archetypes. We have already noted that he pairs Sophia with her masculine counterpart, the Wise Old Man. Jung's more formal name for that archetype is the Logos. His description of the relation between Sophia and the Logos will suggest Molloy's proper role:

> There is no consciousness without discrimination of opposites. This is the paternal principle, the Logos, which eternally struggles to extricate itself from the primal warmth and primal darkness of the maternal womb; in a word, from unconsciousness. Divine curiosity yearns to be born and does not shrink from conflict, suffering, or sin. Unconsciousness is the primal sin, evil itself, for the Logos. Therefore its first creative act of liberation is matricide. . . . (*Archetypes*, p. 96)

The search for the mother and now matricide; the wise Sophia and now the paternal Logos; submission and control—the plot is thickening, as is the exposition of it. Perhaps this is the time to simplify Jung's metaphorical description into a more conventional set of terms.

Molloy is a man seeking his mother and encountering other men and women. More importantly he is a man with psychological problems, and this man seeks or should seek to benefit from his encounters with figures who (and which) embody qualities contained in his repressed feminine nature. In this sense Molloy represents especially the Jungian ego consciousness. That masculine ego consciousness is associated with Molloy's primary psychic nature, his animus. The animus contains a collection of archetypal characters just as the anima does. Centrally important among them is the Logos or Wise Old Man, approximating the person's highest uses of reason.

Jung was fond of imagining the encounter between the Logos and the anima. Sometimes he gave to it overtones of a Biblical creation myth in which Adam brings existence out of the unconscious by means of words or language when he names the animals. As the passage quoted above indicates, the Logos raises the contents of the psyche out of unconsciousness. In so doing it creates enmity between itself and the anima, Nature, the unconscious other half of the masculine psyche. Jung's reference to Prometheus identifies the nature of the resultant suffering; the Logos is punished for its knowledge.

This subject has arisen because Beckett incorporates it in "Molloy," of course. But it is necessary to remind doubtful readers of the word "comic" already introduced. During Molloy's stay with Lousse he is indeed surrounded by and fed by Sophia, the feminine wisdom of the anima. That wisdom is essentially wordless. Molloy reports several times Lousse's failure to make herself understood, as well as her comically conventional and deceitful speeches to the policeman and to the crowd wishing to lynch Molloy for killing Teddy. Certainly Molloy does not help matters; he is evasive of her wisdom as he is of her self. But certainly too, Lousse is essentially like Mag in that neither can communicate verbally, anymore than Nature herself.

We turn to Molloy's masculine Logos, then, for that second creation, the raising of feminine wisdom into verbal consciousness. Or at least the trained and unsophisticated Jungian might expect this result. But Molloy's Logos does not rise to the occasion. Yet repeatedly throughout his stay he turns away from Lousse to speak of his mind. His arrival chez Lousse leads him to survey the contents of his mind—notably empty of any anima—and to review his education. He retreats into his mind to escape Lousse's world. He reacts to Sophie's wisdom by becoming a Skeptic, with help from Arthur Schopenhauer: a topic too complex even to be mentioned here. No mopping up of the eudemonistic slop.

The slow process by which Molloy recovers his reason, signaled in large part by his recovery of language, cannot be traced here either. What all readers can sense is Molloy's exasperating indifference to Lousse, accompanied by his lethargic unwillingness to do anything but accept her hospitality, thanklessly. The man who settled for sucking stones now eats food and guzzles beer or, if they are not immediately available, seeks for them. The man who set out for his mother scarcely mentions her. The man who longed for a fellow or frère now remains indifferent both to Lousse and to her servants. He is a child, a puer aeternus, but he is a self-centered and isolated child. "Aeternus" is Jung's term, of course, not Beckett's. For Beckett time is signaled by change, and even in Lousse's nearly timeless world Molloy changes. His changed thinking causes the next transformation.

That assertion is glaringly oversimplified. Molloy as Skeptic is a topic we cannot discuss here, but Molloy's apathy is immediately relevant. The passions are important for this patient who has been repressing his emotional nature, his anima, all his life, and lately has been evading Lousse by sinking into his faintly rational self. Reason is not necessarily bad. But Molloy must encounter and accept emotionally these images of his anima; all else is either negatively important (the boatman, the shepherd, the police) or irrelevant to the completion of that experience. (Irrelevant material is remarkably difficult to find, in fact.)

Regrettably, Molloy shuns encounters, despite his early warning. His inability to conceive of a satisfactory meeting with A or C certainly contributed to his positive response when he heard the angelus. But since then he has been unable to manage encounters with the police, the boatman, and the shepherd; and though he fell at Lousse's feet he has been negative and unable to manage his words with her since then. Nor has he been able to understand her words (pp. 33f., 49f.). He is at once experiencing and failing the Jungian opportunities presented him.

Instead, he is developing his rational mind. That fact obliges us to point out hastily that the Earthly Paradise provided by Lousse is quite earthly indeed. It presents an idealized Nature in which the physical appetites are satisfied and the psyche is expected to be satisfied thereby. There is no gourmet cuisine chez Lousse, no music, no fine arts, no literature, no rational thought, and none of the theology of Dante's Earthly Paradise.

Let us abandon this hasty visit to the Lousse section, but not before examining Molloy's escape from her world. We must consider at least his recollection of Ruth/Edith, his panicky realization about her and Lousse and Mag, and the one significant souvenir of his stay, the knife-rest.

As noted, the psyche exists in the present. Therefore the sequence of its experiences is the significant sequence, no matter what other sequences are indicated. Ruth/Edith—Molloy is unsure which is her name, and will later substitute Rose—encountered Molloy on the garbage dump much earlier than his descent from the mountainside. But his remembering her at this point in the narrative is the significant fact.

We saw that the Sophia figure is conceived by Jung as at once a form of the mother archetype and a separate form of the anima, although still paired with a son, the filius sapientiae or puer aeternus. Attachment to her distances the masculine ego consciousness from the physical mother. As Jung told us, "the mother-complex . . . is always mixed up with the anima archetype," and that archetype has many forms.

The latest arrival, Ruth/Edith, combines Mag's earthiness with positive sexuality. (Molloy said of Mag that "We were so old . . . that we were like a couple of old cronies, sexless, unrelated," p. 17.) Ruth/Edith is also old, and she appears first on a dump; she is a comic version of what Jung calls the chthonic mother, and like Sophia she has a masculine partner in another instance of syzygy. "The companion of the chthonic mother is the exact opposite [of Sophia's puer aeternus]," Jung writes; "an ithyphallic Hermes (the Egyptian Bes) or a lingam" (*Archetypes*, p. 106). As the three-part moon outside Molloy's window predicted, on his arrival chez Lousse, Molloy's mother has now been joined by the wise grandmother and the seductive daughter.

The arrival of sexuality in Molloy's current life is predictable, at least in retrospect. Shunning Lousse's wisdom while gorging on her food and drink, Molloy developed from the child in the nightgown to the boy wanting a knife and bicycle and then to the adolescent swigging beer and staying out all night (though, cautiously, not out on the town). Time moves him on, and sexuality cannot be evaded. Two Paradises 'twere in one to live in Paradise alone. So Ruth/Edith arrives. "It was she who made me acquainted with love," Molloy reports (p. 56).

In Lousse's garden of earthly delights Molloy has learned the pleasures of eating and drinking. He is initiated into the physical world, the world of the senses. Unsurprisingly, therefore, he decides, just before Ruth/Edith appears, that life is a matter only of "the body's long madness" (p. 56). So his exploration of love with her is similarly presented. When his skepticism wonders, "is it true love, in the rectum?" (p. 57), his answer results from a consideration of the "instant of bliss" derived from a pedicure, a massage, and the experience that ensues "when your frantic member casts about for a rubbing-place" (p. 58). All is physical here.

But we must hurry on. Molloy tells us about Ruth/Edith, and then a remarkably compressed sequence takes place in which the speed of narration acts out the sudden psychic event. Having ignored Lousse, Molloy now joins her to Ruth/Edith by saying that he is "tempted to think of them as one and the same old hag" (p. 59). The next sentence fearfully expands this identification, and the expansion leads instantly to Molloy's flight from Lousse: "And God forgive me, to tell you the horrible truth, my mother's image sometimes mingles with theirs, which is literally unendurable, like being crucified, I don't know why and I don't want to. But I left Lousse at last, one warm airless night, without saying goodbye. . ." (p. 59). Perhaps nowhere else does Molloy show such intensity of feeling. Of course it arises suddenly to be immediately repressed. He moves on, literally, leaving us to make sense of his revelation.

Jung helps, though not quickly. We have heard him speak of the Logos as arising from the masculine ego's confrontation with the anima and as struggling to free itself from the unconsciousness of its maternal womb:

"its first creative act of liberation is matricide." But when he considers the processes of transformation and individuation such bluster gives way to rather different descriptions.

We have noted the Sophia/puer aeternus and the chthonic mother/ithyphallic Hermes syzygies. Jung's split from Freud may have led to his omitting the useful equivalent for Mag and Dan/Molloy: Jocasta/Oedipus. But "it is a psychological fact," Jung says, "that as soon as we touch on these identifications we enter the realm of the syzygies, the paired opposites, where the One is never separated from the Other, its antithesis" (*Archetypes,* p. 106).

"It is a field of personal experience," Jung continues, "which leads directly to the experience of individuation, the attainment of the self." But it ain't necessarily so, of course. The encounter requires one to assimilate the anima images into one's conscious personality, "with the right attitude" (*Symbols of Transformation,* p. 441). Molloy fails. In each of his paired relations he has played a subordinate part (he took from Mag only money, not knowledge). He has exerted his masculine power not to control but to evade.

Jung's discussion of the subject is too extensive even to summarize. It includes the curious claim that access to the anima and achievement of some of its knowledge may lead not to a sense of power but to its opposite. The masculine ego consciousness may sense itself as "a rudderless ship buffeted between Scylla and Charybdis . . . a Prometheus chained to the Caucasus, or as one crucified. This would be a 'godlikeness' in suffering" ("The Relations between the Ego and the Unconscious," *Archetypes,* p. 140f.). In describing the mother archetype's negative qualities Jung comes to Sophia and says: "perhaps the historical example of the dual nature of the mother most familiar to us is the Virgin Mary, who is not only the Lord's mother, but also, according to the medieval allegories, his cross" (*Archetypes,* p. 82). Clearly Beckett has given us a serious psychological revelation here.

But Molloy flees Sophia's Earthly Paradise for the masculine social world on the other side of the wicket gate: "Outside in the road the wind was blowing, it was another world" (p. 60). He carries with him a painful memento of his encounter with the triad of anima figures. He cannot understand it, this short bar with a cross at either end, but we can make some useful interpretations of it. The X—X suggests two unknowns, his unknown present self and the anima, his other half, which he has refused to know. The bar at once links them and holds them apart. His reference to a crucifixion adds another element. No knife encourages the cutting off of the anima from the animus.

Molloy's meditation on this image contains a burst of splendid prose, concluding that "to know nothing is nothing, not to want to know anything likewise, but to be beyond knowing anything, to know you are beyond knowing anything, that is when peace enters in, to the soul of the incurious seeker" (p. 63f.). Considered even in the present sketchy context, that passage reveals itself as mere rhetoric, and evasive at that. Molloy achieves no peace. Indeed, he will later describe his life as a calvary with no hope of crucifixion (p. 78).

"Molloy" is now approximately two-thirds over, but Molloy has already exhausted his best chances. In his three relations with the three versions of his repressed anima, he has failed to come to terms with them, to raise them satisfactorily into his consciousness, to learn about life from them. (One can intuit in the distance a meditative consideration of Molloy's encounters in the context perhaps of Proust's Marcel and his mother, his grandmother, and Albertine. Marcel's achievement, *le temps retrouvé*, sets off painfully the last third of "Molloy.")

Molloy's previous visits to Bally occurred in sunlight, which he found objectionable. Now darkness and rain characterize the town, and his isolation leads him into doorways and a cul de sac and a failed attempt to persuade himself that he is content and should kill himself in order to extend that contentment into eternity. Equally beyond discussion here is the confused passage implying that Molloy spent years in Bally as an adult, miserable in the daylight and little better off at night.

These matters continue his Jungian dream, of course. Reborn from his "god"-mother Lousse and raised through adolescence, he leaves home for the adult male world of Bally and fails yet again. But this time he escapes not to a mountainside but to the seashore, as far away as possible from Bally and his mother (she disappeared when he was with Lousse [pp. 44–56] and will be evaded again on the shore, her maternal bosom replaced by sucking stones).

We recall that Jung divided his archetypes into two classes. One appears in personifications, as we have seen. The second class, "archetypes of transformation," "are not personalities but are typical situations, places, ways and means, that symbolize the kind of transformation in question" (*Archetypes,* p. 38). Bally (clearly masculine), Lousse's house and garden, Molloy's ditches, and the sucking stones are examples. Molloy heaps the cul de sac with such terms: shelter, lodging house, alley, recesses, alcoves, and chapel (p. 6of.). More such images will appear.

As the sucking stones replace Mag, so do the cave by the sea and then the forest. As the policemen and the boatman and the shepherd presented the dualities of the animus, both protective and threatening, so the charcoal burner will offer an isolated version of those qualities. In knocking him down and maltreating him with comic vigor, Molloy acts out a conventional masculine aggressiveness. One might also say that he is rejecting a possible image of his self. In any case, from the charcoal burner as from Mag, Lousse, and Ruth/Edith, Molloy also rejects an offer of affection.

In the cul de sac "I began to think, that is to say to listen harder." Earlier Molloy had listened, inadequately, to Mag, Lousse, and Ruth/Edith. From this point on he will listen to a voice or voices inside his head, and they will become increasingly important. They are connected with thinking (although even that act is made passive by the emphasis on listening). We may usefully recall Beckett's rephrasing of Proust's recurrent metaphor in *A la Recherche:* "the old ego dies hard." Molloy's attempted suicide signals another beginning. Molloy as thinker—not as the Logos but as a rational masculine ego consciousness—begins to create a new identity for himself.

Again, exasperatingly, the subject can only be sketched. The sketch is of the young Descartes, cloistering himself in his *poêle* in Holland to work out his philosophy, for which the relevant idea is obviously thought: I think, therefore I am. The thinking ego replaces the more complex psyche. Hidden from the social world and from his mother, Molloy by the sea will engage in sterile and irrelevant thinking. The celebrated calculation of the problem of sucking stones and pockets is his achievement. Once solved, the problem lacks interest, and Molloy discards the stones. He has provided a comic bit of evidence to support his earlier conclusion after calculating the rate of his farts: "extraordinary how mathematics help you to know yourself" (p. 30).

No evidence can be offered here in support of these assertions about Descartes. Molloy's willingness to go into such detail, about the sucking stones as earlier about the events following his leaving Lousse, was justified by his aphoristic assertion that "homo mensura can't do without staffage" (p. 67). Molloy has resorted to Protagoras. Beckett's own attitude toward this aphorism can be seen in his article "La peinture des Van Velde," where he scorns Claude Lorrain's "staffage" and "le philosophe qui dit: Protagoras avait raison" (*Disjecta,* pp. 122, 132).

Descartes, staffage, the Sophists, mathematics . . . decidedly the world has changed from Lousse's Earthly Paradise. It will come as no surprise, then, that the voice aiding Molloy with his sucking-stone problem by

means of an "illumination"—he should sacrifice "the principle of trim"—
is the voice of that fearsome masculine God whom Jeremiah quotes as
demanding of Judah, "Why trimmest thou thy way to seek love?" (2:33). It
may also be unsurprising that Molloy solves his problem by misunder-
standing God; "trim" means something quite different from "balance,"
which is Molloy's sense of it. The unaided reason is not enough; Molloy's
Cartesian persona is not a source of peace.

A proper application of that odd sentence from the King James translation would be, wordily, this: Why are you seeking emotional satisfaction
in mathematical games (e.g., martingales) when you should be seeking
true love by coming to terms with your mother? (Though the heavily
masculine God of Jeremiah offers himself as a substitute for a woman.)
But Molloy only slowly realizes, by the sea, that "there are other needs
than that of rotting in peace, . . . I mean of course my mother" (p. 75f.).

We cannot accompany him on his slow voyage through the forest,
which he notes as quite unlike Dante's Earthly Paradise, nor can we
discuss his increasing ability to know (his lecture on Bally's swamp or bay,
for instance) and to reason. Repression is weakening, and he is able to
accept that voice in his head and its hypothetical imperative that has been
sending him to his mother. (And then abandoning him, he complains; he
cannot accept responsibility for the completion of the task.) But by now
the anima may be dead.

His Jungian trip toward individualization ends ambivalently. We know
from the opening paragraphs that he reached his mother's room, but his
narrative leaves him in a ditch, waiting as instructed for the help that is on
its way. The voice is not that of the Logos.

"Scenes of my life came back to me," Molloy reports. (He is no enemy
of the commonplace.) That cliché signals a death, of course; another old
ego is dying, but not hard this time, and with the narrative's last sentence
the narrator detaches himself from that Molloy, now in the third person,
who could stay where he happened to be.

He is in a ditch, of course, a final comic image of his mother's womb.
His next incarnation is the Molloy who now inhabits his mother's room
and bed, owns her belongings, and indifferently suspects that she is dead.
"I must resemble her more and more" (p. 7). The encounter with his
anima has ended, and the anima has won, it seems. But there is no victory
here; we recall Mag and the others, and we cannot say that Molloy has
acquired any of their psychic qualities.

There is one central quality possessed by Mag, Lousse, and Ruth/
Edith and echoed by the social worker at the police station and the young

woman on the seashore. The proper term for it must grate, in the bleak context of "Molloy": love. This report cannot enter into that subject. It can only assert that Beckett uses Jungian psychology to present Molloy as failing at life because he fails at love.

Works Cited

Beckett, Samuel. *Disjecta*. Edited by Ruby Cohn. New York: Grove Press, 1984.
_____. *Three Novels*. New York: Grove Press, 1965.
Jung, Carl Gustav. *The Archetypes and the Collective Unconscious*. Translated by R. F. C. Hull. 2nd ed., Bollingen Series XX. Princeton, NJ: Princeton University Press, 1969.
_____. *Symbols of Transformation*. Trans. R. F. C. Hull. 2nd ed., Bollingen Series XX. Princeton, NJ: Princeton University Press, 1967.

10

"Imagination Dead Imagine":
The Imagination and Its Context

James Hansford

First of all, it must be noted that the two terms "outside" and
"inside" pose problems of metaphysical anthropology that are
not symmetrical. To make inside concrete and outside vast is the
first task, the first problem it would seem, of an anthropology of
the imagination. But between concrete and vast, the opposition
is not a true one. At the slightest touch, asymmetry appears.

G. BACHELARD, The Poetics of Space

2.0131 . . . (A spatial point is an argument-place.)

L. WITTGENSTEIN, Tractatus Logico-philosophicus

At the beginning of Part III of *How It Is,* the narrator makes one of his
repeated attempts to describe "my life last state"[1] and does so, as so often
before, in three parts:

> . . . . these last tracts they are the last extremely little hardly at all a
> few seconds on and off enough to mark a life several lives crosses
> everywhere indelible traces

> all that almost blank nothing to get out of it almost nothing nothing
> to put in that's the saddest that would be the saddest imagination on
> the decline having attained the bottom what one calls sinking one
> is tempted

> or ascending heaven at last no place like it in the end

or not stirring that too that's defendable half in the mud half out [.]
(p. 112)

It is characteristic of Beckett's work that there are "three possibilities"[2] to the solution of an epistemological and ontological problem and that these possibilities are not separate. What appears to be a synthesis resolving a dialectical problem only adds to it, creating a trilateral series of propositions that undermines the clarity of the two initial terms. Here, for example, "having attained the bottom" is "what one calls sinking" and "at last" there is "no place like [heaven] in the end." Accordingly, the narrator, having reached neither and "not stirring," is caught in between, "half in the mud half out," divided by the line that traces the separation of mud from "ambient air,"[3] as unable to assert the division as he is to locate the limits of the world within which such a division has reference and meaning.

As the narrator is situated "half in the mud half out," so consciousness is split between knowledge and imagination, the latter "on the decline." The contrast between what is available to knowledge and what is made present to the imagination is characterized on the one hand by what there is to "get out" and on the other by what there is "to put in," what "these last tracts" can yield and what they can be made to contain, what memory and perception can perhaps find there and what imagination can place there. Recovery from the past and discovery in the present are set against uncovering in the future. While there is "nothing . . . almost nothing . . . to get out of it" there is "nothing to put in" and "that's the saddest that *would be* the saddest" (italics mine). That the projection of imagined realities should be referred to here as an "uncovering" underlines the complexity of the imaginative project that, in an analysis of "Imagination Dead Imagine," this discussion attempts to examine.

For the narrator of *How It Is,* the status of images is uncertain. Consider, for example, that of the woman who "sits aloof" (p. 11) at the beginning of Part I; as an image of "life . . . above . . . said to have been mine" (p. 8), of life before partition, it has the characteristics of memory, of recovery, without the certainty of priority; as an image of "life . . . in the light" (p. 8), it has the mysterious genesis of a dream but the narrator lacks the certain knowledge that it has been created anonymously. He therefore discounts both memory and dream: "it was an image the kind I see in the mud part one sometimes saw" (p. 11). The narrator's mental reminder that while remaining within Part III he is describing "part one" and that the image belongs to both parts, typifies the confusion between mental coordinates in the novel. It awakens us to the inauthenticity of partition and prompts us to ask whether "part one" is remembered or imagined in its "present formulation" (p. 141). Even so, just as "my beginnings" (p. 13) are entertained in Part I, so "last images"4 (last or latest?) are presented in Part III so as to accord priority and authority to the distribution of sacks, roles, tenses ("the whole story" [p. 158]) in order to avoid the conclusion that all is present and perpetual discontinuity. "Having attained the bottom" the image is of: "the voice quaqua on all sides then within in the little vault empty closed eight planes bone-white if there were a light a tiny flame all would be white ten words fifteen words like a fume of sighs when the panting stops then the storm the breath token of life part three and last it must be nearly ended" (p. 140).

This image is the vehicle for an attempted depiction of a place and a mode of being within which and from which the "tale is told" (p. 140), from which it may be said "how it is": "clench the eyes I quote on not the blue the others at the back see something somewhere after Pim that's all is left breath in a head nothing left but a head nothing in it almost nothing only breath pant pant hundred to the minute hold it be it held ten seconds fifteen seconds hear something try and hear a few words after Pim how it is quick" (p. 113).

The narrator/narrated5 (the eye/I) of the novel proposes this image of his own inside, of "what little remains" (p. 117), wishing at the same time to remain outside, to become both part of and apart from the image. "Clench the eyes try and see a third" (p. 116) he says to himself. But there is "no alternative" (p. 111) to the confused discontinuity within which and against which he is placed; indeed it is not a position that allows for alternatives. Split between tormentor and victim, the "journey" and the "abandon," the "last images" are projected into "the mud the dark" (p. 114) in an attempt to assert continuity. The vault "bone-white if there were a light" (p. 146) into which the voice moves from the without is a place in which "imagination [is] spent" (p. 111) but which the declining imagination has constructed. "Closed in, as it were, on the outside,"6 it is an imaginative construction "put in" to the flux of forms and tenses; from it consciousness wishes to absent itself: "to the sole end that there may be white on white trace of so many and so many words . . ." (p. 147). The image of "white on white" is only imaginable as a "trace," in the shadow which places figure on ground and thus disrupts continuity. The "so many words" are "a fume of sighs" traced in the panting that they replace. As Derrida reminds us, "[the] inscription [of the trace] . . . succeeds only in being effaced."7 In the act of being inscribed, these traces invite complicity from a consciousness that finds itself replaced on the inside, no longer the "ear in these conditions the gift of understanding . . . the means of noting" (p. 147).

The world of *How It Is,* reduced to a voice speaking in an eternal present, is traced by discontinuous images created and effaced by respiration. Through "images," the narrator attempts to create a continuity from which consciousness can become displaced, and at the same time to create a place within which he can discover himself without relinquishing a position outside himself from which point he provides the context of the imaginative enquiry. But there is an important distinction between the discrete images that are yielded by imperfect memory and perception and those "last images" that are provided in the search for an order of the imagination. External reality in *How It Is,* the "life up above said to have been mine," "all this business . . . of other worlds . . . of sacks . . . of a procession" (pp. 158, 159) is unreachable because it is imaginary; and being imaginary it is not imaginable. Unable to place himself within the context of such a world by invoking, simultaneously, a "not one of us" (p. 151)—who, being displaced on the outside, provides the context that makes that world imaginable—it fragments into velleities.

When the imagination is "spent," there is "nothing to get out of" the by now imaginary world; but the narrator is at once unable to get out of it and unable to find himself placed within it. In constructing an image of his own inside by making imaginable the displaced center of an imaginary world, he is attempting to be outside *discovering* his own inside rather than inside *creating* the outside. Having acknowledged that "the whole story from beginning to end yes completely false yes" (p. 158), and thereby admitted that it has been not so much discovered as created from the threads of memory and perception, the narrator attempts to discover a world at the center of deceased creativity, as though (as he had hoped was true of the world outside) it was already there available to perception and consequently to memory. The paradox of this enterprise lies in the will to discover, for discovery is seen to be a creative activity. This is also the case in "Imagination Dead Imagine" where the discovery of the created image, the attempted uncovering of the imagined object, becomes the partial recovery of all that the image was designed to displace.

"Imagination Dead Imagine" dramatizes the manner in which this will to discover becomes the impulse to create and shows how narrative consciousness "half in" and "half out" of the imagined world—astride the trace of a boundary that both separates and joins the inside and the outside—cannot occupy both positions simultaneously. The narrator is unable to prevent the effacement of the trace and cannot consider either activity separately. It is in "Imagination Dead Imagine" that the distinction between what "these last tracts" can yield and what they can be made to contain is examined further.

The imagination that is "dead, good"[9] is linked to memory and perception, the world of "Islands, waters, azure, verdure," the discrete world of external reality, of troublesome velleities that question the relationship between nature and consciousness. To exclude the world present to the eye it is necessary (as *How It Is* puts it) to "clench the eyes . . . not the blue the others at the back" and to turn to what the mind's eye uncovers. The "one glimpse" is that which is achieved in the blink of the eye, the moment becoming past as soon as the movement is registered. This is why the world does not vanish, it has "vanished," never being fully present because already past, and vanished "endlessly" without the perspective of succeeding moments to ensure both the presence of the moment of vision and its moment of absence.[10]

Having negated both life and imagination as the life of the imagination ("imagination dead") and having rehearsed the procedure to be followed, the omission of the whole process negates that negation by excluding altogether the movement of erasure: "one glimpse and vanished, endlessly, *omit*" (italics mine). However, the life of the imagination cannot be dead; it can only be killed by an act of the imagination. Similarly, the attempted transcendence of such a death through its omission is equally inauthentic; it perpetuates a process that cannot omit *itself* but must always, as negating function, stand "outside of its relation to the positive . . . in that it is what the positive is supposed to be."[11] The narrator of the thirteenth of the *Texts for Nothing* asks, "Is it possible, is that the possible thing at last, the extinction of this black nothing and its impossible shades . . . but it's ended, we're ended who never were, soon there will be nothing, where there was never anything, last images" (p. 135).

While the double negation here is the work of omission, the interpolation of "last images" is that of inclusion. But the space that is vacated is not truly vacant;[12] remaindered by the work of omission, it constitutes a prior text and assumes a consequent reworking of material through inclusion, a project from which the writer can never finally absent himself. The imaginary world of memory and perception is at first discovered. The process of discovery deals with what consciousness can "get out" of outside reality. But because the process of discovery is also an investigative one, consciousness imagines creatively what is present in perception and responds habitually to what is past in memory. Accordingly, what was there to "get out" of the world is replaced by what is "put in" to it and the subject is split between third and second persons, on the one hand unable to "put [himself] in" as object—to include himself in a discovered world—and on the other unable to "get out" of it, to omit himself from a created, an imaginary world for which he is responsible.

Omission attempts to heal this split, for it is at once an omission of the death of the imaginary world as though that world had never been,[13] and at the same time an omission of the creation of the imagined world as though it were already there. While one omission involves the destruction of what is already absent, the other is the making imaginable of what is already present to thought and awaiting discovery.

The split between third and second person forms is very important in "Imagination Dead Imagine," latent in the life of the imagination at the start of the text where life is seen as a series of discrete objects realized imaginatively by the subject. The distinction between "life" and "imagination" is mirrored in the dialogue between the third person narrator and the second person: "No trace anywhere of life, you say, pah, no difficulty there, imagination not dead yet. . . ." The second person, however, to whom the narrator addresses himself, is at best reported as having spoken ("No trace anywhere of life, you say"[14]) so that the report forms part of the third person narrator's disquisition upon the relationship between "life" and "imagination" rather than the latter being a distinguishable response to the former. The frenetic exchange of utterances—reminding, stating, and confirming ("yes, dead, good")—and the imperative form of "omit" destroy both the clarity of a putative dialogue and the singularity of assertive statement.

The space between the second and third sentences ("omit. Till") which is opened up by the necessarily incomplete form of the imperative, also leaves incomplete the movement preceding "till," demonstrating how the end of one movement overlaps the beginning of another. The omission of both these movements (one toward darkness and the other toward light) means that there is no clear "space" between subject and object "that intervenes,"[15] that it inevitably belongs to the "feverish greys" that, it is discovered, feature in the imagined world itself.

The discovered world, "the rotunda," is "all white in the whiteness." Like the "white on white trace" in *How It Is,* it is only imaginable in the trace that places figure on ground, but it is developed here as a content within an enveloping context, the adjective adding to the noun. The half-rhyme "till all," however, shows how tenuous is the linguistic perspective that is being forged. Furthermore, while the movement from "white" to "whiteness" places the rotunda within a context as the description moves from the inside toward the outside, emphasizing the outline of the object, the "all" that is "white" cannot be "all" if it is situated in surroundings that share its whiteness.

The imagined object that is created in "Imagination Dead Imagine" is like Worm's dwelling place in *The Unnamable:* "Quick, a place. With no way in, no way out. A safe place. Not like Eden. And Worm inside" (p. 65). This hermetic world is opened up because Worm "hears the sound that will never stop" and consequently "no longer is." Conceived as a being who is "feeling nothing, knowing nothing, capable of nothing, wanting nothing," "the instant he hears the sound" he is no longer a Being in himself but rather an existent, a vice-exister for whom and in respect of whom the relationship between subject and object, beginning and end, word and world is hopelessly confused: "Then it's the end . . . we know it, we don't say it, we say it's the awakening, the beginning of Worm, for now we must speak and speak of Worm. . . . It's no longer he, but let us proceed as if it were, he at last. . ." (p. 65).

Worm is no longer "still he," already there beyond notions of beginning and ending. In being "he" no longer, he begins to be Other; but his beginning is not so much a commencement as an interruption and his end does not complete a movement because nothing can be said to have begun. "The sound . . . will never stop" and is only said to begin because it interrupts Worm who hears it. The "instant" at which he hears it is both beginning and end, the moment at which both notions come simultaneously into play, the beginning of that which will have no end and the end of that which never began. Before this moment, Worm was always "he"; after it he will "never stop" being Other.

As the experience with Worm shows, the trace of the "instant" that creates a temporal perspective is not therefore a clear line that separates into before and after but rather a momentary line that effaces itself in insinuating the context within which notions of beginning and end come into play. Spatial perspective is also marked by only a momentary line, a line that at once separates and brings together the inside and the outside of the "place" with which Worm has been conceived as coterminous. To situate Being it is necessary to imagine and circumscribe the place of Being. But to imagine Worm, it is necessary to place him on the inside, *within* the context of the imagined space, and to this end consciousness moves inside. Consequently, the place is no longer "safe" and Being is violated. Worm now registers what is outside his hermetic world through the space inside, the space that has been opened up by effacing the trace of separation. And at this point Worm is seen to be not so much coterminous with the place of Being, but rather to exist in the context of the inside, a context in itself replaced by that of the outside from which inquiry began.

The play of inside and outside displaces Being in space as the play of beginning and ending displaces it in time. Simultaneity is seen to be illusory because any simultaneity assumes a consciousness capable of displacing itself in the observation of coincidence and remaining inviolate outside the processes of observation and inquiry. In its search for unity and uniformity, the subject can observe only partial coincidence.

The split within the subject, a part of the inside and apart on the outside, is very clear at this point in the text. Imagined from the outside, the rotunda is conceived as hermetic: there is "no way in." Only its external form inside the total field is posited. But, as Wittgenstein remarks, "If I am to know an object . . . I must know all its internal properties."[16] This is why the sentence as a whole oscillates between third and second person forms, between assertion and command: "No way in, go in, measure." This shows how the trace of separation between the rotunda and the surrounding area is no sooner marked than it is effaced. This being so, the observer opens up a space within the rotunda itself: the movement toward the inside displaces consciousness from a position in which the rotunda traces itself in the context of "the whiteness" and replaces it, in effacing the trace, inside the rotunda's own context, where "all" is "white."

Neither space is entirely vacated; that which is created in the interplay of third and second persons places each person in the context of the other. The attempt to place "white on white trace" is at once to see discontinuity in the presence of the trace and at the same time to assert continuity in its effacement. While the third person narrator discovers the rotunda as an image of discontinuity circumscribed from without (but therefore imagined as a hermetic continuity), the second person observer reveals the rotunda's continuity in being violated from without (but makes it imaginable in its discontinuity by being inscribed from within): "Diameter three feet, three feet from ground to summit of the vault. Two diameters at right angles AB CD divide the white ground into two semicircles ACB BDA. Lying on the ground two white bodies, each in its semicircle" (p. 161).

While it is clear that it is in the second person's suggested or achieved movement from the outside to the inside and vice versa that the disjunction between the two is most apparent, once the second person is active inside or established outside it is very much more difficult to determine whether the descriptions that ensue are a report of what is found or a reminder of what *would be found,* a report of discovery or a reminder concerning an imagined creation.

These descriptions are on the one hand descriptions of the rotunda's internal form (which shares the boundaries of its external form, i.e., the dimensions that would be as easily calculable from the outside as from within) and on the other descriptions of how two-dimensional space within the rotunda can be imagined as distributed, an "effort of the imagination" (*How It Is,* p. 144) not available to outside inquiry. It is clear that "diameter three feet" describes a single measurement from any two points on the contours of the rotunda, but the reference to "two diameters at right angles" reminds us that the measurement of internal space is once again a matter of content and context. The lines that describe internal space do not merely "divide the white ground" as a picture of separate configurations; they also join the object together into a whole centered around the point at which "two diameters" meet "at right angles." But when consciousness reaches for this central point, partition proliferates. One diameter (of "three feet") becomes two ("at right angles"), creating four partially overlapping semicircles. The two semicircles chosen, arrived at with reference to the diameters AB and CD, are formed only by the line AB, and they are united rather than divided because (as is clear from the notation employed to describe them, ACB BDA), points A and B (forming one diameter) figure in both.

These initial investigations into the internal properties of the imagined world duplicate those into its external configuration, for the semicircles are only imaginable separately and together they overlap in the same way as imaginary construction overlaps surrounding space: "all white in the whiteness." Each semicircle (each imaginable part) exists in relation to another, which is the outside of its own inside. What the imagination has provided, mathematics makes imaginable. But this method of confirmation employs an imaginary language to visualize the distribution of space: the "two diameters at right angles," the points along the circumference, do not exist—they are only convenient means of making space imaginable.[17]

In omitting the creation of the imagined world ("omit. Till"), the presumption was that an imagined world would therefore be available for discovery, as though it had always existed, less a matter of an imaginary world than one made imaginable by inquiry. But the imaginary language of mathematics and geometry indicates that the business of making imaginable is more a creative process than the matter of empirical verification it appears to be. But at the same time, the language of geometry is a pure sign system, not creating through signification but attaching names to what is already present and thereby discovered through signification. Insofar as consciousness "discovers nothing but what it has put into [the signs]"[18] the language of geometry is imaginary. But because it functions metalinguistically, "science attaches clear and precise significations to fixed signs"[19] that make real what they signify because the signs themselves are transparent. As Merleau-Ponty points out:

> Whatever stimulates the perceiving apparatus awakes a primordial familiarity between it and the world that we express by saying that the perceived existed before perception. In a single stroke, the immediate data of perception signify well beyond their own content, finding an inordinate echo in the perceiving subject. This is what enables the data to appear to us as perspectives upon a present object, whereas the explication of this object would proceed to infinity and would never be completed. Mathematical truth, reduced to what we truly establish, is not of a different kind. If we are almost irresistibly tempted, in conceiving the essence of a circle traced in the sand which already has all its properties, it is because our very notion of essence is formed in contact with an imitation of the perceived object as it is presented to us in perception, namely as more ancient than perception itself, a self-contained, pure being prior to the subject.[20]

This "self-contained, pure being prior to the subject" is reminiscent of Beckett's description of Bram van Velde's attempt to glimpse "the static thing in the void . . . the visible thing, the pure object"[21] forcing "the deep-seated invisibility of exterior things to the point where invisibility itself becomes a thing".[22] As Beckett goes on to say, "the work considered as pure creation, whose function stops with its genesis, is consecrated to the void."[23] In "Imagination Dead Imagine" creativity is omitted in order to make room for the void, in order to make way for "the object grasped independently of its qualities, in its indifference, its inertia, its latency."[24] But "the explication of this object" is undertaken in such a way that its essence (already present to thought) is superimposed upon by the image and the image becomes subject to investigation as object.

This superimposition cannot be a simultaneous perception of essence and image, intuition and mental representation. Since intuition relies upon memory and thus upon repetition, the image that is discovered as present to thought is only a representation of that which is being lost to memory. Just as memory of the life of the imagination is established only through the representation of habitual response, so the imagination of its death continues with the memory of intuition that is "obscured and obliterated"[25] in the representation as image. This image is consolidated into an object by the supplementing power of the imagination. But the language of geometry, however transparent a system, only signifies the image obscurely. By partitioning the available space and placing one part adjacent to but not separate from another, geometry compels the object to lose both its unity and its clarity. The proliferation of lines and angles highlights the representational nature of the language employed and the narrator's ability to dispense with them exposes the language as imaginary.

That which is imaginable—thought made real in perception—must not transgress the limits of perception. But it is only in attempting to define those limits through an image of its essence that the imaginary can be made imaginable. Because such an attempt necessarily gestures beyond the limits of perception, the process of making imaginable through discovery becomes one of imagining creatively, as the "white on white trace" makes clear. Toward the end of the text the "thousand little signs too long to imagine" show that to imagine a dead imagination leads to a resurgence of the imagination once destroyed. These "signs" show that the work of inclusion, by supplanting the work of omission, goes beyond the limits of the imaginable and returns consciousness to the imaginary world of reality.

Although the subsequent movement outside the cylinder to view the plain rotunda, "all white in the whiteness" replaces the third person as author, this is itself followed by further investigation by the second person observer, and the source of the narrative is once more split in the search for what is imaginable: "go back in, rap, solid throughout. . . ." The boundary separating the inside of the rotunda from the outside is here made concrete by tactile inquiry. Following on from the perceptual observation and the geometric mapping, this is an attempt to determine mass and volume, to make what has been a part of infinite space into the whole of finite space. But at the same time, tactile feelings ("rap") are combined with aural sensations ("a ring as in the imagination the ring of bone") that challenge the solidity that the tactile feelings have established. Albeit solid from the inside, the chamber nevertheless exists within the space that has been made apparent by the echo that opens out on the outside world and returns inside once more. The "ring" sounds within by releasing the echo of the without. In characterizing this sound, the imagination also characterizes the contours of the object that the sound has threatened to efface, but provides a representation in figurative language. Because the observer is dealing with aural and therefore fugitive phenomena, the image of "bone" belongs outside the immediately imaginable world under investigation; it is also a representation of the place from which the imagination stems. Having moved inside, consciousness discovers not another world from which it can return inviolate to the outside. but its own inside. At this point the rotunda is imagined as a skull; it becomes "the vault . . . the little chamber all bone-white," the "ivory dungeon" of the second of the *Texts for Nothing*.[26] In the words of *How It Is,* that which is inside is "in me."[27]

In *How It Is,* the chamber is "all bone-white if there were a light," light being necessary to make "place then most clear," as is shown in *All Strange Away*.[28] But in "Imagination Dead Imagine" "the light that makes all so white [has] no visible source, all shines with the same white shine, ground, wall, vault, bodies, no shadow."[29] There is "no shadow" because there is no point that directs light at the object for it to cast a shadow. To quote *The Lost Ones,* the light "appears to emanate from all sides and to permeate the entire space as though this were uniformly luminous down to its least particle of ambient air."[30] In "Imagination Dead Imagine," as in *The Lost Ones,* there is no distinction made between what sheds light and what receives it. The "ground, wall, vault" do not contain the place of Being—they are the place itself. The bodies too are not apart within it but a part of it. Unlike the "rap" and the "touch" that register the "strong heat" that emanates from the surface of the rotunda, there is "no visible source" of the light and therefore "no shadow," no echo from the object to place parts of the imagined world within a phenomenal field.

Just as in *The Lost Ones* we are referred to "hidden sources," so in "Imagination Dead Imagine" we are reminded that observation and investigation operate in a reasoned manner and that the light source is merely not "visible." Moreover, the objects referred to, as in the earlier sentence "Islands . . ." (which recalled and then erased objects in the imaginary world outside), are placed one in the context of the other by the process of designation. Although it is written that there is "no shadow," the shadow is written about and falls between the objects that are named. The objects remain (and are remains) in the trace of description. "All shines with the same white shine" assumes that there are parts that comprise this all, and these parts have to be set beside each other in order to begin to validate the suggestion that they appear "the same." Whereas the "all white" referred to earlier is singular, "all shines" here is plural. Phenomena are neither independent of the observer nor wholly dependent upon him. The observer's search for clarity and uniformity is essentially a contradictory one: clarity is marked by differences and uniformity by similitudes that can only be asserted by examining differences. Although these differences cannot be clearly traced, neither can they be uniformly erased: the walls are not hot enough to repel contact and not solid enough to muffle sound; while there is light, it has no source; although there is "no shadow," objects are revealed.

There are thus two points of view within the rotunda: one that is imagined (that of the investigator who is present) and one that is imaginary (of which there is "no trace"). The latter conflates cause and effect, surface and substance, and asserts hermetic uniformity; the former traces the relationship between parts and properties in the rotunda. These points of view are therefore intimately but obscurely connected within consciousness, for it is not just a matter of discovering what is already present but also of determining how what is there has come to be present. Although earlier the observer has omitted the creation of the imagined world ("Till all white in the whiteness the rotunda"), this is the question that he now has to include. Just as the "one glimpse" of objects in the imaginary world was neither present nor finally absent, so the genesis of the imagined world is neither discoverable nor capable of being erased. It cannot be traced by conscious inquiry, but neither can it be effaced by the limitations of conscious inquiry.

In the disengagement from the imagined world that follows this examination of conditions within the rotunda, two movements are involved—the first of retreat and the second of ascension: "Go back out, move back, the little fabric vanishes, ascend, it vanishes, all white in the whiteness, descend, go back in." These two points of view outside the rotunda complement the two points of view inside the imagined world. Whereas conscious enquiry of the rotunda's internal properties attempted to imagine another point of view that would circumscribe its own, outside the imagined world consciousness can adjust its position and, by rising above it, circumscribe its earlier point of retreat. In doing so it omits the point to which consciousness had withdrawn, for what is aimed at here is the establishment of a position from which "the sighting of the little fabric" will be a matter of "chance" and not the conscious recreation of an established procedure. In order that the rotunda may be placed and then displaced "all white in the whiteness"—independent of conscious inquiry in other words—consciousness displaces itself to a position independent of that from which conscious inquiry proceeded.

But these two points of view nevertheless remain intimately related to each other. Reentry into the imagined world proceeds along the same route, for its discovery must be guaranteed; it must be discovered at once as though it had always been and at the same time as though it had never before been discovered, as though conscious inquiry had not already foundered against the limits of imaginable phenomena and had been obliged to refer imaginatively to a point of view that could extend them. The rotunda's disappearance is therefore not complete nor is its appearance fortuitous. It remains both present and absent—"all white in the whiteness"—a whole that is yet part of a larger unrealized totality.

This aspect of imaginative inquiry becomes clearer in the subsequent discussion of the phrases "world still proof against enduring tumult" and "absence in perfect voids." For the present it is sufficient to suggest that the view from the without accords with the view, yet to be imagined, of the within, that on emergence the rotunda "vanishes" in the light and on reentry "vanishes" in the dark. While there is "still no trace" of the source of the fluctuating light (although the phenomena are variously perceptible), so the positions outside are no more omniscient than those inside and from them the rotunda is no less variously disposed.

On reentry the rotunda is characterized by "emptiness, silence, heat, whiteness" and conceived as a hermetic place emptied of objects and governed by properties that assert stability and avoid problems of causation. But reentry begins an inevitable movement toward plenitude. Not being coterminous with the object of investigation, the inquiring consciousness must clear a space for itself inside, a space that is opened up by the injunction "wait," an admonition that, accompanying a movement toward darkness, disrupts the appearance of uniformity. In order to imagine the death of the imagination it is obviously necessary to erase what has been imagined. In *All Strange Away* it is suggested that "dark must be in the end"[31] but even there it is necessary to see what is in the dark. to imagine "all strange away" in the light so that what is "in dark alone" is "as though in light." There is, as Beckett puts it, "need for light as in long light for dark." But whereas in *All Strange Away* the "mere delay" of the words moving "down again" disturbs the consonance of the movement toward darkness and the tendency of other phenomena toward entropy, in "Imagination Dead Imagine" the temperature falls "at the same time" and reaches "its minimum, say freezing point, at the same instant that the black is reached." This, we are told, "may seem strange," and later we are again informed that the stability of the extremes in temperature may also "seem strange, in the beginning." This suggests that habit will serve to make imaginable what is variable and uncertain, coercing light and temperature into simultaneity and closing the gap between past, present and future by projecting memory as habit.

The lengthy description of the movement of the light and temperature that occupies the long middle section of the text shows us the attempt to locate phenomena in relation to two extremes. But we should recall here the displacement of the outer limits of being there in *How It Is* with the narrator "half in the mud half out" when learning of "the convulsive light," of the stability of the extremes being only "as long as they last," of observation undermining the temporal and phenomenal certainties—"the black dark or the great whiteness, with attendant temperature"—in attempting to locate the intervening periods within the imaginable framework.

"If there were only darkness all would be clear. It is because there is not only darkness but also light that our situation becomes inexplicable."[32] Although it is suggested in *All Strange Away* that "dark must be in the end," it is also necessary to "say dark and light here equal in the end that is when all done with dead imagining and measures taken" for the movement from "the very sill of black . . . till at last in and black" lasts "any length" and is impossible to time. Although Beckett asserts via Bruno that "the maxima and minima of particular contraries are one and indifferent," and thus that "minimal heat equals minimal cold,"[33] the stability of the extremes is undermined as the contrasts between light and shade and heat and cold throughout the intermediate periods and passages become increasingly difficult to locate. When, for instance, a pause in the light and heat occurs "at some intermediate stage . . . then all vibrates, ground, wall, vault, bodies, ashen or leaden or between the two as may be." Although the vibration is a microcosmic appearance of the larger vibration between the two extremes, the oscillation between two intermediate and adjacent points is so rapid as to be incalculable and therefore unimaginable. The "all" is fragmented and the bodies are either "ashen" or "leaden" or "between the two, as may be." "These feverish greys" prey upon the imagination that attempts to put into them an imaginable clarity but which gets out of them only an unimaginable plethora of possibilities.[34]

Examining the "pauses of varying length . . . between end of fall and beginning of rise" and "between end of rise and beginning of fall," it is discovered that they vary between "the fraction of the second to what would have seemed, in other times, other places, an eternity." It is highly significant that the pause should be that of "the fraction of the second," for Beckett's use of the definite rather than the indefinite article does little to increase the clarity of such a supposedly imaginable moment. This is a moment similar to that later in the text at which the "eye of prey" murmurs "ah, no more in this silence and at the same instant . . . the infinitesimal shudder instantaneously suppressed." The murmur of the observer and the "shudder" of the inhabitants occur "at the same instant" and yet, as written, they follow each other. They may overlap, but they cannot be said to occur simultaneously. Similarly, the "shudder" (like the "vibration" earlier) is "instantaneously suppressed." The moment of its occurrence, the space between its appearance and disappearance is no more imaginable than it is possible to time the interval between the murmur and the shudder, between action and reaction. "The fraction of the second" is as unimaginable as what is posited as the opposite extreme, "an eternity." The sentence "It is clear from a thousand little signs too long to imagine, that they are not sleeping" sets beside "a thousand little signs" (which are too discrete to make imaginable) "an eternity" that is too long to imagine. In the one, memory is unnecessary; in the other, it has no place. In between, memory as habit attempts to make the future imaginable by recalling the past, but the process of momentary and continuous observation places the inquiring consciousness as both part of the "enduring tumult" and apart from it, situated in a position from which the "world [is] still proof" against it.

That the world should "whatever its uncertainties . . . return to a temporary calm" suggests a movement back from the rotunda toward that "absence in perfect voids" in which it is "rediscovered miraculously"[35] and its sighting purely "a matter of chance," after which it is "no longer quite the same." The tumult is of the world, which is "still proof" against it only if the imagination sets consciousness "against" the world by placing itself in a certain imaginable relation to it, and at the same time displacing itself as absent from it: in other words, only if the inside and the outside are separate and yet simultaneous. The world is itself a perfect void only if it is not present; but it asserts its presence by the making present of conscious inquiry. It also asserts itself in the rotunda that, on the return of the observer, is "no longer quite the same, from this point of view." "This point of view" cannot be finally specified. While at any moment "there is no other," it differentiates itself from another from which phenomena are "no longer quite the same." ("Absence in perfect voids" is clearly not a presence from which there can be a point of view and is therefore not self-contradictory.) The unexplained movement from absence to presence is described as one in which the rotunda (which can only exist from a point that sets surface against depth, sound against echo, light against shadow) is "rediscovered miraculously," as "a matter of chance." Perfect voids are not imaginable because they have neither inside nor outside and are not conceivably imperfect. Having omitted the sighting "all white in the whiteness," on return "externally all is as before" despite the chance encounter, and despite the fact that the rotunda is once more included in the surrounding area. But the imagination of life emerges through what is imaginable and moves inside to what is imaginary. This is why the point of view is fixed but always changing, why although there is still "storm" it is never "the same." This is why "its whiteness merg[es] in the surrounding whiteness" and why the world that is "rediscovered" is nevertheless a different world.

A further crucial instance of the opposition within consciousness between that which forms part of and that which sets itself apart from phenomena in the world concerns the "left eyes" of the inhabitants that "at incalculable intervals suddenly open wide and gaze in unblinking exposure long beyond what is humanly possible." This statement is written at once from the point of view of one who is himself "humanly possible" and at the same time from an unimaginable source that transcends it. Because the observer is unable to time the interval between opening and closure, because he is himself constrained to close his "eye of prey," he can only conclude tacitly that the period of "unblinking exposure" is "an eternity."

As we shall shortly see, it is particularly significant that there should be two inhabitants, and that, as with the light and the heat and the imaginative enterprise as a whole, the attempt should be to coerce differences into simultaneity. But "never the two gazes together except once, when the beginning of one overlapped the end of the other, for about ten seconds." We are concerned here with three eyes: those of the two inhabitants and that of the observer. Although he is unable to make imaginable the period of an individual gaze upon the world and upon the witness of that world (in other words, himself), he is nevertheless able to measure the period between the point at which one eye, in opening, joins the other, and the point at which the other closes. Because they overlap during this period, he is able to isolate this period from the closure of one on one side and the other on the other.

But the individual gaze is "too long to imagine"; accordingly, the blink is too short. It takes place, like the "infinitesimal shudder," "in the fraction of the second," the momentary closure of the eye overlapping with the momentary disclosure of the bodies. This period is described in the past tense ("overlapped") as having already happened, just as the momentary "glimpse" of the imaginary world "above in the light" was said to have "vanished." What has been captured by the imagination or lost in the imaginary asserts itself only momentarily against the "enduring tumult" and the attempt to validate such moments has already been discredited. Similarly the contrast "between [the inhabitants'] absolute stillness and the convulsive light . . . is striking, in the beginning." At the "beginning" the observer can note the difference, but now it is impossible. The contrast was only possible, furthermore, because habitual response could assert it, only possible "for one who still remembers having been struck by the contrary." The "beginning" is therefore displaced both by the memory of previous confusion and by the variable perception of present tumult. A stable term of relation no longer serves to locate any other. The present tumult precludes even the attempt at asserting differences in what has become an imaginary (because forgotten) world. The three stages of perception—the moment of perceiving difference, the moment of placing it within memory and the moment of having forgotten the difference— show not only how the imaginary becomes imaginable through memory as habit but also how it once again becomes imaginary as observation fails to locate phenomena within a habitual framework. Not only the products of memory but the process of memory itself becomes past.

It is important that there should be two inhabitants and that narrative consciousness should attempt to relate one to another in order to make a whole. It has already been noted that the diameter AB that divides the available space and separates the two bodies also joins them together as it knits together the two halves of the rotunda. Just as the line forms part of both semicircles, overlapping both, so one body is not clearly set apart from another. Neither, however, do they together form a whole when what is visible of them is only a part. Since both of them are lying on their right sides, both expose only their left eyes to view; although they are "back to back" they are also "head to arse." The bodies are only "whole and in fairly good condition, to judge by the surfaces exposed to view" and "the faces too" are assumed to be "the two sides of a piece," an assumption that could be made more conclusive if one were to expose one side of the face and the other the other. In the attempt to view the "world still proof against enduring tumult," the process of inspection and inquiry, as has been commented upon in detail elsewhere in Beckett criticism, "is not easy."[36] Inspection here only reveals that one of the bodies is that "of a woman finally" whose "long hair of strangely imperfect whiteness" impedes both the subsumption of the figure into the surrounding whiteness and the recognition of this "strange" detail as a sure "trace of life." This assertion of difference between the woman and the ground against which she figures (and of difference between her and her "partner") undermines further the suggestion that the parts are interchangeable, each part doing duty for the whole. The whole is indeed greater than the sum of its parts, the imaginary greater than the imaginable; in the same way, the position of the third person narrator encompasses that of the inquiring observer. But the role of the observer cannot be subtracted from that of the third person so as "finally" to throw into relief the composition of the whole. The third person narrator's final injunction "Leave them there, sweating and icy. There is better elsewhere" becomes from this perspective a discourse on what he has mistakenly supposed to be a problem resolvable by recourse to an alternative. Although "life ends," the imagination of life still remains. This remainder can neither be erased nor clearly formulated as "life necessarily."[37] Although there is "nothing elsewhere" and "no question now of ever finding again that white speck lost in whiteness," there remain interpolated questions regarding what can be imaginatively included. Although these possibilities fall initially into two groups—that in which the bodies are still and the world in tumult and that in which the bodies are still and the world at rest—it is possible that the bodies are not still. But it cannot be imagined "what they are doing." While the imagined world is described negatively in the attempt to extrude variable phenomena, the world of the imagination denied at the end of the text is released as a possibility that includes them. Just as it is necessary to assert the death of the imagination ("yes, dead, good") so it is inevitable that one can do no more than deny that it is alive.

Notes

1. *How It Is* (London: Calder and Boyars, 1964), 7. All page references to the text are from this edition.

2. *The Unnamable* (London: Calder and Boyars, 1975), 130. All page references to the text are from this edition.

3. *The Lost Ones* (London: Calder and Boyars, 1972), 40. All page references to the text are from this edition.

4. *Texts for Nothing* "XIII," in *No's Knife* (London: Calder and Boyars, 1967), 135. All page references to the text are from this edition.

5. This is Beckett's phrase, used in a letter to Hugh Kenner. See Kenner's *A Reader's Guide to Samuel Beckett* (New York: Farrar, Straus and Giroux, 1973), 94.

6. G. Bachelard, *The Poetics of Space,* trans. M. Jolas (Boston: Beacon Press, 1969), 215.

7. Jacques Derrida, "The Retrait of Metaphor," translated by the editors of *Enclitic, Enclitic* 2, 2 (Fall 1978): 29.

8. This is a point made by J. E. Dearlove in her essay "The Voice and Its Words: *How It Is* in Beckett's Canon," *Journal of Beckett Studies* (Summer 1978): 57.

9. "Imagination Dead Imagine" in *No's Knife,* 161.

10. See Jacques Derrida, *Speech and Phenomena and Other Essays on Husserl's Theory of Signs*, trans. D. B. Allison (Evanston, IL: Northwestern University Press, 1973), particularly chaps. 4 and 5, "Meaning and Representation" and "Signs and the Blink of an Eye."

11. Hegel's *Wissenschaft der Logik*, 1: 541–42, quoted by H. J. Schulz, *This Hell of Stories* (The Hague: Mouton, 1973), 13.

12. It is this "space that intervenes" ("Recent Irish Poetry" [1938], republished in *The Lace Curtain* 4 [Summer 1971]: 78) that Beckett believed the work of the van Veldes struggled to state, and it is this space that makes its appearance following the sundering of the relationship between subject and object. It is, then, necessary for the artist to glimpse in "the absence of relation and in the absence of object the new relation and the new object" ("Peintres de l'empêchement," *Derrière le miroir* 11 and 12 [1948]: 7, quoted by J. Pilling in his translation in *Samuel Beckett* [London: Routledge and Kegan Paul, 1976], 20).

13. "[N]o more blue the blue is done never was the sack the arms the body the mud the dark the living hair and nails all that" (*How It Is*, 114). In earlier draft versions of the text in French, "omit" first appeared as "leave unsaid" (RUL ms. 1541/1) and as "leave out" (RUL ms. 1541/2). Both mss. are in the Reading University Library Beckett Archive (RUL).

14. In an early draft of the text in French (RUL ms. 1540/1) "dites-vous" was "dites-vous, dis-je."

15. "Recent Irish poetry," 78.

16. *Tractatus Logico-philosophicus*, trans. Pears & McGuiness (London, Routledge and Kegan Paul, 1961), 2.01231, p. 9.

17. "Imagine what needed, no more, any given moment, needed no more, gone, never was" (*All Strange Away* [London, John Calder, 1979], 9). *All Strange Away* was *I Imagine*, said Beckett, written "about 1963/64 . . . on way to *Imagination morte imaginez*" (Beckett to James Knowlson, quoted in editorial in *Journal of Beckett Studies* 3 [Summer 1978]).

18. M. Merleau-Ponty, *The Prose of the World* (London: Heinemann, 1974), 5.

19. Ibid., 4.

20. Ibid., 123. See also his discussion of the parallelogram as a "possible triangle" and the "equivalent meanings between them" (104–5).

21. "La peinture des van Veldes, ou le monde et le pantalon," *Cahiers d'ant*, 20 and 21 (1945–46): 352. Quoted by Pilling in his translation in *Samuel Beckett*, 20.

22. Ibid., 354.

23. "Peintres de l'empêchement," 4.

24. Hegel, *Encyclopaedia of the Philosophical Sciences*, in W. Wallace, *Hegel's Philosophy of Mind* (Oxford: Oxford University Press, 1971), 203.

25. Quoted by E. Donato, "The Ruins of Memory: Archaeological Fragments and Textual Artifacts," *Modern Language Notes* 93, 4 (May 1978): 575–96.

26. *No's Knife*, 78.

27. *How It Is*, 146.

28. *All Strange Away,* 16.

29. This unexplained presence of light is a frequent topological feature in Beckett's late writing. See *All Strange Away,* 8, and *Ghost Trio* in *Ends and Odds* (London: Faber and Faber, 1977), 41.

30. *The Lost Ones,* 39–40. However, "No other shadows then than those cast by the bodies pressing on one another wilfully or from necessity as when for example on a breast to prevent its being lit or on some private part the hand descends with vanished palm" (p. 40). See below for a discussion of the intimate relationship between the observer and the light source as a second "point of view" within the rotunda.

31. *All Strange Away,* 23.

32. "Beckett by the Madeleine," interview with Tom Driver, *Columbia University Forum* 4 (Summer 1961): 22.

33. "Dante . . . Bruno. Vico . . . Joyce," in *Our Exagmination round his Factification for Incamination of Work In Progress,* (London: Faber and Faber, 1972), 6.

34. "Whether all grow black, or all grow bright, or all remain grey, it is grey we need, to begin with, because of what it is, and of what it can do, made of bright and black, able to shed the former, or the latter and be the latter or the former alone. But perhaps I am prey, on the subject of grey, in the grey, to delusions" (*The Unnamable,* 17). Grey is both subject and object here. Consciousness, itself grey, is surrounded by the object of the discourse's subject. As the two overlap, one is not distinguishable from the other and the third term, consciousness of the world, shares both places—the place of narration and the narration of place. See the essay by L. Janvier, "Place of Narration/Narration of Place," in *Samuel Beckett, a Collection of Critical Essays,* ed. Ruby Cohn (New York: McGraw-Hill, 1975), esp. 108–10. The following few remarks are worth quoting in full: "Writing, who can say he is building? Or having written that he has mastery over place? In a dwelling, who shelters whom? Words are not dwellings: speaking, I am always outside myself. And yet the theatre of words is a dwelling; they create space, an enclosure, an absolute exterior that is within, a tomb. In the inmost part of this enclosure is myself, that other" (109–10).

Alongside an early draft of the text in French (RUL ms. 1451/1) Beckett has written "Observation instead of experience"; whether this is an assertion, command, or reminder and to what part or parts of the text it refers can, as in the text itself, only be guessed at.

35. The suggestion of the miraculous is evident early in the text; the English "one glimpse and vanished" is from the French "fixez, pff, muscade" (i.e., "muscade" referring to a conjuror's vanishing ball).

36. See, for example, J. E. Dearlove, "'Last images': Samuel Beckett's Residual Fiction," *Journal of Modern Literature* 6: 1 (February 1977): 106–10.

37. From Beckett's 1974 poem "Something there," in *Collected Poems in English and French* (London: John Calder, 1977), 63.

Watt: Music, Tuning, and Tonality

Heath Lees

Literary critics have been understandably diffident when dealing with the references to music that abound in Beckett's work and have wrongly supposed that Beckett, often described as a "competent amateur musician," manifests a correspondingly amateur knowledge of music and musical matters in his writing. Such a diffidence, and such a misapprehension, are especially to be regretted in the case of the novel that most requires one to confront technical issues: *Watt*. Susan Field Senneff's "Song and Music in Samuel Beckett's *Watt*"[1] and Eric Park's "Fundamental Sounds"[2] both address the problem of music in *Watt* combatively. But Senneff makes some musical errors and miscalculations, while Park oscillates nervously between a technical and a metaphoric usage of a few very important musical terms. And both writers fall into the trap of crediting Beckett (or themselves) with only a limited understanding of music and thus fail to appreciate how continuously the musical themes are exploited in the novel. The imagery of tuning and untuning, for example, has been virtually ignored, yet it pervades the work, provides a musical parallel to the often-quoted existence of the ladder, and is, as I hope to show, a penetrating commentary on music itself as a unique modality. It is the purpose of this essay to explore these issues fully for perhaps the first time.[3]

All the available evidence, properly interpreted, suggests that had Watt learned to respond to the nonliteral language of music his mental catastrophe might have been avoided. By embedding specifically musical material in the novel, Beckett subtly demonstrates that Watt is exposed to musical stimuli that exert a diminishing influence upon him. Musically speaking, the novel might be described as a *diminuendo al niente*—a fading into nothing—and symptomatic of Watt's failure to achieve what Murphy too fails to achieve, Attunement.

Watt's existence, it is clear, depends on the properties of reason—the ability to enumerate, to codify, to order and compare; in sum, to provide a framework of "meaning" for his perceptions. And for this "meaning" to exist it must for him be expressible in words, indeed his world collapses when events are no longer fully accounted for in words (The Galls) or when words seem no longer to fit objects (pot, man) and finally when his own words become distorted and incoherent (nilb, mun, mud). But against this obsessive equation of words with meaning, the novel investigates the possibility of musical experience as a no less significant mode of perception, a purely musical universe unsullied by the ordinary linguistic fidgeting with significance, systematization, and sense, and yet one that carries its own meaning within its own specifically musical framework.

As James Acheson has shown,[4] Beckett was deeply and permanently influenced by the writings of Schopenhauer. Schopenhauer writes challengingly, if fancifully, on the subject of music, nowhere more so than in a passage quoted by Acheson: "[Music] is perceived . . . in and through time alone, with absolute exclusion of space, and also apart from the influence of the knowledge of causality . . . ; for the tones make the aesthetic impression as effect, . . . without obliging us to go back to their cause."

Such a description corresponds well with Beckett's own description of Proust's "impressionism." "By his impressionism," says Beckett, "I mean his non-logical statement of phenomena, in the order and exactitude of their perception, before they have been distorted into intelligibility in order to be forced into a chain of cause and effect."[5]

In Watt music is presented as having precisely this "impressionistic" potential—the promise of intelligibility without the necessary concomitant process of distortion. Watt's increasing inability to form an aesthetic relationship with music is indicative of his refusal to surrender the Cartesian chain that binds him to a view of the world in terms of cause and effect. Whereas Watt's existence depends on retracing the ordered series of causes, music, in Schopenhauer's view, makes its own effect "without obliging us to go back to their causes." Watt gradually proves himself quite unable to come to terms with music, and in time his ears become deaf to the invitation that music seems to offer.

Schopenhauer's description of the ranges of musical voices or parts in a composition is of particular interest in connection with Watt: "Those musical parts nearer to the bass are the lower of these grades, the still unorganised, but yet manifold phenomenal things; the higher represent to me the world of plants and beasts. The definite intervals of the scale are parallel to the definite grades of the objectification of will, the definite species in nature. The departure from the arithmetical correctness of the intervals, through some temperament, or produced by the key selected, is analogous to the departure of the individual from the type of the species."[6]

The theme of tuning (Schopenhauer's "temperament") and tonality ("the key selected") is fundamental to the understanding of *Watt*. But the very relationship that Schopenhauer proposes between music and the world of "unorganised but yet manifold phenomenal things" on the one hand and of "plants and beasts" on the other, also leaves its mark on the novel. The Threne (p. 33)[7] for example, has a disorganized, rumbling-and-grunting bass, with inexplicable interjections of a blasphemous or coarse nature, while the soprano is clearly heard, and even given some fully written-out music in the Addenda.[8]

For Schopenhauer, the realm of plant life shares with music the immediacy of the "aesthetic impression": "The plant reveals its whole being at the first glance, and with complete innocence, which does not suffer from the fact that it carries its organs of generation exposed on its upper surface. . . ."[9]

In *Watt*, we may recall, before the singing of the Threne, there are parallel intimations of the secret vibrancy of Nature and Watt's bed of "wild long, grass, the foxgloves, the hyssop, the pretty nettles, the high pouting hemlock" (p. 33). A much smaller—and less poisonous—catalogue of flowers precedes the Frog Song (p. 135), and later still only desultory mention is made of shrubs and trees at the point where the Descant Song is adumbrated but fails to appear (p. 223). Watt's perceptions of plants and of music are presented as parallel experiences, whose significance is not to be extracted by "sweet reasonableness" but rather, in Bergson's phrase, to be "entered into." Watt is faced with a series of invitations to aesthetic encounter; but the invitations themselves gradually lose their already tenuous hold on Watt as the novel progresses. The brief survey of his ever-diminishing response to music that now follows is also intended to serve as a reminder of the main musical occurrences in the novel. For reasons of space, some of the interesting but minor references have been omitted.

At the appearance of the Threne (p. 33) Watt waits, Belacqua-like, in the ditch and hears a choir either inside of himself or outside, he is not sure; but he senses a reality of relationship between himself and the music.

At the close of the song the narrator notes: "Of these two verses Watt thought he preferred the former." The reason given for his preference is grounded in the primacy of "meaning" over aesthetic effect, though at this stage Watt's thoughts do admit a halting possibility of some correlation: "Bun is such a sad word, is it not? And man is not much better, is it?"

The next musical encounter—the Frog Song (pp. 137–38)—appears much more detached from Watt's experience, firstly because it is not an actual event but a recollected one, and secondly because Watt seems to be aware only of the principle of order that underpins it. It is also worthy of note that whereas some composed music is given for the Threne (even if it is relegated to the Addenda), the Frog Song is given as a mere pattern of words. It seems significant in this connection that Beckett himself should not actually use the term "song" to describe the incident nor ever state that the frogs actually "sing." I have retained the designation Frog Song in order to demonstrate later that there is an element of specially musical significance in the passage—indeed the Frog Song, in a musical context, is crucial to the process of Watt's "untuning." But it is obvious that the words of the frogs, only minimally musical in themselves, are not subjected to any type of musical dynamic by way of barring or phrasing, and that the silent beats are represented by dashes rather than by rests. Insofar as it appears as a musical experience at all, the Frog Song unquestionably takes place outside of Watt. There is, surely symptomatically, no linking phrase in the manner of "he heard." The man and the song are not related, merely juxtaposed.

The third song is referred to in the Addenda simply as "Descant heard by Watt on way to station" and in brackets the numeral IV is added, presumably to prevent the reader from confusing it with the Threne in chapter I, also heard "on [the] way to [the] station." The single line of introduction given in the Addenda is the narrator's only attempt to fix the song in time and space since perusal of chapter IV reveals that the song does not in fact appear in the text of that chapter. The implication, I take it, is that the song is sung, but that Watt, now so out of tune with his environment, does not hear it, despite the information given in the Addenda. Page 223 contains the obvious juncture for this song; the root and branch of Nature appears again, "not unpleasant," reference is made to "the place," the bough drags backwards and forwards despite the fact that there is no wind, and Watt is again overtaken by weakness. "But it passed, and he pursued his way, towards the railway-station." Here, it would seem, Watt's musical awareness has finally failed him. Like the conniving caricature that passes for Mr. Louit, Watt, too, has now "no ear for music."

As for the music and the plants, so too for the "voices that Watt hears," voices that act as premonitions of music, playing out their gradual diminuendo al niente. They sound first before the Threne (p. 29), while Mr. Spiro is waxing eloquent. Though unintelligible, the character of these voices can at least be elicited. They sing, cry, state, and murmur, and Watt's attempt to construe meaning from them consists of simply framing their mode of expression in mathematical permutations—though even that fails as an ordered system.[10] But the voices are there, Watt can hear them, and can attribute some element of tone to them.

A less clear "little voice" is heard by Watt (p. 91) after the exposition of the twelve possibilities entertained by him in connection with the problem of Mr. Knott's food. This voice is dimmer, more enigmatic, almost mocking. It uses something of the incremental technique found in folk song, allied with a knockabout, music-hall type of lyric, of a kind that Beckett has admitted he far prefers to opera since it "at least inaugurates the comedy of an exhaustive enumeration."[11] Watt is unable, however, to tell whether this "little voice" is joking or serious. And by the time Watt is on the point of leaving Mr. Knott's house, sound has diminished still further: "the pleasant voice of poor Micks . . . was lost, in the soundless tumult of the inner lamentation" (p. 217). In the railway station waiting room, having recently passed "the place" where the Descant Song may conceivably have been sung, Watt's voices return momentarily: "He lay on the seat, without thought or sensation, except for a slight feeling of chill in one foot. In his skull the voices whispering their canon were like a patter of mice, a flurry of little grey paws in the dust. This was very likely a sensation also, strictly speaking" (p. 232).

The closing silence following Mr. Case's departing footfalls is described as "a music of which Watt was particularly fond," and but for one whispering voice that Watt ascribes to a woman he once knew, the last references to music are all less than tangential to Watt's experience, including Mr. Case's book, ironically entitled "Songs By The Way" which, we are told, he had forgotten to leave behind. The final inclusion of sound is that of the goat dragging its (Cartesian) chain and "pale"—the "pale music of innocence" (p. 174)?—into the distance, with the fading clatter forming the al niente of the inevitable diminuendo.

The novel's treatment of the voices, of the experience of music, and of the encounter with Nature all suggest that if Watt had accepted the invitations offered by music all might have been well—or at least for the best possible. But increasingly he ignores it and Attunement for Watt proves as impossible as it had been for Murphy. Murphy's strained crescendo of failure in "music, MUSIC, *MUSIC*" has now become a diminuendo of failure from *MUSIC* to an empty, fading clatter.

But in *Watt* the failure goes deeper, for Beckett contrives in a variety of ways to demonstrate that not even music is the ideal, purely musical language, intelligible yet undistorted. On the contrary, says Beckett, music itself is distorted and incomplete and, like language, forced to surrender its natural life on Western humanity's altar of systematic reason.

To understand the musical context in which Beckett makes this clear, it is necessary to look at the unpublished draft (B) of *Watt* where the following passage appears:

> In what month this was he could not tell. It was when the yew was green, dark green, almost black. It was on a morning white and soft, promising sunshine, threatening rain. It was to the sound of bells, of church bells, of chapel bells, ringing deep and slow, ringing high and swift, in commemoration of some memorable occasion in the life of their Lord, or of His family, or of His numerous followers. Deep and slow, high and swift, so that for every three peals of the former there were no fewer than five of the latter, and that the third and fifth, the sixth and tenth, the ninth and fifteenth, the twelfth and twentieth, etcetera, strokes, on the one hand of the reformed, on the other of the aboriginal clapper, produced a chord, a charming chord, a charming charming second a comma sharp, a charming charming third a comma flat, assuming that the bell-ringers began to ring their bells at precisely the same moment, and that they continued to ring them at intervals in each case identical with the initial interval, and that Quin's [Knott's] residence was precisely equidistant from the two [space] . . . of worship, a combination of circumstances seldom united, and it was on a morning that the milk-boy came singing to the door, in his shrill voice to the door his ["tuneless" scored out] harsh song, and went singing away, having poured out the milk, from his can into the jug, with his usual generosity. The strange man's name was Phelps. He resembled Arsene in structure. (Draft [B], p. 241)

The image of the yew suggests the farthermost edge of winter, before the expected bright green of the new growth. Watt, too, may reasonably expect that the arrival of Phelps (Arthur) signals a change in the present darkness of his own *Winterrëise* through Mr. Knott's world. Even if the dawning day hardly betokens "the unsoiled light of the new day . . . the day without precedent at last" (p. 64), still there is a feeling of promise, a suggestion of hopefulness. Is not that something?, as *Watt's* narrator would say. The printed text reads:

> He did not know when this was. It was when the yew was dark green, almost black. It was on a morning white and soft, and the earth seemed dressed for the grave. It was to the sound of bells, of chapel bells, of church bells. It was on a morning that the milkboy came singing to the door, shrilly to the door his tuneless song, and went singing away, having measured out the milk, from his can, to the jug, with all his usual liberality.
>
> The strange man resembled Arsene and Erskine, in build. He gave his name as Arthur. Arthur. (p. 148–49)

The relative optimism of the draft has been decisively altered here; the "charming" peal of bells[12] is now placed in a context that reminds us that the earth is being "dressed for the grave." The fascination with the bells and their interfering series seems to have disappeared in the printed text, but if we turn to the Frog Song we can see that the actual intervals reappear there, since the lower two frogs sing at a distance of five and three, numbers whose addition gives the interval with the top frog—eight.[13]

Commentators have experienced difficulty in assigning any really musical meaning to the song, Susan Senneff, for example, concluding that it is little more than "a humorous interlude of noise." Certainly the song can be related to its environment in ways other than musical ones. There is an oblique numerical relationship between the earlier permutations of Tom, Dick, and Harry and the permutations of the three croaks of the song. The numbers used for the servants' coming and going—two years and ten years—yield the numbers eight and five and hence three when subjected to the reductive processes of division and subtraction. The song begins on a coincidence of the three frogs and ends (or begins again?) on another such coincidence. The song can, therefore, be interpreted as an agent of transition between the inevitability of separateness (the individuation of Tom, Dick, and Harry) and the possibility of meeting (the meeting of Watt and the fisherwoman). One cannot help here but recall that the meeting in *Murphy* between Murphy and Celia is described in the continuous musical transition from serenade to nocturne and finally albada.

Yet this line of inquiry leaves one feeling dissatisfied. The inexorable coherence of the song seems somehow illusory. Arithmetically, the song appears to be completely worked out; one writer has even described it as "computerized."[14] Yet Beckett may well be teasing the reader when he puts the all-important exclamation point after each of the terms "Krak!" "Krek!" and "Krik!" A mathematician would see the exclamation point as a factorial sign and would quickly become aware of the unfinished effect that Beckett achieves ($3! = 3 \times 2 \times 1$: $4! = 4 \times 3 \times 2 \times 1$ etc.). The terms of the series seem to be fully and logically worked out, yet the factorial sign suggests that further operations in respect of each term have yet to be made. In other words, the linear logic is followed impeccably, but the implied harmonic depth of the terms themselves remains unexplored. Attunement eludes the grasp again.

If the song is shifted from the mathematical to the musical context and combined with a reading of the quoted section from the typescript draft (B), a wholly new possibility that is merely hinted at in the mathematical context becomes apparent in the musical dimension. Beckett chooses to conceal this dimension by dropping two technical terms in the final version. The first of these terms is the word "interval."

In musical practice, intervals are counted by including both the outer framing notes in the calculation. On the paradigmatic scale of C major, the interval of a third from the tonic produces the note E; the fifth is G; and the eighth (octave) is of course the higher C. The acoustic relationship within the octave from top C to bottom C is $2/1$, i.e., within any one time interval the upper C has exactly twice as many vibrations as the lower C. All the Cs on, for example, a piano are fixed from bottom to top in this constantly doubled relationship. But the consequent, basic Western division of the octave into twelve roughly equal steps is actually only a convenience, arising out of centuries of musical experiment and generated by the desire to repeat the series on every note of the division. It results in the ability to move from one scale series to another (modulation) but only by paying the price of having some intervals slightly mismatched.

Beckett's awareness of the difficulties and compromises that are bred into the Western scale system emerge more clearly when we turn our attention to the second "technical" term in his typescript, the seemingly innocent word that implies a metaphor but which is a proper musical designation—the word "comma." It would not be overstating the case to say that only two groups of people use this word in music. The first—very small—group comprises those musicians whose work takes them into the theory of acoustics. The second—much larger—group (and here Watt comes swimming back into our ken) is made up of piano tuners. For the art of piano tuning lies in the ability to reconcile the mathematical reality of acoustics with the musical necessity of an equally partitioned octave, repeatable at any pitch. To achieve this, the notes have to be tampered with (the Western scale is called a "tempered" scale), and the note that sounds most tampered with is the third, when set within the frame of any octave and its fifth. These figures of three, five, and eight are of course the ones that Beckett supplies for the bells and then transposes in a spatial context to the frogs. The comma—its full designation is the "Pythagorean comma"—is the difference between tuning twelve perfect fifths as opposed to tuning seven perfect octaves. If one were to start at the bottom note of the piano (A) and tune the whole series in fifths in the "correct" mathematical ratio (3/2) one would arrive at a top note somewhat sharper—"a comma sharp"—than would be obtained by beginning on the same note and tuning upwards for each A in the octave ratio of 2/1 (see figure).

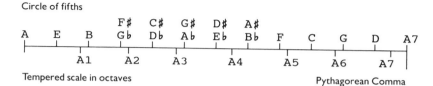

Circle of fifths

To reconcile this anomaly of musical nature, much discussed by the Greeks in their experiments with one sounding string, the mathematical "degrees" have to be put aside and the string's natural sounding modes have to be slightly distorted, with the consequent out-of-tune-ness being spread as imperceptibly as possible over other notes within the octaves. The present systematic division of the octave into twelve notes (i.e., including black notes) means that from the bottom of the keyboard each fifth note has to be "plotted" as an *almost* perfect fifth so that after twelve of these (the circle of fifths) the system can coincide on the starting note, seven octaves above.

Just as the fifth has to be "tempered" within the octave, so too the third has to be tempered within the fifth, necessitating other tiny adjustments in the notes round about; but once the intervals of third, fifth, and octave have been established from any given pitch, the basic (though slightly distorted) concord of the key has been set into the pattern known as doh-me-soh-doh. Without this slight distortion of natural sound, the seven-times-repeated notes that make up a piano keyboard would not be possible. To quote from Grove's *Dictionary of Music and Musicians:* "It so happens that if from any given note we try to tune three series of notes

. . . one in octaves, one in fifths and one in thirds, we shall never reach a unison again between the notes of any two of the series."[15]

This information is marshaled here in an attempt to suggest that, far from being just a symbol to the effect that "physical events . . . do not interact but coincide" (Kenner) or even a "literary anti-romantic mockery" (Senneff), the Frog Song is crucial to the understanding of the inevitability of Watt's failure. Against the background of acoustic theory, the song becomes an ironic sign of the fact that even in music itself Attunement is more illusory than real. The intervals of third, fifth, and eighth, the very basis of Western tonal concord, will never properly cohere unless fixed in a predistorted musical system. Musical "order" demands a continuous tinkering with natural sound to make the tonal system repeatable for different keys and therefore amenable to the form of series—the triumph of ratio over musical matter. Western music relies for its effect of discord resolving into concord not on musical truth but on musical compromise, the kind of compromise that is to be found in a preestablished, sleight-of-ear system that piano tuners, for example, are paid to create. Watt's ear for music fails him not just because sensibility is overwhelmed by sense, but because the Western musical system of tonality is based on an element of distortion in order to achieve that system. It is, so to speak, a trick. In Wattian terms, Art *is* Con; tuner, piano, and pianist are all doomed.

It will be observed that thus far I have ignored the "incident of note" in which the Galls arrive at Knott's house to "choon the piano."[16] But I think it is clear from the above discussion that temperament (in the musical sense, as the word is used by Schopenhauer) demands a much more important place in the interpretation of the novel than it has yet been accorded. As will be seen, the Galls loom quite as large in relation to musical theory as they do in relation to Watt's own untuning—the beginning of what Arsene would call his "existence off the ladder."

Specific musical references in the narration of this incident can now be studied more closely and their proper importance gauged. The most obvious references are to do with the apparatus of the piano, but two other musical objects are mentioned in the description of the music room into which the Galls are conducted: a bust of Buxtehude and a ravanastron. In the early handwritten draft (A) these two objects appear as part of the description of the second picture of Erskine's room, the picture "representing gentleman seated at piano," and it seems likely that in Beckett's mind this picture would have been painted in Mr. Knott's music room. In the draft it is actually made clear that the picture is of Mr.

Knott's father, who, among other things, holds a degree of Bachelor of Music from the University of Kentucky.

Both the bust of Buxtehude and the ravanastron have perplexed critics, and the reasons offered for their appearance have been at best half-hearted. Coetzee[17] finds only this to say of Buxtehude: ". . . the bust of divine Buxtehude, to hear whom Bach walked two hundred miles." The ravanastron defeats him entirely. "Perhaps we are supposed to find it funny, but we cannot be sure we have caught the joke until we know what a ravanastron is (and the N.E.D. will not tell us)." Coetzee goes on to suggest that the two objects are simply the recondite, slightly pathetic props of an "insignificant retired musician." That Beckett intends this as an overtone is easily acknowledged, but by this time we may be wary of accepting any of Beckett's musical allusions in *Watt* as being "simply" one thing or the other.

Dietrich Buxtehude was born in 1637 and died in 1707. Coetzee is right to draw attention to his influence on Bach (1685–1750) because Bach did embark on the pilgrimage to Lübeck to attend the famous concerts in the Abendmusik series held there on Sundays. But Buxtehude was not the only organist who influenced Bach—he made it his business to hear other famous virtuosi organists of that earlier generation, notably Reinken. The important thing for this discussion is that Buxtehude was the most famous of the pre-J. S. Bach school of north German organists whose virtuosi fame was made possible by their development and exploitation of the tempered scale. Buxtehude is in fact the best-known representative of the composers who, at the turn of the seventeenth century, were moving the musical center of gravity away from the modes of the old vocal music to the newly worked out tunings, scales, and keys of instrumental music. The musical achievement of Bach's *Well-Tempered Clavier*—the forty-eight preludes and fugues written in the major and minor forms of two of each of the twelve divisions of the octave—was made possible by the daring experiments of the earlier keyboard composers, particularly the earlier generation of organ composers in Germany, of whom Buxtehude is the best-known exponent. Bearing in mind Beckett's apparent concern in *Watt* with the way the tuning system of Western instrumental tonality has been altered by a ruse ("ruse a by," as Watt would say), one is not surprised to find Buxtehude laid low in the early manuscript (A), where the bust is described as being "under the piano, on its side."

The ravanastron is representative of a much older, non-Western musical tradition. Beckett's minimal description of it is dirgelike: "A ravanastron hung, on the wall, from a nail, like a plover" (p. 71). With its long neck from which a tuning peg extends downward at an angle, and at the other end a rounded sounding board, the instrument has the appearance of one of the spike-beaked, limicoline family of birds. The nail reminds us that this bird can no longer fly or sing. It may be that Beckett is here referring to the symbolic death of music as a source of tribal dynamism, and he has used this image before when he described Mr. Ticklepenny in *Murphy* (p. 86) as having "hung up his lyre." Certainly the ravanastron is crucified onto a wall, by means of "a red nail" in draft (A) (p. 50), and a rejected, unnumbered page describes it as "a scarlet nail."

Coetzee is correct to claim that the ravanastron cannot be found in the N.E.D., but it can easily be traced in dictionaries of old instruments. In the fifth edition of *Grove's Dictionary of Music and Musicians* it appears in the entry for the banjo family—not such a surprising link, perhaps, when it is recalled that Mr. Knott's father graduated from a university in Kentucky, where the banjo tradition still flourishes. The relevant sentences read:

> It is known that in India an instrument called the Ravanastron has been in use during the whole of the Christian era and for a thousand years or more before it. This was an instrument with one string stretched over a long wooden arm or neck, at the end of which the string was fixed, being fastened at its other end to a peg, or key for the purpose of tuning. At the end where the string was immovably fixed the arm had fastened to it a sort of circular wooden frame, over which was stretched parchment or vellum vibrating so as to reinforce the resonating power of the string when the latter was set in motion.[18]

The writer goes on to assert that similar instruments were known in Africa, Asia, and Egypt, but one of his most interesting observations appears slightly earlier, when he comments that the existence of such an instrument testifies to the expertise of "those who knew how to stretch strings over sounding-boards of whatever kind and how to determine the required intervals by varying the required lengths of the string." One may be at liberty, therefore, to conclude that the ravanastron, or something much resembling it, was the basis for the Pythagorean experiments in tuning. Perhaps it was with such an instrument that the mathematical relationships of sound, their conflict with musical actuality, and the existence of the "Pythagorean comma" were first discovered. At any rate, Beckett has succeeded in bringing us back to the distortion of the Western musical system, by his juxtaposition of the pioneering Buxtehude on the one hand, with his famous technique made possible by the equal tempered scale, and the rudimentary sound-string of the ravanastron on the other. Though centuries apart, both represent stages in "the tale of man's effort to resolve the irremediably discordant."[19]

Against this background of acoustic theory and musical history, the Galls' "incident of note" works in a typically Beckettian Chinese box type of series. The objects in the music room are connected with stages in human acoustic exploration. The tuners represent the ability to impose a predetermined system on natural sounds, yet the state of the piano renders this impossible, and the incident itself throws out an insuperable challenge to Watt's systematically grounded powers of reasoning. Watt is as defeated in trying to tune the Galls into his concept of meaning as the Galls themselves are in trying to tune the piano into their tempered system. Galls and Frogs are connected, we may say, not just by the obvious Roman pun and the Anglo-Saxon jibe but also by the ruse of the Western tonal system.

But the incident of the Galls is in many ways an inversion of the Frog Song. For the Galls have a handful of notes (terms) that cannot be tuned to the series, while the frogs have a meticulously cogent series that is, in its musical implications, at variance with the order of the terms. In this connection Beckett's choice of nine notes remaining for the piano tuners is an interesting one, since musical inversion within the octave is calculated inclusively, using the figure of nine. The inversion of a second is a seventh, of a third is a sixth and so on. The main musical suggestion of a piano with only nine notes remaining could be the ability to turn things upside down. This would certainly be in accord, if one may be pardoned the phrase, with other elements in the novel. And yet in the narration of the incident of the Galls it is implied that an element of tuning has gone on, that some work has actually been done on the piano: "While Watt looked round, for a place to set down his tray, Mr. Gall Junior brought his work to a close. He reassembled the piano case, put back his tools in their bag, and stood up" (p. 72).

Furthermore, on two slightly later occasions, Watt recalls actual tuning happening: "of two men, come to tune a piano, and tuning it . . ." (p. 74). And again: "and of the piano they had come all the way from town to tune, and of their tuning it. . ." (p. 77).

Aside from mere contradiction, two choices are possible: first, that the hammers and dampers do in fact coincide to give a recognizable series of nine notes. This seems unlikely in view of the exchange between father and son:

"Nine dampers remain . . . and an equal number of hammers."

"Not corresponding I hope. . . ."

"In one case."

But it could be argued that there is actually a pun here, and that the "case" refers to the piano case that has been mentioned in the preceding sentences and that the only correspondence the hammers and dampers possess is that they are part of the seven-octave compass of the piano. The absurd suggestion of tuning the piano by dividing the range of all the notes in its "case" by seven would of course yield the irrational, rolling decimal ending of .285714, part of the inexorable lamentation of the Threne.

A second, and admittedly more likely, solution is the normally accepted one, that only one note can be sounded ("in one case"), and that any tuning by the Galls was in order to determine an absolute pitch rather than any relative pitch. But in music, just as relative pitch contains discords that have been tampered with, so too absolute pitch is really only a notional concept, carrying with it an element of discord and ambiguity that requires the Western system of tonality to resolve it.

In the final pages of this essay I intend to align the notional concept of absolute pitch with the Threne, and the discordant effect of it with the second picture in Erskine's room; these are the two remaining mainly musical references in the novel. (The Descant song may, for all practical purposes, be omitted since my discussion is concerned primarily with Watt's experience of music or musically related incidents, and Watt does not really hear the "exile air" that constitutes that song and theoretically appears in chapter IV).

In the late 1930s there was much discussion over the setting of a universally accepted standard of pitch. In 1939 an international conference established standard pitch as middle-A equal to 440 cycles per second. The tradition in England and America has tended to a higher pitch while in France there was a slightly lower standard, set by decree in 1859 at 870 vibrations (435 cycles) per second. The Beckett reader will remember that the infant Murphy, slightly at variance with historical fact in 1938, does not sing "the proper A of International Concert Pitch, with 435 double variations per second, but the double flat of this" (i.e., a tone lower).

It might be thought that with the establishment of standard pitch and the perfecting of the tuners' convention of the tempered scale the system became unambiguous. But absolute pitch can be made, as it were, to sound higher or lower, to "feel" different depending on the context of the scale or key in which it appears. This phenomenon goes back to the instrumental tuning of a scale, where the slightly distorted notes produce the double function referred to by musicians as enharmonic change. Every note serves two purposes in the system and may be described in two ways: G-sharp is also A-flat; A-sharp is B-flat, and so on. It is worth noting that the enharmonic change from one note-name to its alternative was referred to in the seventeenth century as "breaking the circle" (of fifths). Singers and string players are not so limited by the fixity of the notes as keyboard players are, and will tend to make an A-flat sound a little lower than a G-sharp, as implied, not by an absolute pitch, but by the tonality or underpinning key system obtaining at the time. In short, there is really no steadily maintained absolute pitch in Western musical performance, but rather a series of small adjustments to changing tonalities in the course of a piece of music.

To a musical ear the key of C-sharp major can sound brighter, more buoyant than the key of D-flat major, though on the piano the notes C-sharp and D-flat are forced in equal temperament to coincide on the one note. That Beckett was fully aware of this particular aspect of musical ambiguity is clear from the handwritten draft (A) of *Watt*, where the music of the Threne is described: "Watt heard the music in D-flat minor but it was probably in C-sharp minor for Watt was inclined to hear A with a flat" (Draft [A], p. 228). The implication is that like Murphy—indeed like most people—Watt is unable to focus his ear clearly toward an absolute pitch since for Watt that absolute pitch, to make "sense," would need to be clarified by the enveloping musical system of key.

This predicament and its link with *Murphy* is further evinced in the Addenda where the music to the Threne appears. This naturally invites comparison with the fragment of melody that Beckett sketches in the early handwritten draft (A). The key signature of the early version is represented by five flats, which corresponds with the tonality of D-flat (major, however, not minor). But in the music as given in the Addenda (Grove Press text) the tonality is clearly B-minor, i.e., a tone lower, which according to the evidence is how Murphy would have pitched it. Characters in early Beckett tend to inherit Murphy's musical infirmity: Arsene has to break off his rendering of "Now the Day Is Over" because his opening pitch was misjudged ("haw! I began a little low perhaps") (p. 57).

Musical theory, then, leads us to the conclusion that relative pitch (the division into scale) depends on systematic distortion, and that even absolute pitch is distorted in our perception, since these perceptions are colored by the same system of key and changing tonality. Even the possibility of being in tune with one theoretical, absolute note is doomed to fail in musical practice. Interestingly the only solution left, that of the best possible compromise between absolute and relative pitch, is denied by Beckett's Threne. If the music were to be at least cogent and consistent with respect to scale and the implications of a tonally conditioned pitch, would not that at least be something? Alas, we find that Beckett distorts even the pitch-identifying feature of the key signature, as Senneff has noted, with E-sharp and C-sharp, which is very nearly correct, but not quite: the E-sharp should be one degree higher, to become F-sharp.[20] Similarly, the unpublished manuscript sketch in the handwritten draft (A) uses the key signature for the correct pitch mentioned there—D-flat—but not for the correct key mode since five flats import the major tonality although Beckett has specified minor. Adding insult to musical injury, he makes some of the flats appear wrongly disposed: three a little too sharp, one a little too flat.

The music of the Threne, not surprisingly against such a background, also tends to avoid any sense of key and keynote. Every phrase falls to what the key signature implies will be the tonic—the note B—except for the last phrase, that is an implied (but not strictly accurate) inversion of the main phrase, and then careers off onto the leading note of the key, setting up a contradictory effect of expectancy on what should be the final cadence, and so "according to the caprice of its taking place" destroying the validity of the notional governing pitch.

Some attention needs now to be given to the description of the second picture in Erskine's room since it supplies further insight into Beckett's knowledge of acoustics. The chord that the figure (Mr. Knott's father) is taking such physical pains to sustain with his right hand is "that of C Major in its second inversion" (p. 250), and Watt has "no difficulty in identifying" it as such. In the earliest manuscript version Beckett scored out the words "of c major in its first inversion" and substituted "second." The first inversion would be the notes E, G, and C, which in the scale of C major would be notes 3, 5, and 8, forming the intervals with bottom C that I have already discussed with respect to the Frog Song. But the use of the second inversion has the effect of transposing the E an octave higher, the notes appearing in the order G, C, E. Apart from the technicality of octave displacement the intervals remain unchanged in relation to the bottom note, but the order of the notes shows that Mr. Knott Senior is concentrating hard on discerning the notes of the harmonic series, or overtones.

Any fundamental note (one can hardly help here but recall Beckett's description of his writing as a matter of making "fundamental sounds . . . as fully as possible") generates a series of overtones appearing in a certain mathematical relationship. Using the note C as a fundamental note, and playing an octave in the left hand, a pianist will naturally generate the overtones G, C, E, G (B-flat), C . . . of which the first three are being sustained in the right hand by Mr. Knott Senior who has removed his left hand to cup his left ear toward the sound source. I have placed the B-flat in the series in brackets since it is slightly out of tune with the other notes in the relationship and there are other, similarly flawed, notes farther up in the series. The sound that is being heard is the gradual dying away of the concord of C major, and the figure is paying close attention to the gradual appearance of the enharmonic overtones of which B-flat is the least remote. This provides the acoustic context in which to set Beckett's description of the "extraordinary effect on musical nature by faint cacophony of remote harmonics stealing over dying accord" (p. 251).

Less well known is the fact that the "faint cacophony" sounds most clearly when the sounding medium is of the attack-and-decay type like a piano (or even a bell!), or a string plucked rather than bowed. When a note is struck on a piano, it is instantly consigned to history. Short of actual repetition, it cannot be continuously maintained in time. The string of the piano reverberates in decreasing function, and dies. Friction, acting between the air and the vibration through the air, exercises a natural diminuendo al niente, and as the diminuendo is taking place, the gradually distorting, coloring effects of the out-of-tune overtones may be perceived—hence the element of discord that so-called "absolute pitch" inevitably contains.

However, the process of bowing a string or blowing a wind instrument largely overcomes this decaying, distorted effect, since the player supplies more than enough energy to sustain the note and so overcomes the action of friction on the vibration. The note sounded by a piano cannot be continuously sustained in this way, notwithstanding the monumental force that Mr. Knott Senior is exercising at the keyboard. Increased resonance can certainly be imparted to a piano string by removing the dampers over the string, that is, by depressing the right-hand-side pedal, and this Mr. Knott Senior is doing, using all his might, the weight of his body, and both his feet. But try as he might, all his efforts to overcome the element of disharmony are doomed (as the Galls could have told him) to fail. He would have been better to have tried to bow the string of his ravanastron; but the ravanastron is essentially not a bowed instrument but a plucked one, so the problem would remain. Besides, in the face of the constantly evolving Western musical systematization, the ravanastron has long since ceased to sing.

Throughout *Watt's* music, the quest begun in *Murphy* for Apmonia or

Attunement is thwarted. The notion of true pitch is thrown into confusion; the coherence of an underlying key system is denied and the patterns of scales themselves are revealed as a manipulation of acoustic fact—a mere expedience wrought at the hands and ears of Western musicians in league with the tuners. The experience of Western musical composition does not after all offer a real solution to the problem of "intelligibility without distortion." The diminuendo al niente of *Watt* (and of Watt) is inevitable not just because Watt is what he is, but also because Western music is what it is.

Notes

1. Susan Field Senneff, "Song and Music in Samuel Beckett's *Watt*," *Modern Fiction Studies* 10 (Summer 1964): 137–50.

2. Eric Park, "Fundamental Sounds: Music in Samuel Beckett's *Murphy* and *Watt*," *Modern Fiction Studies* 21 (Summer 1975): 157–71.

3. I have been greatly aided in my examination of the music in *Watt* by access to the early drafts of the novel, thanks to the generous cooperation of the Humanities Research Center, the University of Texas at Austin, and of course to Mr. Beckett himself who kindly authorized that access, and granted permission to quote certain passages from those drafts. The drafts are three in number, the first (A) in holograph form, a second (B) in edited, typed version, and a third (C) that includes substantial parts of (B) along with another 163 pages of handwritten material.

4. James Acheson, "Beckett, Proust and Schopenhauer," *Contemporary Literature* 19 (Spring 1978): 175–76.

5. Samuel Beckett, *Proust* (New York: Grove Press, 1931), 66.

6. Arthur Schopenhauer, *The World as Will and Idea,* trans. R. B. Haldane and J. Kemp (London: Kegan Paul, Trench, Trubner and Co., 1909), 3: 334.

7. Beckett, *Watt* (New York: Grove Press, 1959). All succeeding references to the novel are to this edition.

8. The appearance of the music in the Addenda is itself tortuous. Some editions present the complete sentence of introduction with the music (Olympia, Grove, and Italian). Others retain the introductory sentence but omit the music (Calder, Swedish, and Spanish), while the Minuit and German editions both omit both. The Norwegian translation contains both, and the music is rewritten in another hand, innocently "correcting the mistakes" of key and time-signature.

9. Schopenhauer, *The World,* 1: 204.

10. See John J. Mood, "The Personal System—Samuel Beckett's Watt," *PMLA* 86 (March 1971): 255–65, for a survey of the distortions and incompleteness of Watt's permutations.

11. Beckett, *Proust,* 71.

12. The bells in the draft are important not merely for their contribution to the

seductively optimistic tone of the passage, but also for the additional imagery they provide of a circle with a moving center, an image that recurs in one form or another throughout the book proper. The music in the Threne with its seemingly aimless repeats has something of the character of a peal of six, imperfectly rung.

13. The actual intervals have been confused thanks to a mixture of inclusive and exclusive counting. Senneff (p. 142) counts the top series correctly to give 8, but then counts only the dashes, to arrive at the figures for the two lower frogs as 4 and 2. In *Samuel Beckett, A Critical Study* (London: John Calder, 1961), 86, Hugh Kenner falls into the opposite trap by counting both croaks twice to give a figure of 9, 6, and 4. Yet both give the 360 figure for the total—a total arrived at by including the first term and excluding the recurrent term; the musical system of counting bars rather than intervals is to be adopted, giving figures of 8, 5, and 3, and 360 total. Park (p. 170) gives the correct figures for the series.

14. H. Porter Abbott, *The Fiction of Samuel Beckett: Form and Effect* (Berkeley, CA: University of California Press, 1973), 59. The frogs are erroneously ascribed to Murphy and the exclamation points omitted.

15. *Grove's Dictionary of Music and Musicians,* ed. Eric Blom, 5th ed. (London: Macmillan, 1954), 8: 374. The *New Grove Dictionary of Music and Musicians,* ed. Stanley Sadie, 6th ed. (London: Macmillan, 1980) has a much shorter—and, for our purposes, less obviously relevant section—on the subject of tuning. The acoustic facts of the varied temperings of octaves remain unchanged of course, and the articles on Temperament and Interval repeat the prime importance of the manipulation of the octave, fifth, and third in the Western system of tuning.

16. John Pilling has offered the welcome suggestion that the sudden appearance of Dublin accent on the word "choon" is more than a colourful music-hall overtone but an initial clue to this very process of tuning and untuning. It would seem very typical of Beckett to tune the word "tune."

17. J. M. Coetzee, "The Manuscript Revisions of Beckett's *Watt,*" *Journal of Modern Literature* 2 (November 1972): 474–75.

18. *Grove's Dictionary,* 5th ed., 1: 402. *The New Grove* omits references to the ravanastron.

19. Park, "Fundamental Sounds," 162.

20. It is interesting to observe that the symbolist painter Joan Miró, in a fragment of music in the painting "Carnival of Harlequin" (1924–25), has one dislocated sharp in the "key-signature" and this is again an E-sharp, as in the Threne. The three notes included in the painting are very similar to the first three notes of the Threne. (Is there another play here, this time on the word Threne itself?) Beckett would no doubt have seen Miró's painting, but a discussion of the symbolists' ideas on music in the context of Beckett's sources lies outside the scope of this present essay. Dougald McMillan's essay "Samuel Beckett and the Visual Arts," in *On Beckett: Essays and Criticism,* ed. S. E. Gontarski (New York: Grove Press, 1986): 29–45, provides illumination on many of Beckett's various incorporations from the visual arts.

12

Quoting from *Godot*: Trends
in Contemporary French Theater

Anne C. Murch

In its 1979–80 season, the National Theater of Strasbourg (TNS) featured a play inspired by Samuel Beckett's *Waiting for Godot*. The text of this play was made up of extracts from the dialogue of the original French version. Such an event obviously constitutes a striking demonstration of the status achieved by Beckett's play in Western culture. But it also throws light on some of the changes that have occurred in Western drama since the end of World War II. The present article will examine these two phenomena.

The first performance of *En attendant Godot* in Paris, at the Théâtre de Babylone in 1953, was received with indignation and scorn. The scorn and the indignation were reminiscent of the treatment meted out to that other revolutionary play, *Ubu-Roi,* at the Théâtre de l'Oeuvre in 1896. Yet, a quarter of a century later, *Godot* continues to be performed throughout the world. Starting from the stage and the shelves of bookshops it has reached amphitheaters and classrooms, first as a prescribed text in universities, then as a text for secondary school students. Reaching an ever wider public in terms of cultures, age groups, and social classes, it seems to have thrived on, rather than suffered from, the delicate process of translation and interpretation. It has successfully survived the linguistic and cultural differences/distortions that such a process unavoidably entails. This very resilience confirms its universality.

What seems to have occurred in this singular rise to fame is that the dramatis personae first given life by Beckett's writing, then, as it were, given a second birth through their incarnation on stage, have rapidly left the narrow precincts of art to become, perhaps subliminally, part of the collective imagination of our time. They have become crystallized into living images that Western or Westernized human beings in the troubled second half of the twentieth century recognize: they are moved by them and they identify with them. Pozzo and Lucky as the master and the slave, functionally interdependent, are to be found in all walks of life. Estragon and Vladimir, as the ineffectual, likable, incredulous losers bonded in friendship, waiting for the miracle which tomorrow must bring, are also present everywhere.

The personae may have become somewhat simplified in the process. Their metaphysical dimension has lessened as the period has turned its back on metaphysics. Their comic-strip features have been exaggerated as the world has turned to ever more simplistic, manicheistic representations of itself. And the detached quality of their irony has sometimes been overshadowed by their simpler, rough-and-tumble humor, so that the physical "gags" are better remembered and better understood than some of the subtleties of dialogue. But the characters still stand firm as representatives of an existential malaise, epitomes of human floundering in the prison of time and space, troubled by the riddle of mortality, the focus of a bewilderment and pain daily experienced and rejected. Thanks to their powerful *iconic*[1] quality, they can be used as *models* to give concrete expression to instances in the here and now of a plight whose universal dimension they initially articulated. They have become, it seems, a cross between archetypes and stereotypes, inviting identification over a wide spectrum of existential situations.

An early example of this, and one which has been much quoted, was the immediate success of the play with the inmates of San Quentin Penitentiary. The dramatis personae, prisoners of the human condition, were received as *icons* of the prisoners in the penal institution. The personae's general plight became equated in literal terms with the life imprisonment that was their audience's *particular* fate. Hence the immediate identification.

Another instance of this process, operating in reverse this time, was seen in an Australian production of the play in Melbourne (Alexander Theatre, Monash University, March 3–20, 1976; director: Peter Oyston). In this particular case it was the *staging* that iconized the particular and the specific. Beckett's abstracted personae were made to fit the realities of the Australian outback. Vladimir and Estragon were presented as "no-hopers" wandering aimlessly in the bush, deafened by the roar of omnipresent cicadas, clinging to each other in a hostile environment that emphasized the rejection of people. Pozzo became the *icon* of the colonial oppressor; Lucky, an Australian aborigine, the colonial slave. The audience, entirely white and urban, had no difficulty in transcending the regionalist *parti-pris* and identifying with the plight of the personae. It was experienced as their own malaise in a rootless culture in which they groped unsuccessfully for some life-giving, structuring principle in a big city, urban but not urbane.

Beckett's play, through a wide range of differences in stage realization and audience reception, has come to offer a structured substitute for the apparently unstructured complexity of raw experience in any one reality. The substitute at once simplifies and clarifies this reality. It takes its place in the collective imagination and operates as a *stereotype*. I am henceforth using the term *stereotype* as positive and implying in my context the presence of an archetypal element. The antipodean "tampering" with the play in the Monash production was minor by comparison with the much more radical "tampering" undertaken in *Ils allaient obscurs sous la nuit solitaire*, the title of the Strasbourg production.[2] In the latter the performing space was a disused hangar, rented by the company in order to free itself from the traditional architecture of its own theater. The spectators were forced to walk across the actors' performing area to their seats when the hangar door was finally opened. The whole length of the hangar, and about half its width, was used as the performing area. The remaining space accommodated a few tiers of wooden benches for the spectators. The wide performing area thus set up was lost in fog (this artificial fog spread through the hangar while the spectators waited to be let in; water had been poured on the concrete floor across which they had to walk). The fog remained during the performance, though it began to disperse toward the end. The lighting was dim throughout, with no use of light effects of any kind. All the light originated from the props themselves. Surrounding a vast empty area in the center, the set consisted of a neon-lit bar on the left with large windows through which could be seen a barman, endlessly washing and drying glasses and serving some newlyweds who were the only people entering the bar. There were two cars parked diagonally by the curb in front of the bar, the main facade of which was perpendicular to the audience; the bar occupied a street corner; a number of parking meters were aligned on the pavement. Facing the bar on the opposite side of the stage were two shops, apparently closed, but with their display-windows lit; in one of them a television set was turned on, as was the set displayed in the bar opposite. Another shop, neon lit and glass fronted, stood along the back of the stage; but from what could be glimpsed through the fog, it turned out to be a dentist's consulting room with patient's chair, drill, and the usual equipment. Between the bar and the shop opposite, and closer to these, a row of stacked supermarket trolleys divided the performing area, structuring the space with the props of a consumers' society already hinted at in the rest of the set. Against the back wall and to the right, a door was just noticeable, with two lighted windows high above it.

This space, marked by diffusion, and therefore quite unlike the traditional concentration of dramatic space, was animated, not by four actors and the brief appearance of a fifth one (as in Beckett's play), but by ten actors. Four of them bore the names of "Gogo," "Didi," "Lucky," and "Pozzo." The others were: "the owner of the Citroën," "the barman," "the bridegroom," "the bride," "the man with the Ricard," and "the man with the clubfoot." The dialogue, consisting of extensive quotes from the original, was distributed in segments among the ten actors, not necessarily following the order of the original. The circular structure of Beckett's play was retained, though it was much less readily apparent due to the fragmentation of the dialogue. Perhaps in order to compensate for this, the circularity was underlined in powerful visual terms in the finale, where all ten actors filing across the stage suddenly stopped, frozen in suspended animation, in a grim version of a game of "statues" in which no move forward could allow the player to reach his goal. The action, as in Beckett's play, was marked by repetition and deterioration. However, the clear binary repetition engineered through the two-act structure of the original was abandoned here. The show was performed without interruption. The repetition appeared fragmented over the microstructures.

In Beckett's *Godot,* the deterioration is shown mainly through the changes suffered by Pozzo and Lucky in Act II. Pozzo has gone blind, Lucky can no longer sing or dance, much less, presumably, think. The change is presented by Beckett as wrought by life itself, by a fate common to all humanity. The perspective changes in the TNS play, which introduces the following added *peripeteia:* Pozzo and Lucky disappear through the door at the back of the stage into the area indicated by the lighted windows; the play continues without them (as in the original); then a huge explosion is set off in that area, sending bricks and rubble flying in all directions; out of the wreckage cries for help are heard, answered by Vladimir and Estragon's memorable statements about being called at last; when Pozzo and Lucky are finally dragged out of the ruins, they are in the same condition as the pair in Act II of Beckett's play. The explosion is associated with an act of terrorism by the audience. In other words, the deterioration is ascribed here to a human agency at a particular moment of history, rather than to humanity's condition viewed in universal terms and apparently transcending history.

The deliberately makeshift nature of the space used by the TNS points to a rejection of the format of bourgeois theater, in which a privileged audience may view in comfort a show put on for its entertainment and/or edification. The TNS production undermines the dichotomy of stage and auditorium, in an attempt to elicit from the audience a less complacent reaction. The response of several spectators to the explosion suggests that the project had succeeded: they asked each other in troubled voices whether this was part of the show, or an explosion in earnest; feelings of shock and unease were shared by all. The thin, shifting line between appearance and reality had gone, jolting the audience into an awareness that would have been unthinkable within the traditional theater architecture. The extension of the performing area altered both the interaction between the characters and the interaction between the characters and their space. Only one section of the area was used for a performance by the actors at any one time, except in the case of the final frieze. The principle of a concentrated "dramatic" time-space, emphasizing the importance of the characters, was replaced by a loose space in which the actors' presence seemed a transgression: the lines they uttered, the gestures they made, were immediately swallowed up by that space and reduced to insignificance. Estragon's statements in Beckett's play, "Ce n'est pas le vide qui manque," were here made concrete in the scenography. In this respect the TNS production is representative of a strong trend in contemporary theater style, which tends to favor the physicality of the stage as a transmitter of *signs,* over the actor as the source of the all-important dialogue.

In the Strasbourg version the setting of Beckett's *Godot* has changed from "a country road" to a suburban landscape; the tree, an ironic reminder of nature even in the original, has been eliminated. The change reflects a change from the abstracted, timeless, metaphysical clowns of Beckett's play to the present-day urban dwellers of disintegrating cities. The passage from the rarefied, neutral set to one displaying the signs of consumption and technology also points to a change of focus in terms of the relative importance of humans and the nonhuman furniture of the world. The plays of Robert Wilson carry this growing trend to its logical conclusion, erasing the human hero and replacing him by technology, presenting the new hero attended by a bevy of human puppets.

The stage lighting of the TNS was also significantly different. The waning daylight was replaced by the neon lights from the shops and the bars; no additional lighting was used. The semiotics at work here are unambiguous: the creatures on stage receive light from the worlds of consumption and technology only; they are conditioned by a cultural bondage whose interruption would spell their doom. The fog pervading the whole set reinforced the ghostlike character of the humans groping in it—as they grope along, directionless, through their lives.[3]

Finally, Beckett sets the action of his play in the evening; his characters await the arrival of night which will bring temporary oblivion. In Pautrat's play the night has already come, but it has not brought relief. Night is no longer a time for rest and sleep, for tending the wounds inflicted by the day; under the man-made lights, which are never extinguished, aimless living continues. The demands made on humans in the Strasbourg version are ever greater, the returns ever smaller, and human compliance appears boundless. From the 1950s to the 1980s, theater has more and more tended, it seems to me, to portray the sigh of resignation, rather than the cry of protest, the dull hopelessness of life rather than the lucid appraisal of it.

The Strasbourg choice of preexistent material as subject matter for a play is itself of considerable significance. "The Dramaturg" explained in the program notes that the play was neither an adaptation nor a new staging of Beckett's play, but rather a work for the stage grafted on to extracts from Beckett's text. He was concerned to present "not an original or wiser version of the play, but a faithful, black picture of our time, following the tone set by all of Beckett's works."[4] In achieving this the remarkable iconic quality of the Beckettian stereotypes was further vindicated. Beckett's play and his personae were used as mediators, truer than life, to reach out to, and to describe, the ever more elusive reality of our times.

This use of preexistent material may be seen (as in certain comparable Brecht plays) as a kind of vast *quotation* from a product of the incriminated culture. The product itself is incriminating, but in universal terms. Here it is inserted more pointedly in history. Quoting is usually a privileged terrain for irony. Not so here, where it is used both referentially and deferentially. Yet it would obviously be wrong to see it simply as a homage to a writer, for the "grafting" is also a transgression of the cultural taboo that sets up works of arts as sacred and untouchable. The quoting, here, acknowledges the fact that Beckett's work, by its exceptional resonance, has broken free from such constraints. It confirms its passage into that category of the collective imagination in which it appears truer than life. But in addition to being a comment on the work's impact, the process of quoting is clearly a comment on life itself. Offering the "show of a show" as a *faithful picture* of that life, it suggests that life itself has become a show that can only be apprehended through the mediation of the spectacular, i.e., the mediation of the alienating culture. A society celebrating its own finality in narcissistic fascination, vampirizing in so doing the individual and his or her natural environment, is mirrored in a theater about itself—a theater delighting in quoting itself.

Here again the TNS play, far from being aberrant in contemporary terms, acts as a paradigm of a trend to be found in plays by many present-day dramatists. Their invention stems not from the observation of nature, or from the workings of society, or from the now-discredited individual psychology, but from the reflections arising from, and the inspiration provided by, secondary sources: cultural artefacts, including dramatic texts.[5] This process of self-quotation is not, of course, limited to theater: it is self-evident that there has emerged in our time, not so much an art for art's sake, as an *art about art,* which acts as a comment on, an access to, but also a shield from, a reality whose remoteness and complexity are experienced by humans no longer as a challenge, but increasingly as a threat.

The most striking alteration effected by the TNS play is, of course, the atomization suffered by the dramatis personae, now ten in number. The Beckettian motif of the couple has proliferated and in the process the gruff tenderness linking Gogo and Didi has disappeared. The four pairs, two of which are now heterosexual, operate according to the bare imperatives of power in a shifting master-slave rapport. Between them, physical violence erupts suddenly and subsides likewise, in short bursts. The maimed personae seem to react to stimuli beyond their control and beyond even their awareness, as if caught in a dimension of discontinuity, a disconnected present. The most powerful exemplification of this occurred in the episode of the "rape" of the bride that the TNS introduced into the play. Dressed in her wedding gown, standing in the rain, pressed against the wall of the bar, the bride was subjected by the bridegroom to a brief coitus, his aggression followed by her flight into the night, leaving behind the bridal veil to be trampled mindlessly underfoot and reduced to a muddy, torn rag.

In the TNS play the characteristics embodied in Estragon and Vladimir are distributed over three pairs. The man with the clubfoot and the man with the Ricard, living in one of the cars, have assumed Estragon and Vladimir's tramplike quality and their physical infirmities. The two heterosexual pairs feature chiefly the grimness of the couple association.

They represent two stages of the couple in time. The wistful allusions of Beckett's pair to better times known in the past are now belied by the stage impersonation of the bride and bridegroom, whose youth and youthful compact are presented as no less hopeless. If the repeated reference to waiting is restricted to the older doubles of Didi and Gogo, this in no way distracts from the utter failure of their younger doubles. Significantly, the leitmotif of waiting shifts from *waiting for* to just *waiting*. The mode of waiting, transitive in Beckett, has become intransitive here.[6] Accordingly there is no messenger as such, although the lone, silent barman constitutes an avatar of the missing messenger—or even a degraded incarnation of Godot himself. He dispenses the solace of warmth, light, and alcohol to the privileged few, here the bride and bridegroom, i.e., the young. The bar is a derisory version of the stable yearned for by Beckett's tramp. Perhaps the bar, heavenly stable on earth, stands for all that was once waited for, for all the grand hopes of earthly fulfillment proffered by the messianic ideologies of social justice and affluence. The owner of the Citroën appears as an offshoot of the pair retaining the names of Pozzo and Lucky, and it appropriately falls to him to voice the philosophizing ascribed to Pozzo in the original. He appears as a kind of seedy, disillusioned "guru," a familiar specimen in the modern urban fauna.

In the Strasbourg version the Beckettian stereotypes have been weakened, split up, and their charisma destroyed. Allowing the spectator a measure of identification, Beckett's *Godot* gave his own feelings of despair and bewilderment a face, confirming him still in the notion of a personal identity, however precarious. The TNS play bears witness to the crumbling of even that residual, desperate, useless, and hopeless notion of identity and singularity—of that lost persona. The Beckettian stereotype remained lucid and ironic, the irony led to dignity of a kind. There is little irony here, little dignity in the atomized stereotypes;[7] they are shown as completely dominated by their cultural environment and their apparently mindless behavior and relationships. They are at once bewildered and angry—out of phase: like shadow-puppets barely silhouetted against the dim light, whose manipulator has lost control of the rods, yet somehow still manages to jerk them into bursts of convulsive action, brief acts of bravura followed by more despondency and powerless resentment.

Intent on presenting a "faithful, black picture" of our time, the play, in atomizing the personae, reflects the further deterioration of the individual in our time, his more deeply problematic status in the culture which manipulates him—a manipulation which begins to show signs of faltering. Indeed the TNS play offers a striking demonstration of a process that is widespread throughout contemporary theater: the disappearance of the character. The demonstration is especially striking in this instance because the audience is constantly receiving a double message: one from the atomized personae moving about the stage and the other from the Beckettian characters *in absentia*. The loss of power suffered by the original personae is ever present in the minds of the audience as the comparison is set before their eyes through the quoted dialogue. The TNS play achieves a telescopic rendering of the startling passage from the death of God to the death of humanity, the former embodied in the dialogue, the latter in the exploded original characters.

As far back as the late plays of Strindberg and the German Expressionist theater of the twenties, the dramatic character was subjected to a process of fragmentation; but the fragmentation, the result of an *Ich-Dramatik,* was as much an affirmation as a questioning of identity in crisis. The fragmentation witnessed in theater since no longer asserts or defends that *Ich,* but rather celebrates its demise.

The TNS play also sheds light on the dialectic obtaining between drama (here representative of literature and art in general) and critical activity. For concurrently with the ever-increasing attacks waged on the dramatic character by the playwrights themselves[8] in this, the "age of suspicion,"[9] a critical approach has developed that ceases to take the personae in their individual situation as valid units for the analysis of a play's structure. This critical reappraisal finds its most coherent expression in the exponents of a *semiology of theater.*[10] As early as 1963, Roland Barthes in his *Racine* stated that characters were mere "masks, figures gaining their differences, not from their social identity, but from their place in the general configuration in which they are caught" (the "configuration" being that of the play).[11] Patrice Pavis, in his *Problèmes de sémiologie théâtrale,*[12] urges: "We must abandon the anthropomorphic position which makes us posit that the character is at the center of the action, while the decor is relegated to [the status of] passive characterization" (p. 101). Anne Ubersfeld, in her *Lire le théâtre*[13] likewise states that the autonomy of the subject is to be excluded; according to her, when this autonomy appears "it can only be [as] an illusion or a trick serving a reductive ideology." These critics may be taken as an index of the growing consensus that only the basic subject-object relation is meaningful.

The "character" discredited as a functional model is replaced in a semiological theater by the concept of the *actant,* a term taken from narratology. The actant, in a given play, may be an abstraction, or a collective persona, or a group made up of several characters. A character, in turn, may assume, simultaneously or in succession, different actantial functions. An actant may even be scenically absent. The actant is never "a substance or a being, it is an *element in a relation*" (Ubersfeld, p. 79). The interaction of the actants orients the play toward its conclusion; it is the actants that move the characters, and not vice-versa.

This critical approach shifts critical analysis from an animate to an inanimate vortex—from humans as the independent engineers of their fate in an anthropocentric construct to humans as a meeting-ground of forces, some internalized, with which they interact. Or, as Pavis puts it: "each character is a transformation and an externalization of the actantial code" (p. 92). Furthermore, the belief in a meaning preexisting in the dramatic text and merely actualized—or betrayed—by the performance, is also rejected. This erroneous belief, due to a "logocentrist attitude" must be replaced by "an approach [which considers] theater not only as the staging of the word, but also as the *verbalization of the stage*" (Pavis, p. 12, my emphasis).

This actantial model is clearly the inspiration behind the TNS version of Beckett's play. The TNS breaks down the original personae into their components, then redistributes some of their physical, gestural, and verbal characteristics to create new stage incarnations. They dispose of the parent generation, retaining their names as a kind of *in memoriam* for some of their offspring. This, a disrespectful treatment in the eyes of the old-time theatergoer and critic, follows the logic of the actantial model in demystifying the importance of the characters as such. The original Beckettian personae were already highly problematic, with none of the individual psychology beloved of bourgeois drama. Now they become mere shadows of shadows, whose precarious hold on reality is further weakened. At no time can this pale progeny be mistaken for the motivating forces of the play—for the *actants*. The spirit of the TNS adaptation is congruent with the dominant critical ideology of our time, and must have been influenced by it.

The TNS play, fragmenting the dialogue of the original, changes its status. The quotation is presented as a montage. The conventional tendency to endow dialogue with individual psychology is checked, the temptation to interpret it as an expression of autonomous subjects removed.

Since the dialogue is played down, the nonverbal elements of the message are developed and diversified. The language of the stage, the set, the lighting, the gestures and movements of the actors, costumes, the sound effects, the music, the semiotic aspect of the dialogue as sound as against its semantic dimension, are all painstakingly emphasized as the quoted dialogue becomes a "verbalization of the stage" in Pavis's terms. The theory is reinforced by the praxis that, in turn, is vindicated by the theory. Nowhere are the changes wrought upon the original by the TNS more illustrative than in the treatment of the pair retaining the names of Pozzo and Lucky, which is worthy of comment on three main counts: (1) the nature of Lucky's burden; (2) the nature of the violence suffered by him; and (3) his monologue and the reaction it elicits:

(1) Lucky's burden in *Godot* is the timeless burden of man's oppression by man. With the TNS it becomes specific and socioeconomic: Lucky's suitcase has been replaced by a supermarket trolley which the exhausted drudge pushes and drags with great difficulty. In the dim light of the stage the trolley with its inseparable retainer also connotes a child's perambulator, with a suggestion that the precious life-burden has been replaced by the gross burden of merchandise. The original suitcase still features among the props: the female Didi carries it. It points to her personal subjection within the couple. The transfer of the sign from Lucky to her is itself a statement to the effect that all couples are variations on the Pozzo-Lucky compact.

(2) The new Pozzo does not display the physical viciousness of Beckett's character. He appears a gentle, thoughtful man in speech and manner. The only time he actually uses force on Lucky is when he compels him to drink water until the slave chokes. This, however, is done in order to keep him alive; with laudable intent in other words. Yet Lucky is subjected to a far more refined form of violence, which can dispense with brute force. Pozzo's courtesy toward his *knouk* hides a subtler form of repression, which has become institutionalized. In this conception slave and master alike are reconciled with, and secure in, the order of things; they no longer expect, in fear or hope, a transformation of that order. Pozzo's gentle ministering to Lucky as he wipes his brow epitomizes the careful ministering of the prevailing powers to the complacent masses tamed by consumption—even when the consumption amounts to the prescribed quenching of an obligatory thirst.

(3) Lucky's monologue, a climax of the letdown in Beckett's play, is usually staged in accordance with the author's painstaking directions. The tempo is marked by acceleration and leads to a convulsive crescendo. The semiotic level of the physical speech is privileged, the semantic level played down. Any attempts to give precedence to the meaning of the speech by spelling it out tend to fail in dramatic terms as they weaken the climax and lessen the pointedness of the frenzied response to the monologue. In the TNS production, thanks to the montage, it has been possi-

ble to give the monologue an entirely new impact. Lucky is seated on the pavement throughout the speech, propped up against the facade of the bar; the monologue is carefully enunciated, in a thoughtful, educated voice; the ka-ka-ka phonemes take the form of wild stutters, the repetitions appear as a natural effect of the fastidiousness of thought and speech; there is nothing frenetic or hysterical about the delivery, and it does not climax in uncontrolled acceleration. The subtext surfacing in the silences and superficial nonsequiturs is fully actualized; the tone is one of lucid, illusionless, intelligent appraisal of the totally adverse fallout left by the explosion of knowledge witnessed by our times.

Changes have also been made in the reactions wrought by the speech on the other characters. These, multiplied as we have seen, attempt to listen at first to the free entertainment provided by Pozzo; but they quickly tire of the effort required; one of them lights a cigarette, another follows; soon they turn their backs on the disappointing performer, and form a circle punctuated by the red dots of their cigarettes. At first they jeer at Lucky, then they forget him altogether, indulging in the fleeting conviviality of their circle, exchanging a few words, laughing intermittently, smoking. Lucky, meanwhile, painstakingly pursues his diagnosis of failure; and when exhaustion finally overtakes him, reducing him to silence, he slumps further into the night, with his chin resting wearily on his thin chest. Later Pozzo, in his quiet, knowing voice, informs Gogo that he may remove Lucky's hat "as he will no longer think now . . ."—a far cry from the original "gag" in which the hat has to be forcefully removed in order to put a stop to the threatening logorrhea.

The frenzied, climactic character of the episode in Beckett's play has been replaced by one of calm and resignation in Lucky, boredom and unconcern in the onlookers. The same "defusing" process is used in the sequence in which Lucky dances the dance of the net. The dance is performed by him in a sitting position, the movements reduced in scope and limited to his arms and hands: clearly the hold of the net has tightened over the years, leaving him less room for movement. The dance elicits no unease or bewilderment in the spectators, merely an eruption of hilarity shared by all—noisy, prolonged, mindless, and physical—and the episode is forgotten.

Lucky's monologue and the reaction to it on stage become a vignette for the whole TNS play: both the play and the monologue attempt to raise the consciousness of the audience—and fail. The monologue, in being given such prominence, presumably contains a plea to the audience not to dismiss it as their doubles on stage have done. But the plea is half-hearted, the utterance merely an echo, quoting what already amounted to bravura in the original: its appeal is aesthetic, rather than rhetorical.

The TNS experiment, intrinsically interesting as it is, should not be conceived of as standing alone. Rather, it is an illustration of a growing trend. Three more examples of this semiologically conscious theatre may be quoted from my own experience during the 1979–80 French season. In all cases, the theory of the actant has been heeded in the dramatic praxis.

A montage on Molière entitled *Molière Molière* was performed in Paris by the Théâtre de la Jeune Lune as an open-air show in August 1979. There were two moments when the actantial model came clearly to the fore. In the monologue of *The Miser* the famous lines were no longer spoken by one actor impersonating the character or subject. This miser was in the center of the stage surrounded by half a dozen or more other actors. The miming of the scene and the distribution of the dialogue among the actors were such that the driving force behind the miser's behavior became actualized. The actant(s) took precedence over the character and his personal obsession. Miserliness was exposed not primarily psychologically as an individual failing, but rather in its sociological aspect in a society where acquisitiveness constitutes a virtue. Secondly, the seduction scene in *Tartuffe,* which was part of the montage, featured a similar approach. On stage, in addition to Elmire and Tartuffe, were half a dozen actors wearing masks and long, black robes, who were present throughout the seduction scene. The mimicry of these scarecrows standing in a threatening, grimacing group behind Tartuffe showed them up as his doubles and his mentors. Thus physical embodiment was given to the actant at work through Tartuffe, the influential faction of the power-hungry bigots who pursued Molière himself. Here again the autonomy of the character was exposed as "an illusion" through the actualization of the other element of the relation, the real force at work through him. In both cases the concrete actualization of the abstract actant made explicit the ideology implicit in the plays, grounding them firmly in history.

In the autumn of 1979 the Théâtre de Lucernaire in Paris offered a theatrical adaptation of Flaubert's *Un coeur simple.* Had it tampered with Flaubert's prose merely in order to extract a dramatic dialogue from it, it would have been of little interest. Instead, it reproduced the text without any changes, the creative effort being directed at the forces at work in the narrative—at the actants. These, elements of the code, were acted out in preference to the characters of Félicité, Madame Aubain, etc., who belong to the *message.* The text was apportioned accordingly, not to the characters following the dictates of superficial realism, but to these actants given stage incarnation. Here again, the ideological context and subtext of Flaubert's *conte* were made visually explicit in a rendering in which the ideological stage of the time was verbalized through the text, rather than the verbal element staged.

A third example was four Molière plays (*L'école des femmes, Tartuffe, Don Juan, Le misanthrope*) staged by Antoine Vitez.[14] Vitez's production highlights the change in theatrical style in France away from a naturalistic rendering. He retains the text in a position of preeminence, but at the same time he introduces an extensive gestural element in the performance. This "body language" is neither a gratuitous concession to fashion nor a superficial acknowledgment of the dictates of theatricality. Instead, it gives expression to what is left unsaid in the dialogue, namely its hidden dominant ideology and the way in which the characters accept it, reject it, struggle with it. This, mostly unknown to the characters themselves, caught in spontaneous ideology (so that it is fitting that it should not surface in the dialogue) is shown critically through the physical messages their bodies send out. It is thus possible to show at once the false, or at least biased, questions that the characters ask themselves and the real questions that the play lays open to the spectator's scrutiny. In this way the audience is offered a double, *dialogical*[15] decrypting. Vitez's practice cannot be divorced from his theory, which it vindicates. Belonging to the mainstream of French theater, his work may serve as a fitting example of the growing acceptance of a new style of dramaturgy and a new kind of criticism.

I have dwelt at some length on this aspect of the TNS rendering of Beckett, because the contrast it highlights is consistent with the process of change in French theater over the last thirty years. The theater of political commitment featuring humanity as an active agent of history (Camus, Sartre) was superseded, as disillusionment set in on the political scene, by the "theater of the absurd," which was contemporary with Beckett's first plays. This brought with it the return of "universal man" alienated in the cosmos and seemed to ignore his place in history. However not all theater followed that trend. Standing alone, and perhaps closest to Artaud's vision, was Jean Genet's theater of ceremony. And partly under the influence of Bertolt Brecht, there has emerged a theater with socioeconomic preoccupations, applying the ideological tool of historical materialism to demonstrate the lessons of history (e.g., Adamov, Cousin, Gatti). This theater, often laboring under difficulties because of its didactic aims, only occasionally succeeds in capturing the imagination of its public. The allegiance it forms is often the result of its ideological stand, rather than its dramatic qualities. It sometimes seems as if its subject matter, not always theatrical, might be treated more felicitously by the mass media. These, however, controlled by the state apparatus, only churn out the dominant ideology. With universal man, that figment of the bourgeois humanist tradition, largely discredited, and people as victims of history not finding their voice in drama, theater seems to have reached a dead end. It has been reduced to turning to itself for its themes—to quote from *Godot*. But the quotation can itself become a new statement. As such, it also casts light on the direction drama is taking thematically. Using Beckett, the TNS play reinserts universal man into history—but reinserts him no longer as a maker of history, but as a disillusioned resigned victim of the historical process. A victim, not so much alienated in a faulty consciousness of his society, as aware of it, yet wearily bowing to its inevitability. A victim, catatonically absorbed in the daily routine of couples, of waiting, of consuming, still. Crushed by history, but gently so, nearly painlessly so, so far. However, the shattering explosion featured in the TNS play suggests the end of deceptive gentleness, the beginning of searing pain. These already feature, for instance, in the recent plays of Michel Vinaver, showing the victim trampled down by worsening socioeconomic conditions and uttering a muted cry of bewildered pain.

The now frequent phenomenon of "quoting" in theater may be linked with the increased dominion of a culture alienating the individual from him- or herself and the world. Extensive quoting, in a creative work, however interpretive and critical, acknowledges this alienation in submitting to the power of the cultural mediation which only mediates back to itself. Such a process points to a refinement, but also an impoverishment, of invention. Furthermore, its appeal is necessarily limited—the quotation used as subject matter only fully speaks for an audience conversant with the original; there is a real danger of theater becoming a cult for the initiated few. One might view in the same light the present favor enjoyed by the classics of the repertoire and see them as subjected to similar limitations. They do not escape the principle of quoting because of the cultural mediation required for their full understanding.

The struggle of theater over the last few years confirms its state of crisis. We may indeed be reduced to "quoting from *Godot*," and we may be tempted to accept that in our bankrupt cultures the truly seminal power of theater is also spent. Except that, as a rose is a rose is a rose, theater is theater is theater, conjuring up in the multilayered complexity of its signs the memory of a human's mythical appurtenance to the world;

briefly healing, through the physical immediacy of its message, the mediate character of contemporary personal experience of this world: reincarnating the individual through the flesh and blood of the ritual of performance, even when the starting point is quoting from *Godot*.

Notes

1. "The iconic is that which exhibits the same quality, or the same configuration of qualities, as the object denoted—for instance, a black spot for the color black; onomatopoeia; diagrams reproducing relations between properties" (O. Ducrot and T. Todorov, *Dictionnaire encyclopédique des sciences du langage* [Paris: Seuil, 1972], 115). (This is my translation, as are all subsequent translations, unless stated otherwise.)

2. With, as its subtitle, "D'après *En attendant Godot* de Samuel Beckett." The director was André Engel, the "dramaturg" Bernard Pautrat. I shall henceforth refer to it as the TNS play.

3. "Un monde s'éteint, un monde au regard las qui ne voit, du présent, que son rideau de brume" (Pautrat, program notes).

4. "Variations sur deux thèmes, l'attente, le couple, afin de proposer, non de la pièce une version originale et plus intelligente, mais de l'époque un tableau juste, noir, à quoi l'oeuvre entière de Samuel Beckett donne lui-même le ton" (Pautrat, program notes).

5. In Arrabal's *The Tower of Babel* (shown at the Odéon in 1979 in a remarkable production by Jorge Lavelli) a large proportion of the dialogue is made up of quotes from Cervantes, St. Theresa of Avila, and Che Guevara; Arrabal's own dialogue is characterized by clichés taken from the cultural vortex. The whole of the dialogue is undercut by the adoption of a grossly derisive tone. A play such as Tom Stoppard's *Rosencrantz and Guildenstern are Dead,* based on *Hamlet,* follows a similar process of quotation, though in a very different spirit. Ionesco's *Macbett* and Edward Bond's *Lear* are other instances that come to mind.

6. As Pautrat states in the program notes: "l'époque attend, mais elle n'attend plus rien."

7. With the exception of Lucky, as we shall see later.

8. For a recent study of these trials, see Robert Abirached's *La crise du personnage dans le théâtre moderne* (Paris: Grasset, 1978).

9. Natalie Sarraute, *L'ère du soupçon,* (Paris: Minuit, 1953).

10. Using, among others, for its theoretical elaboration in France, the findings of Souriau, Gouhier, Propp, Greimas, Mauron, and Barthes.

11. Quoted in Patrice Pavis, *Problèmes de sémiologie théâtrale* (Quebec: Les Presses de l'Université du Québec, 1976), 94.

12. Ibid.

13. Anne Ubersfeld, *Lire le théâtre* (Paris: Éditions Sociales, 1978), 82.

14. Created by the Théâtre des Quartiers d'Ivry at the Avignon Festival in 1978, since shown throughout France and Europe, with its latest repeat season at the Théâtre de la Porte St. Martin in the autumn of 1979.

15. By this is meant the simultaneous presence of two voices inside the same literary text, exposing a contradiction (Ubersfeld, 97). The most obvious example of this is Vitez's treatment of the female roles in Molière, gesturally exposing woman's state of subjection in a patriarchal society, which requires a "dialogical" reading.

13

"Imaginative Transactions"[1] in "La Falaise"

James Hansford

The first draft of "La Falaise," entitled "Pour Bram," was begun on January 6, 1975, and the final typescript is dated March 26, 1975.[2] Although written as a *témoignage* to accompany a 1975 exhibition of Bram van Velde's paintings, and despite the feeling that the text describes a painting or the painterly, Beckett apparently had no particular van Velde canvas in mind;[3] indeed "La Falaise" is a recognizable incursion into a "skullscape" while being at the same time a homage to an artist whom Beckett has always admired and with whom he has always felt an affinity.

"La Falaise" is a "skullscape" in two senses, for the landscape in the text contains at one point "un crâne entier" and more generally the text enacts the movements and impulses of the eye (or, as it becomes, the mind's eye) as it searches for a "rapprochement" with the object of its consciousness. In doing so the subject faces the "empêchement" that Beckett recorded in his 1948 essay on Bram and Geer van Velde. In that essay, "Peintres de l'empêchement," Beckett distinguished the brothers' assaults upon and by the object by suggesting that for Geer the object was invisible and unrepresentable because of what it was, while for Bram it was equally inaccessible, but because the subject was what it was.[4] In his 1976 poem "Neither," Beckett asserts that both "self" and "unself," both subject and object are "impenetrable" and that movement "to and fro" is "by way of neither."[5] This route or passage, described at the end of the poem as an "unspeakable home," is surely the same area to which he referred in the 1934 essay on Irish poetry as the "space which intervenes" following the "rupture of the lines of communication."[6] The artist is "absent . . . / from self and other," hovering in no-man's land. It is a topic to which Beckett returned in a short text of 1966, again on the occasion of a fine art exhibition, this time of the Israeli artist Avigdor Arikha: "Seige laid again to the impregnable without. Eye and hand fevering after the unself. By the hand it unceasingly changes the eye unceasingly changed. Back and forth the gaze beating against unseeable and unmakable. Truce for a space and the marks of what it is to be and be in the face of. Those deep marks to show."[7]

Of course the final emphasis here upon being "in the face of" such an "empêchement," rather than upon the subject-object dichotomy as such, is different from that in the earlier essays (and also from the later poem "Neither"), but the predicament for the artist remains essentially the same. The object (the "unself") is "impregnable" because the "eye and hand" of the artist "unceasingly changes" its constitution and disposition; and the artist in his turn is "unceasingly changed" by the attempt at representation. The "fevering" of artistic endeavor (a condition sketched as early as the Proust essay) is a perpetual movement rendered even more unsteady by the process of attempted rapprochement.

"La Falaise" depicts this movement without in fact attempting to clarify the formal conflict between subject and object which the poem and the art essays try to encompass. Although the paintings of Bram van Velde provide a suitable occasion for Beckett's own incursion into a "skullscape" ("my skull shell of sky and earth," as he wrote in an early poem, "The Vulture"[8]), in "La Falaise" it is the artist's or observer's "fevering after the unself" that is recorded and the subject as vulture who finally provides the center of attention. The "shell of sky and earth" is presented at the very beginning of the text with the window apparently serving synecdochially as the eye witnessing the scene:[9] "Fenêtre entre ciel et terre on ne sait où." It is not enough, however, simply to equate the window with the observing eye, however often Beckett may insinuate such a parallel elsewhere in his writing.[10] Beckett wants us to see a window, rather than to see it as the observing eye, wants us to be aware that the narrator is "under . . . glass," like the "I" in the second of the Texts for Nothing.[11] Early drafts of the text make it clear that the window is very much there and that the eye is "derrière la vitre," and also indicate that the window needs to be circumscribed in a manner familiar to us from the Têtes-mortes of the 1960s: "Quatre mètres de haut sur deux de large la fenêtre s'élève loin du sol." The window in "La Falaise" serves very much to frame the view, as the edges of a canvas serve as the constraints surrounding the art object:

"L'inspection la plus rasante par rapport au plan de la fenêtre n'apprend rien à ce subjet." While it is true in some measure that in revising the drafts Beckett was, as John Pilling has said, "jettisoning irrelevant details,"[12] details that make little alteration in kind to what we have in the finished version, it would certainly be a mistake to overlook this initial presence of the window. The text begins (like Beckett's early poem "La mouche"[13]) by showing the window as the agent that both separates and joins observer and observed. Moreover, a little later in the text it becomes clear that the observer's position behind the window (and consequently within a dwelling that commands only a restricted view of the outside world) leads to difficulties in arriving at an accurate picture of what is seen, within a wider context, which remains unperceived.

Most importantly, the disappearance of the window after the first sentence and the increasing attention paid first to the eye itself (finally in evidence as the vulturine "l'oeil de voler") and then to the eyes within the skull glimpsed in the cliff, make it clear that the presence of the window is part of the dynamics of the piece. In "Imagination Dead Imagine," narrative consciousness is split between a third person narrator and a second person observer who at the start of the text is present only as the object of the narrator's imperations ("go in, measure") or only as having reportedly spoken ("No trace anywhere of life, you say").[14] Similarly, in "La Falaise," we must see the window as a preliminary means of access to, or emblem of separation from, the object and controlling incursions upon it. Just as in "Imagination Dead Imagine" the observer ultimately becomes an object to the presiding third person narrator, appearing in the text (and the rotunda) as "the eye of prey,"[15] so in "La Falaise" "l'oeil de voler" becomes very much in evidence toward the ending of the piece. The subject has gradually become an object and supplanted the original object that the observing subject has begun to resurrect. The "coronal" of the skull and the "orbites" within it increasingly constitute, or insinuate themselves as, a mirror image of the subject. This gradual process causes the original object to disappear along with the cliff from which it had emerged and against which it had been set. All that remains is a blank surface ("les blancs lointains"), the very surface that confronts the subject at the start of the text. As the narrator of "Imagination Dead Imagine" put it, "no question now of ever finding again that white speck lost in whiteness."[16]

It is clear at the start of "La Falaise" that both observer and observed are imprecisely constituted. The absence of a pronominally identified narrator is characteristic of much of Beckett's '70s fiction (notably *Still* and *For to End Yet Again*), in which it is accepted that the search for self is unconnected with the question of pronominalization as such; indeed, that the search for a pronoun when there is, as the Unnamable put it, "no pronoun for me,"[17] only results in being "far" from a constituted self. The imprecision of any relationship between observer and observed is a direct result of the instability of both the terms. In the opening sentence "Fenêtre entre ciel et terre on ne sait où," the unspecific personal pronoun "on" is mirrored both phonetically and semantically in the use of "où" which indicates only a vague area to which attention is being directed. This stresses the difficulties of focusing clearly on the subject-object confrontation. It is only the window that stands out as a specific object. While the window is an object in its own right, it is more importantly a means through which the subject may perceive and organize more compelling objects of attention that as yet totally elude his grasp. The window is very much the "way of neither . . . self . . . [nor] . . . unself" as recorded in the poem of 1976.

The cliff that becomes visible ("à quelques kilomètres de la fenêtre" in an early version) is nevertheless "incolore." It was originally described as "irréelle" and as "crayeuse"; but the most suggestive of the comments omitted from the final version is the remark that the cliff "a l'air faite par l'homme." This reminds us, as nothing in the published text does, that van Velde's paintings provided the occasion for "La Falaise," a reminder that Beckett no doubt thought distracting and unhelpful. But there is a more compelling reason for the omission of this intriguing detail; whereas recourse to the painted surface (a recourse implicit in Beckett identifying the cliff as "couleur de craie" in an early draft) provides an opportunity of winning a point of perceptual purchase on the object—very much a central concern in the text—it shirks the more compelling problem surrounding the "deep-seated invisibility of exterior things" that Beckett had identified as crucial in the work of the van Veldes thirty years before in his art criticism of the 1940s.[18]

In fact it matters little whether the source of the cliff's unreality is connected with the world of man-made objects or not, if the observation is as much a projection of the subject's need to establish relationships as an account of what is indisputably there. And it is clear that attention soon shifts (as with the sighting of the "tent the colour of its surroundings" in As the Story Was Told[19] and the rotunda in All Strange Away and "Imagination Dead Imagine") to more readily available means of establishing contour and reference. In particular, the eye exhibits a profound need to separate figure from ground rather than remaining content with dissolving the problem (and blurring the distinction) by recourse to the painterly. Inspection along a vertical axis does nothing to clarify the view, however: "La crête échappe à l'oeil où qu'il se mette. La base aussi." This is to be explained by the fact that the window provides only a partial and selective aperçu; the viewer remains somewhere between "ciel et terre." But inspection horizontally is more successful: "Deux pans de ciel à jamais blanc la bordent." A just discernible contour enables him to delineate the width of the cliff, which now figures against the ground of the sky.

But a problem arises in having detected two patches of sky within the total frame provided by the view from the window, a view which it was hoped would be that of an "endscape": "Le ciel laisse-t-il deviner une fin de terre? L'ether intermédiaire?" Perhaps there is *another* cliff, further sections of cliff lying alongside the view provided by the window; what the window or the frame of the canvas excludes evidently becomes an integral part in determining what is there. The observer therefore needs to place his or her view within a much wider context even while hoping that no inspection beyond what is in front is required. Responding to this need, the eye behind the window sees both the sky and the cliff as the ground against which the frame of the window figures.

The observer's sudden impulse to reassessment is epitomized by the number of questions asked at this point in the text, which strike a very different note from the short, declarative statements earlier in the piece. The observing subject is beginning to see his or her own processes of observation as themselves objects of inquiry. Indeed both the tone and the situation remind one of the conclusion of "Imagination Dead Imagine," in which two voices speak where previously there has been only one: "Leave them there, sweating and icy, there is better elsewhere. No, life ends and no, there is nothing elsewhere."[20] The "white speck lost in whiteness" of "Imagination Dead Imagine" has been transformed in "La Falaise" into the sea birds that are perhaps "tout claire pour paraître." The narrator has already remarked "D'oiseau de mer pas trace" as an expression of his need both to witness some sign of life in an otherwise "irréelle" scene and to confirm that the scene is indeed an "endscape," the cliff forming "une fin de terre" by giving straight onto open sea.

Although there are no traces of such life, it is suggested that such traces may be invisibly there, present as part of the ground although thus far absent as figures set upon it, existing negatively. The suggestion appears to provoke in the viewer the need for an ostensibly more promising sign of life, a human face. But once again, it is the *question* of its existence that is posed: "Enfin quelle preuve d'une face? L'oeil n'en trouve aucune où qu'il se mette." In a text about ending, Beckett's use of "enfin" is characteristic here,[21] and the syntactical proximity of "face" and "l'oeil" alerts us to the progressive mirroring of subject and object that is gradually being willed into being but that has yet to occur definitively.

Because nothing of the kind is forthcoming the eye gives up its effort: "il se désiste et la folle s'y met." In the lengthier drafts it is clear that the imagination, the mind's eye, takes over: "Licence ainsi donne à l'imagination." To draw back what the narrator of the long-unpublished novel *Dream of Fair to Middling Women* referred to as the "still flat white . . . warpless music"[22] and to reveal what is present beneath the hermetic surface can only, we must infer, be achieved by drawing the lids across the eyes. In a different context, and with different problems to tackle, the narrator of *Company* describes this process well: "This at first sight seems clear. But as the eye dwells it grows obscure. Indeed the longer the eye dwells the obscurer it grows. Till the eye closes and freed from pore the mind enquires, What does this mean? What finally does this mean that at first sight seemed clear?"[23]

A point of purchase on the cliff is finally ("enfin") provided by "l'ombre d'un corniche." Interestingly enough, it is not actually the ledge itself that is visible but its shadow; the object is being conjured into being negatively. It is as though imaginative vision transforms the landscapes once scrutinized by normal stereoscopic vision into photographic negatives. While there were no shadows of sea birds visible to the "eye of flesh" because the light was too bright for anything to appear, the light of the imagination (while strong enough to prevent the appearance of the ledge itself) permits the shadows of objects to figure against the impassive white surface. The muted light of the imagination unearths details comparable to those in photographic negatives—hence the emphasis in many of the late texts upon seeing in the dark. In "La Falaise" (unlike, for example, in "Horn Came Always") it is very much in inner space that "such *images develop*" (my emphasis),[24] although the observer in the later text has a similarly "unbroken plane" in front of the mind's eye.

At this point Beckett makes clear that "Patience" is the faculty that is needed to allow features to appear, and that questioning insistence either keeps objects (like the absent sea birds) embedded in the surface or distracts the observer away from the scene by the frame of reference that the window provides. And it is "Patience" that allows for the resurrection ("s'animera") of what an early draft referred to as "lot d'ossements humains," "des restes mortels" of the final version. Nevertheless, the skull that appears along with the "débris" it accompanies is very much the bare bones of humanity, something like the shadow of a real human face or a shape discernible under an x-ray: "Un crâne entier se dégage pour finir. Un seul d'entre ceux que valent de tels débris." It is in the hope that this imaginative projection will obviate the need for further inquiry that inspection fixes upon what has struggled into being. The syntactical proximity of what is essentially becoming ("se dégage") and ending ("pour finir") suggests that, having been vouchsafed this emergent vision by patient submission, the eye nonetheless wishes to control it. It must be an active concentration rather the passive submission that operates as the skull "tente encore de rentrer dans la roche," thereby anticipating the skull and the skullscape that "pour finir encore" will "glimmer," not for the last time, in *For to End Yet Again*.[25]

Before the skull disappears, however, a further vision is kindled into life: "les orbites laissent entrevoir l'ancien regard." In earlier drafts Beckett stressed both that the glimpse gave "une idée" of the old gaze and that the "orbites" were "beautés."[26] One may recall here the proposition Beckett made in *Proust* to the effect that "Imagination, applied—a priori—to what is absent, is exercised in vacuo and cannot tolerate the limits of the real."[27] For just as the shadow of the ledge implied the presence of the ledge itself, so the vacant orbits of the skull bring to life "l'ancien regard." Through the examination of something akin to a photographic negative, the imagination then "develops" it into a positive image, to fill in spaces which are empty just as it had constructed "un crâne entier" from the "lot d'ossements humains" (as an early draft has it).

But it should be stressed that this further imaginative transaction is of a different order from that which allows for the presentation of negative images. Just as in "Imagination Dead Imagine" the image that can be imagined becomes the "thousand little signs too long to imagine,"[28] in "La Falaise" the impulse to develop the image into a positive picture disrupts the whole procedure. In "Imagination Dead Imagine" the "white speck" of the rotunda is finally "lost in the whiteness";[29] in "La Falaise" at this point it is not only the skull that disappears but the cliff also: "Par instants la falaise disparaît." *Both* figure *and* ground vanish, revealing the vacant space upon which the cliff had been established and upon which the details that had been brought into precarious existence had figured. The imaginative impulse that momentarily fleshed out the vacant eye sockets has insinuated a further figure *within* the cranium to appear. It is not so much a patient passivity as a movement *toward* the object (like that suggested in the penultimate sentence of "La Falaise"), the impulse "vers les blancs lointains." The transaction is of a quite different order from that which allowed the figure of the cranium itself to appear. The *imaginable* construct of bone has been superseded by something approaching the imaginary creation of living tissue; the subject has become aware that he is imagining and now sees himself projected into the object.[30]

Beckett said in *Proust* that subject and object are "automatically separated by the subject's consciousness of perception" and that "the object loses its purity"[31] (he refers elsewhere in *Proust* to the "impure subject"[32]). In "La Falaise" the object withdraws under the gaze of the subject. The *Proust* volume regards the issue in a moderately affirmative spirit and speaks of a "reduplication" that is "at once imaginative and empirical, at once an evocation and a direct perception, real without being merely actual, ideal without being merely abstract, the ideal real, the essential, the extratemporal."[33] But in "La Falaise" the emphasis falls squarely on the collapse of imaginative inquiry in the face of its own image. The object reminds the subject of his own need, the need as Beckett described it in his 1938 review of Denis Devlin's *Intercessions,* "that is the absolute predicament of particular human identity."[34] It is as though we are being returned to the opening scenario of the text, before a window looking out onto a featureless beyond. But at the end of "La Falaise" the window is not the only figure in sight: there is also "L'oeil de voler": "Alors l'oeil de voler vers les blancs lointains. Ou de se détourner de devant."

The scene at the end of "La Falaise" is once more "entre ciel et terre on ne sait où," with the blank canvas framed only by the impulse to clarify what lies within its purlieu. The incursion of something like an "eye of prey" ("voler" implies both flight and theft) has precipitated the disappearance of what signs of life have been glimpsed. Narrative consciousness, aware of itself as an object, has displaced the original object of its inquiry, a situation we also find at the conclusion of both "Imagination Dead Imagine" and *Ping.* A superfluity of need (most dramatically and chaotically enacted in *All Strange Away* with its sudden shifts of attention and contorted syntax) displaces the object and foregrounds that need.

This movement of the eye toward the desiccated scene is quite inimical to the state of passivity during which it was hoped that "patience" would bring the scene to life. The inaccessibility of the object as it attempts to merge once again with the ground will be even more apparent if it is assaulted. As the poem "Neither" outlines it, the movement from self to unself is "as between two lit refuges whose doors once neared/gently close," leaving the subject displaced and dispossessed. In "La Falaise" the subject is left with two alternatives, the two possibilities cited earlier in the piece: either to concentrate on what is in view or to look elsewhere. As normal vision reasserts itself once more, this uncertainty returns again.

The text ends without any of the singularity of an "endscape"; "les blancs lointains" are beyond notions of beginning and ending. Impelled by the searching eye, they will perhaps once more throw up features that will begin in order to end. Alternatively, it may be possible to search elsewhere for another "endscape" outside the frame of the window.

The retreat from the blank planes, however, is also a return (as the repeated use of "de" as preposition and suffix in "de se détourner de devant" serves to remind us). For the reader, the single solid paragraph—a block of language—is itself a clifflike surface upon the page, "that something itself" as Beckett wrote of *Work in Progress*.[35] The reader is as unable to habituate him- or herself to its contours and structure as was the observing eye faced with the cliff's crest and base. In reading and reconstructing visual and imaginative experience, the reader's eye moves "vers les blancs lointains" upon which Beckett has inscribed the record of a perpetual struggle. "La Falaise" leaves us with a wandering subject, a self unsure of its constitution because the unself has remained essentially impenetrable; but sure of its need to constitute itself by a further rapprochement while at the same time conscious of its desire to relinquish necessity.

Notes

1. Beckett uses this phrase in the course of a short critique of allegory in his review of Jack B. Yeats's novel *The Amaranthers*. The review is entitled "An imaginative work!" and was published in *The Dublin Magazine* 11 (July–September 1936): 81; reprinted in *Disjecta* (London: John Calder, 1983), 89–90.

2. The drafts are in Reading University Library (RUL), mss. 1396/4/34–1396/4/40. The published text is in *Celui qui ne peut se servir de mots* (Montpellier: Fata Morgana, 1975). All references to versions other than the published text are to ms. 1396/4/35 (unless otherwise indicated). This is the first of the drafts in typescript.

3. Beckett thought the text not worth translating into English. Both pieces of information I have, courtesy of Beckett himself, are from John Pilling.

4. "Peintres de l'empêchement," *L'herne* issue on Beckett, ed. Tom Bishop and Raymond Federman (Paris 1976): 67–70; reprinted in *Disjecta*, 133–37.

5. In *Journal of Beckett Studies* 4 (Spring 1979); reprinted in *As the Story Was Told* (London: John Calder, 1990), 108–9.

6. "Recent Irish poetry," *The Bookman* (August 1934): 235; reprinted in *Disjecta*, 70–76.

7. Beckett's English translation of "Pour Avigdor Arikha," in Victoria and Albert Museum catalogue, February–May 1976 (Paris: Galérie Claude Bernard, 1967); reprinted in *Disjecta,* 152.

8. *Collected Poems in English and French* (London: John Calder, 1977).

9. The point is made by Peter Murphy in "Language and Being in the Prose Works of Samuel Beckett" (Ph.D. thesis, University of Reading, 1979), 528; published as *Reconstructing Beckett*: Language for Being in Samuel Beckett's Fiction (Toronto: University of Toronto Press, 1990).

10. For example in *Embers* (London: Faber and Faber, 1959), where Henry narrates how Bolton "starts playing with the curtain, no, hanging, difficult to describe, draws it back . . . then towards him again, white, black, white, black" (p. 38). As Paul Lawley explains ("*Embers*: An Interpretation," *Journal of Beckett Studies* 6 [Autumn 1980]: 9–36, reprinted as chapter 7 in this volume), the "skull-room" has its "window-eyes (hanging-lids)," p. 20. In *Company,* once the eye has closed, then "the mind too closes as it were. As the window might close of a dark empty room. The single window giving on outer dark." *Company* (London: John Calder, 1980), 30.

11. *No's Knife* (London: Calder and Boyars, 1967), 77.

12. "La falaise," in *Frescoes of the Skull,* with James Knowlson (London: John Calder, 1980), 185.

13. *Collected Poems,* 43. The window is clearly a barrier: "entre la scène et moi / la vitre / vide sauf elle. . . ."

14. *No's Knife,* 161.

15. Ibid., 164.

16. Ibid.

17. *The Unnamable* (London: Calder & Boyars, 1975), 122. "All the trouble comes from that" he says "that, it's a kind of pronoun too, it isn't that either, I'm not that either." Beckett returned more explicitly to the problems of pronominalization in *Company.*

18. "La peinture des van Veldes, ou le monde et le pantalon," *Cahiers d'art* 20 and 21 (Paris, 1945–46): 854. Reprinted in *Disjecta,* 118–32.

19. In *Gunter Eich zum Gedächtnis* (Frankfurt: Suhrkamp Verlag, 1975), 10–[13]. Reprinted in *As the Story Was Told,* 103–7.

20. *No's Knife,* 164.

21. In "Pour finir encore," the word "enfin" is translated as "In the end," in "For to end yet again," *For to End Yet Again and Other Fizzles* (London: John Calder, 1976), 11.

22. Quoted by Lawrence E. Harvey in *Samuel Beckett: Poet and Critic* (Princeton, NJ: Princeton University Press, 1970), 262. *Dream of Fair to Middling Women* has been published (London: John Calder, 1992).

23. *Company,* 29.

24. *For to End Yet Again,* 34.

25. Ibid., 11.

26. Ms. 1396/4/36 (RUL).

27. *Proust and Three Dialogues* (London: John Calder, 1965), 74.

28. *No's Knife,* 164.

29. Ibid.

30. The moment is not unlike that in *Film* (New York: Grove Press, 1969) when E confronts O: "Gradually that look" (p. 44), and is to be contrasted with the eyes in *Still 3* which are "in imagination from the dead" but which are "not looking," *Essays in Criticism* 28, 2 (April 1978): 156–57. Sartre's discussion of "The look" in *Being and Nothingness* (New York: Pocket Books, 1966), 340–400 and Jacques Lacan's analysis of the gaze as "the subject sustaining himself in a function of desire," in *The Four Fundamental Concepts of Psychoanalysis,* trans. Alan Sheridan (London: The Hogarth Press, 1977), 86, are of interest in this respect.

31. *Proust,* 74.

32. Ibid., 92.

33. Ibid., 75.

34. "Denis Devlin," *transition* 27 (Paris, 1938): 289; reprinted in *Disjecta,* 91–94. See also "Les deux besoins," *Disjecta,* 55–57.

35. "Dante . . . Bruno. Vico . . . Joyce," *Our Exagmination Round his Factification for Incamination of Work in Progress* (London: Faber and Faber, 1972), 14; reprinted in *Disjecta,* 19–33.

14

Beckett and the Temptation
of Solipsism

███

Ileana Marcoulesco

Esse est aut percipere aut percipi.
GEORGE BERKELEY

Of all philosophical positions and forms of speculation known to human-kind, solipsism is perhaps the most extreme and paradoxical. The re-markable thing about affirming the existence of the *solus ipse* as the only known and testable instance and source of existence for the universe is that this affirmation seems to be reached as an ultimate logical conclusion of both idealism and empiricism—two otherwise irreconcilable philo-sophical doctrines.

There are few, if any, consistent doctrinaire solipsists in the Western tradition while they literally abound in Eastern philosophical systems. The best-known instances of solipsistic talk (not always considered as such) are offered by George Berkeley and, closer to our days, by Husserl and Wittgenstein. While Beckett is certainly not indebted to the last two (at least not in this respect), he owes as much to Berkeley as to some logical persuasions of his own. Berkeley, in his turn, owed a lot to Locke's description of ideas and even to Hume's relational concept of matter. Unlike Locke, however, the Bishop of Cloyne flatly denied the existence of a material substance. He wrote: "All I can do is to frame ideas in my own mind. I may indeed conceive in my own thoughts the idea of a tree, or a house, or a mountain, but that is all. And this is far from proving that I can conceive them existing out *of the minds of all spirits*."[1]

Few thinkers, writers, and ordinary individuals resonate with the idea of solipsism to the point of, say, enjoying its inner attractiveness or repulsiveness, consistency, and paradoxality. Among these, Samuel Johnson, in a letter to Berkeley, confessed: "The reading of your books has almost convinced me that matter as it has been commonly defined for an unknown *Quiddity* is but a mere non-entity. That is a strong presumption against the existence of it, that there never could be conceived any manner of connection between it and our ideas. That the *esse* of things is only their *percipi*. . . ."[2]

The laconic dictum *esse est aut percipi aut percipere* summarizes the impossible central solipsistic position, without properly enlisting adherents in the Western hemisphere. It nevertheless haunted several powerful and critical minds, among them Fichte, Wittgenstein, and Husserl, no less than Husserl's progeny: Sartre and Merleau-Ponty. None of these philosophers, however, succumbed for more than a fleeting moment to the temptation of absolute, mad, contrary-to-fact consistency. Solipsism as qualifier is, in philosophical parlance, an insult, and even the suspicion of flirting with it stigmatizes one with ignominious guilt.[3] As a consequence, anyone even slightly contaminated by it will retreat into philosophically more sound positions by trying to deploy his or her own kind of realism, be it phenomenological (*cum corpore, cum conscientia*), transcendental, communicational, empirical, dialectic, scholastic, etc.

Not so with Beckett who, fortunately, not being a philosopher, could experiment with the dangerous central dictum of solipsism at will.

But if philosophical solipsism is no more than a provisional, ephemeral, almost fictional stage in the development of an argument, it appears in Beckett's work as one of the leitmotifs that stamp his artistic construct with the indelible emblem of an impossible wager. A singular rhetoric will betray this obsession, a rhetoric of the first person singular (sometimes plural)—soliloquy.

Film—a metaphysical visual joke about perceiving and being perceived, and therefore being thrust into being without consent—acts no longer on the Cartesian split of mind and body, but on the more sophisticated opposition between the Transcendental Ego and the constituted self.

The aporia in *Film* consists actually in the unbearability of being "perceived" (*percipi*)—presumably by oneself, but the perfect neutrality and admissibility of *percipere*, e.g., the room as perceived by O is normally perceived, described as bearable. It is the perceivedness of O by E that is agonizingly painful, this very form of *inspectio sui* à la Geulincx. The split in *Film* might also be expressed as one between the "for itself" (*pour soi*) and the "in-itself" (en-soi) in Sartrean terminology; this will be then the fear of reification leading to the pathological flight of the subject in front of the camera. The camera is objectifying, casting, constituting Buster Keaton as an image. It makes visible, it sustains in being, it "creates"; but that may be a secondary, "evil" creation. The character has our sympathy and tries to escape the camera, this obstinate voyeur engaged in an eternal pursuit of its "object," by violently "bracketing" that object's individuality, subjectivity, inner privacy, soul.

Philosophically, Beckett descends from Descartes, although there are quite a few important allusions to Greek and medieval philosophy scattered in his work; but as far as the subjectivistic close-in is concerned, one cannot go further in time than Sr. du Perron, who already appears as master-model in the early poem, *Whoroscope*.

The Cartesian track has been explored exhaustively, in all its implications, especially in Morot-Sir's "Beckett and the Cartesian Emblems."[4] My contention is that from *Murphy* on—and Murphy is acknowledged as both a prototype for future incarnations and as a Cartesian hybrid (not to say centaur, or chimera)—the Cartesian ontology is refracted through occasionalism, mainly that of Geulincx, according to whom the *cogito* is an assertion of powerlessness associated with an incessant and painful introspection; the ego, unlike the Cartesian subject of *cogitationes*, is at best an occasion for, and not an underlying substructure of, thinking. Geulincx spills out treasuries of ratiocination only to prove in the end the spirit's impotency to probe into the abyss of matter and of itself. While acutely aware of the Cartesian problematic, occasionalism is also a conviction about its insolubility and, because of that, has indefatigably, obsessively, insisted for years, as in a hopeless waiting (Simone Weil), on incomprehensibility and its correlate, the miracles in the universe. Beckett's moods, even in *Murphy,* but certainly more so in *Watt,* sound infinitely more akin to the agnosticism and pessimism of a Geulincx than to Descartes's apodictic certainties, But even Murphy, once his *conarium* (pineal gland) is reduced to zero though ascetic practices, allows himself to be "kicked," both *in intellectu* and *in re,* and is therefore shaken off his solipsistic posture.

Another pillar of Beckett's solipsism seems to arise from his artistic minimalism that directly leads to the last, minimal, and actually non-reducible, residue of all subjectivity: the ego. This irreducibly is both a comical occurrence and a willful choice. So in *Image:* "je dis me comme je dis je comme je dirais il parce que ça m'amuse je me donne dans les seize ans. . . ."[5]

At the risk of appearing pedantic in projecting a favorite grid upon the reading of Beckett, I would advance that he operates in his work one of the most thoroughgoing phenomenological reductions. His aporetic, the systematic deconstruction of language and of meaning, but especially that of reference, is akin to the tedious and sometimes outright inexplicable steps of the Husserlian *épochè,* as well as to a ladder of successive purifications in any genuine mystical system, as, for instance, that of Advaita Vedanta. This is not to say, however, that Beckett is intent upon reductions or purifications in a teleological way, with a purpose of gaining anything: certainty, salvation, heaven, or hell. Phenomenological reduction comes spontaneously to the artist in quest of essences, of simplicity and, in turn, it yields pure formal translucency. By uncluttering the natural landscape, the artist arrives at bare figures and scarce colors; successive eliminations, far from hurting the mysterious meanings, let them shine through. Sometimes the illumination is produced by baring the descriptions, speeches, and stories of all their elemental components and leaving intact their genitor: the "I" that speaks. That way, the universe will appear to vanish or be kept in being by a mouth, traversed by a verb or two, which even then seems to transcend its power of generation.

Credibility in the evanescent structures of the universe borrows its evocative strength from the ego that lends it intention and intentionality, direction and vectoriality. Outside the "I" that one can vaguely guess behind the enfeebled syntactic and semantic game, little prods us to pay attention: an I, seldom a we. Sometimes only fleeting images that, we know for sure, are shreds of memories, imaginative rags; yet somebody's. Moreover, this asymptotic pole of the artistically suspended universe tends constantly to negate itself: isn't that the only way to silence the whole "blooming, buzzing confusion," to at last annihilate Being?

Solipsism might be stirred up by the existential anguish expressed by Heidegger in quite classical fashion: "Anxiety individualizes Dasein and thus discloses it as *solus ipse.* But this 'existential solipsism' is so far from the displacement that results from putting an isolated subject-thing into the innocuous emptiness of word-less occurring, that in an extreme case what it does is precisely to bring Dasein face to face with its world as world, and thus bring it face to face with itself as Being-in-the-world."[6]

One step beyond that, however, and the attempt to supersede anguish brings about the nihilation of the ego itself. This is the deeper sense of Beckett's mysterious play with the: "not-I"—a repeated negative—which exorcises anguish, as in the mouth of Mouth, in *Not I.* The same juggling with an "I/not-I" pointing both to the ultimate instance of construing the universe of discourse followed by its cancellation, is to be found in the *Unnamable,* where a constant irony about, and rejection of, the I are exhibited:

> Where now? Who now? When now? Unquestioning. I, say I. Unbelieving. Question, hypotheses, call them that. Keep going, going on, call that going, call that on. . . . I did nothing. I seem to speak, it is not I, about me, it is not about me.[7]

> Ah yes, all lies, God and man, nature and the light of day, the heart's outpourings and the means of understanding, all invented, basely, by me alone, with the help of no one, since there is no one, to put off the hour when I must speak of me. There will be no more about them.[8]

To transcend the state of solipsism, the *solus ipse* must be killed or at least bracketed. In *Company,* this situation obviously obtains: a super-instance—the Voice—addresses the character in the dark, describing its spatiotemporal coordinates. But the whole is an act of the imagination; quick, hushed silence is required in the mysteriousness of the process. One *may* say that the Voice is the Transcendental Ego, absolutely impersonal, addressing a third, an Alter Ego. The emergence of any third appears as highly improbable, or in any event, exceedingly difficult. There are two: the Voice and the one, whose reference frame is spelled out by the Voice, and whose mind is passive to the point of not even reaching to the Voice. The voice recites the litany of the little boy, and of his mother, hand-in-hand, in the presumably Irish landscape; the voice speaks of the blue of the sky, and of the day when the other saw the day, and of the father's regrets about it, themes familiar from *Texts for Nothing, Fizzles,* and other opuscules. But in *Company,* a subtle advance takes place, which, one could say, is the investigation of the need *not to be the only one* left in the world. "Inventing the voice and the hearer and himself. Deviser of the voice and of its hearer and of himself. Deviser of himself for company. Leave it at that. He speaks of himself as of another. Himself he devises too for company. Leave it at that. Confusion too is company up to a point."[9]

Company offers in a nutshell the most extreme, and extremely advanced, modern literary shape of solipsism together with Beckett's central "trouvaille," a philosophical one, if anything, about the necessity, the duty even, to live with and within the "mess" (le gâchis). The piece is about loneliness (and sole-ness too), a loneliness engendering another loneliness, in order to dispel loneliness. An Ego generating an Alter Ego and another, and so on up to the genesis of the "blooming buzzing confusion" of the world as the end of any alterity. The vast parable of solitude grows into hyperbole when the comic overtones start taking over. What could possibly "enhance company"? Within this feverish activity led by the author for centuries, that of "the conjuring of something out of nothing,"[10] resonates a voice, even one's own, perceived as not one's own, a different voice received as mysteriously different, imagination, confabulation, even prayer—with a slight shade of self-mockery. The black (of darkness) apt at keeping company. Some shades at least. Some postures more capable than others. But which ones? Some locomotion modalities, although they too might remain unidentified. Apparently because they might foster some possibilities of meeting. Whom? A dead rat, for example. Fine example of company: a long ago dead rat.

In the impossibility of fighting loneliness coupled with the need for company, Beckett touches on his usual *aporia* at a most delicate point of the phenomenological balance. The "I" that speaks is obviously alone; at the same time, in the mode of constituting its world in imagination, it must seek the company of others, of *an* other at least. The first such to be taken seriously is the body: in its "spectral bone-whiteness," it is the first real companion to the "I." The others, as we have seen, are possibly aural phenomena, not far from the hallucinatory, the voices a poet hears, emanating from behind one's own, or from within, but nonetheless pure and disembodied. Finally there are the even less real, sometimes mock companions, like the sea, or the tide, the dead rat, or like the vanishing woman in *Company* who, by the way, seems to carry the mood obverse to that of the woman in *Premier amour.*[11]

This concrete literary experience in solipsism is floating amid a sea of pessimistic if not outright nihilistic moral connotations. Obviously, meditating on the evils of mankind, one may emerge as a solipsist—a pathway current in Oriental metaphysics. The idea that every other is a projection of self transcends, however, the implicit moral meditation and takes one abruptly into a hard-to-accept ontological statement. But Beckett had anticipated this aporetic demonstration through symbols much earlier, in the poem "Echo's Bones,"[12] in *Murphy,* and in *Watt.* Only a reader capable of accepting this progression or regression of thought from the search of sole-ness to its less-than-conditional final assertion, can take at all seriously an opus like *Company.* Yet *Company,* along with the stress on the counterfactual of absolute solitude, paradoxically populates the world of the writer and the reader with innumerable phantoms, all results of the phantasmagoric capacity of the I to proliferate and create more similes to itself. Modern solipsism, in shifting emphasis from the everyday experience of the person in the street to an "author in search of characters" or of subject matter, proves undeniably subtler, more elusive but also more "realistic," if this word be permitted, than classical solipsism. It is a solipsism of language and meanings, not one of being and knowledge.[13]

But why speak of solipsism? Isn't loneliness sufficient as a critical category? The paradox of solipsism exhibits almost literally the same shape as that of Beckett's ultimate and most profoundly stated *aporia*: impossible, therefore unavoidable. I can't, therefore I shall. It espouses the same logical form as Tertullian's: *credo, quia absurdum.* . . .

While it is impossible to think of myself as the sole source of being, this thought is inescapably true for the poetic universe, the only one delivered by the writer, in any event; and it is rigorously correct, both experientially and logically. Thus the absurd lies at the core of Beckett's dramaticules, not as sheer *non sequiturs,* cultivated nonsense and flat denials of meaning, but as *the* logical paradox that moves the writing hand out of its inertia. What logic and reflection affirm, ordinary experience is sure to deny. If we accept Locke's rambling thought that "the mind, in all its thoughts and reasonings, hath no other immediate object than its own ideas, which alone it can contemplate";[14] we must also admit as evident "that our knowledge is only conversant about them."[15] It appears thus that the possibility of a would-be *pragmatic* solipsism is at the very roots of modern philosophy, and not at all a postmodern contraption. It is true, however, that the wager of transmogrifying an abstract epistemological argument into the stuff of prose, drama, and poetry was won by Beckett, our contemporary, with far-reaching consequences for the notion of art itself. By that I mean solely that Beckett stands at the frontier between the minimalist experiment in art and its self-cancellation altogether.

Thus, the craving is for a real close-in, and then again for an expansion to the size of the universe as if the skull once folded in upon itself in deep reverie or reflection could later, at will, produce or reproduce the whole universe. A passage from *The End* mimics that: "The sea, the sky, the mountains, and the islands closed-in and crushed me in a mighty systole, then scattered to the uttermost confines of space."[16]

Even though the roots of Beckett's solipsism can be found in classical British empiricism, they do not lie there exclusively. His skepticism is equal in power and stringency to that of a Sextus Empiricus or a Nagarjuna; Beckett's pessimism is of Buddhistic intensity, whether acquired indirectly through Schopenhauer,[17] or independently conceived, or both. His version of cosmic pessimism is coupled with an abhorrence of self and the sheer mystical bent to destroy it whenever feasible. The solipsist character par excellence, Murphy, who is also the prototype for all future egological characters in Beckett's prose, sleeps well for the first in a long time when he succeeds in conferring upon the self he hates the aspect, even to Ticklepenny's expert eyes, of real alienation.[18]

Another concomitant or perhaps mandatory correlate of solipsism is minimalism, which I would characterize in Beckett's art as the conscious progression toward experiencing and producing the minimal structures still able to account for an aesthetic effect. In this perspective, the *solus ipse* (taken in the act of writing) emerges as a minimal, vestigial structure, a bedrock source of difference, the last irreducible residue (of subjectivity) out of which the universe—dilated *or* contracted at will—can be engendered.

Similarities between Beckett's progressive simplification of the world and the phenomenological reduction have been pointed out by Hesla[19] and others; it is a procedure he shares with many, especially with painters in the abstract-expressionist tradition. Yet none of these artists has eliminated the outer world or deconstructed so systematically every objective meaning. "Beckett climbs one more rung in the ascetic ladder" as Jean-Louis Mayoux aptly remarked.[20] The parallel with Husserl's requirement for his *époché* is striking indeed.

Each time Beckett stages pure voices, void discourses, rather than polyphonic narratives and descriptive paragraphs, it seems, *bel et bien,* that it is the Transcendental Ego who speaks, who constitutes himself a body, (mostly a mutilated one), then some kind of persona whom he immediately addresses in the second person, and following this—why not?—a whole bunch of Alter Egos: the Murphys, the Molloys, the Malones, the Watts; and, upside down, the Worms, the Mahoods, and the Macmanns: *a whole intersubjective community of monads,* as Husserl would call it. All this, however, only to retreat once more into the inaccessible Jar of the Unnamable, or a primordial Womb, Skull, or Tent; yet no sooner is "monad" uttered—whether Leibnizian, without windows, or phenomenological, somewhat more open to communication—than we are relapsing into the world of absolute closure, self-containment, and self-sufficiency of solipsism.

A rather unique combination of the static and dynamic in the metaphor of the skull, a "hollow sphere hermetically closed to the world without,"[21] and the "inside of my distant skull where once I wandered, now I am fixed, lost for tininess or straining against the walls,"[22] as the Unnamable would have it. The padded cell, like the hollow sphere or the empty chambers, the huts, the caves and the cabins, or, more archetypically, the caskets, are all privileged *places* that release the imagination and hence the creative power to produce *or* to annihilate the world. This is the case in *Endgame.*

In *Watt,* the Kafkian incident of the piano tuners—the Galls, father and son—as related by Watt, takes on the value of a symbol for a solipsistic and apriori constitution of meaning. After the younger piano tuner declares the piano doomed, and they both depart, the narrator starts wondering why the incident did not die in Watt's mind but "continued to unfold, in Watt's head, from beginning to end, over and over again, till it developed a purely plastic content, and gradually lost in the nice processes of its light, its sound, its impacts and its rhythm, all meaning, even the most literal."[23] Whatever had happened that day, "the scene in the music-room, with the two Galls, ceased very soon to signify for Watt a piano tuned, an obscure family and professional relation, an exchange of judgments more or less intelligible, and so on, if indeed it had ever signified such things, and became a mere example of *light commenting bodies, and stillness motion, and silence sound, and comment comment.*"[24] The passage suggests the filmic constitution of a perceptual noema, where some allowance is still made for "comment on comment" but with a definitely artistic, uninvolved point-of-view, that of the mind that entertains perceptions and *percepi*s; the "I" in rapid, and less rapid, motion.

This "fragility of outer meanings" discovered by Watt passes further into *no meanings* whatsoever, into the very annulment of the pursuit for meaning. The incident of the Galls that was converted into images "rather belonging to some story heard long before, an instant in the life of another, ill told, ill heard, and more than half forgotten,"[25] plays in the narrative the miraculous role of abolishing, for Watt, all possibility of the preexistence of any "outer meanings" altogether, even of objective correlates of meanings, simultaneously with the occurrence of events, or the encountering of objects.

Watt is a drama of "surds," of utter incommensurability; that of Watt to his task; of Knott to his image; of language to feeling; of emotion to reality. No wonder it ends, for Watt at least, in the paraphrastic distortion of his language, a total glossolalic effect. It is true that in the end, all the incredible inversions in Watt's speech are straightened out, deciphered, made sense of. But what of Mr. Knott, the master and end-goal of Watt's pilgrimage? Was he discovered? Seen? Understood? Did he succeed in taking away Watt's doubts, down-to-earth habits, empirical convictions, changing him in any way? Well, in this universe of total "surds," "Mr. Knott needing nothing, if not, one, not to need, and two, a witness to his not needing, of himself knew nothing. And so, he needed to be witnessed. Not that he might know, no, but that he might not cease. . . ."[26]

Actually, to make things more comical, Mr. Knott needs to be witnessed permanently, that is why he is careful to keep two valets, one on the going, one on the coming, lest he be faced with extinction by not being watched. . . . This is the supreme irony directed by Beckett against the very Berkeleyan emblem of solipsism, as there are other ironic treatments of the Leibnizian monadology. The wager of solipsism which, at times, looks sterner and more earnest than, say, Tertullian's paradoxes, Kierkegaard's fear and trembling, or Pascal's emotional wager of faith, takes on definitely the hue of a literary jocular device, being saved thereby from physical impossibility if not from ridicule.

Telling as these stratagems and devices are in Beckett's art, it would be preposterous to try and inflate his flickering meditations to the size of a philosophical self-conscious thesis, or to dissolve his work into a mosaic of metaphors each signifying a philosophical dilemma, an argument, or a counterargument. Solipsism is not really thematized by Beckett, but only lightly touched upon, toyed with, and, in the end, deconstructed as surely as any other formal or informal intellectual proposition that occurs to him; the term *solipsistic* itself appears in the texts qualified in ironic or even oxymoronic ways. "Seedy" (Murphy), "peripatetic" (Belacqua), "in love" (*First Love*), etc.[27] But even as it becomes more qualified, it is negated as such, i.e., as pure solipsism. Philosophy can be read into the Beckettian text as the willy-nilly accompaniment of the drive to think, along with the impossibility to think, one's lived experiences, as the trace, or *gramme* (Derrida) and/or any allusion to it; yet never as the thing itself; humor pulverizing everything, even the hardest of philosophical dilemmas, into a shining cloud of stardust.

Notes

1. G. Berkeley, *Principal Dialogues and Philosophical Correspondence* (Indianapolis: Bobbs-Merrill Co., 1965), 145.

2. Ibid., 215.

3. Indicative of this stigma is the curious fact that in a 340-page book on *Berkeley: Critical and Interpretive Essays*, ed. Colin Turbayne (Minneapolis: University of Minnesota Press, 1982), the word solipsism does not occur even once; "solitary man" is mentioned, however, as the seventeenth-century image from which Berkeley tended to deviate toward a philosophy of action of sorts.

4. Edouard Morot-Sir, "Samuel Beckett and the Cartesian Emblems," in *Sam-*

uel Beckett: The Art of Rhetoric, ed. Edouard Morot-Sir, Howard Harper, and Dougald McMillan III (Chapel Hill: University of North Carolina Press, 1976).

5. Samuel Beckett, *L'image* (Paris: Les Éditions de Minuit, 1988), 11.

6. Martin Heidegger, *Being and Time,* trans. J. Macquarrie and E. Robinson (New York: Harper and Row, 1962), 233.

7. Beckett, *The Unnamable,* in *Three Novels by Samuel Beckett* (New York: Grove Press, 1965), 291.

8. Ibid., 350.

9. *Company* (London: John Calder, 1980), 74.

10. Ibid., 34.

11. In *Premier amour,* the mood was toward a "monadic" relationship to life, in Peirce's terms, a pure beatitude of sound, color, with almost no "shock of individuation." In *Compagnie,* it seems that Beckett really won the "battle of the soliloquy" of which he used to speak in *Mercier et Camier.*

12. Clearly, there is an early talk of the skull, and prefiguration of the close-in universe, while the "I" sees itself as "The Vulture": "dragging his hunger / through the sky of my skull / shell of sky and earth" ("The Vulture," in *Poems in English* [New York: Grove Press, 1961], 21).

13. A. D. Nuttal in *Common Sky: Philosophy and Literary Imagination* (Los Angeles: University of California Press, 1974) gives the following elaborate classification of solipsistic devices met in literature: intermittent, epistemological, methodological, communicational, of meaning, and doctrinaire. While Wittgenstein and Husserl are evidently of the doctrinaire type, they also tend to back off its ultimate consequences. Hume, Bradley, Wordsworth, and Eliot are said to have created fancy chimeras, centaurs, out of sheer solipsistic fear or unease.

14. John Locke, *An Essay Concerning Human Understanding,* ed. J. W. Yolton (reprint of the 5th ed. [New York and London: Dutton, 1961]), 1:23.

15. Ibid.

16. *Stories and Texts for Nothing* (New York: Grove Press, 1967), 72.

17. Schopenhauer, however, hated solipsism, and thought that all its representatives belonged in the nuthouse.

18. "And in effect Murphy's night was good, perhaps the best since nights began so long ago to be bad, the reason being not so much that he had his chair again as that the self whom he loved had the aspect, even to Ticklepenny's inexpert eye, of real alienation. Or to put it perhaps more nicely: 'conferred that aspect on the self whom he hated'." *Murphy* (New York: Grove Press, 1957), 194.

19. David Hesla, *The Shape of Chaos* (Minneapolis: University of Minnesota Press, 1971).

20. Jean-Louis Mayoux, "Comment se tenir compagnie?," *Critique* 402 (1981): 1105–7.

21. *Murphy,* 107.

22. *The Unnamable,* 34.

23. *Watt,* 74.

24. Ibid., 75.

25. Ibid., 72.

26. Ibid., 208.

27. Eugene Kaelin has exhaustively listed all the instances where solipsism occurs in Beckett's work in his *The Unhappy Consciousness: The Poetic Plight of Samuel Beckett* (Dordrecht, Holland: Reidel, 1981). Kaelin's thoroughness in phenomenological description and analysis is admirable; however, I cannot agree with his conclusion that, "sooner or later (e.g., in the stories) the Solipsist will die" (p. 58). Like every other philosophical posture and structure of nihilation in Beckett's prose, solipsism is cyclically revived and obliterated, without ever disappearing as a metaphoric correlate of artistic activity. The artistic drama unfolds exclusively within the confines of one's skull. And this is not, by any means, an impoverishment: let us not forget that, roughly speaking, the number of neurons in one fully developed brain equals that of the stars in our galaxy.

Bibliography of Books, Portions of Which First Appeared in the *Journal of Beckett Studies*

Ben-Zvi, Linda. *Samuel Beckett,* English Authors Series. Boston: Twayne Publishers, 1986.

Brienza, Susan. *Samuel Beckett's New Worlds: Style in Metafiction.* Norman, OK: University of Oklahoma Press, 1987.

Cohn, Ruby. *Just Play: Beckett's Theater.* Princeton, NJ: Princeton University Press, 1980.

Connor, Steven. *Samuel Beckett: Repetition, Theory and Text.* New York: Basil Blackwell, 1988.

Dearlove, J. E. *Accommodating the Chaos: Samuel Beckett's Nonrelational Art.* Durham, NC: Duke University Press, 1982.

Doll, Mary A. *Beckett and Myth: An Archetypal Approach.* Syracuse: Syracuse University Press, 1988.

Fitch, Brian T. *Beckett and Babel: An Investigation into the Status of the Bilingual Work.* Toronto: University of Toronto Press, 1988.

Knowlson, James, and John Pilling. *Frescoes of the Skull: The Later Prose and Drama of Samuel Beckett.* New York: Grove Press, 1980.

Murphy, P. J. *Restructuring Beckett: Language for Being in Samuel Beckett's Fiction.* Toronto: University of Toronto Press, 1990.

Rabinovitz, Rubin. *Innovation in Samuel Beckett's Fiction.* Urbana: University of Illinois Press, 1992.

Toyama, Jean Yamasaki. *Beckett's Game: Self and Language in the Trilogy.* New York: Peter Lang, 1991.

Zurbrugg, Nicholas. *Beckett and Proust.* Totowa, NJ: Barnes and Noble Books, 1988.

Contributors

James Acheson is senior lecturer in English at the University of Canterbury in Christchurch, New Zealand. He is coeditor of *Beckett's Later Fiction: Texts for Company,* editor of *The British and Irish Novel Since 1960,* and author of two forthcoming books, one on Beckett and the other on John Fowles.

Thomas J. Cousineau is associate professor of English at Washington College and the author of *"Waiting for Godot": Form in Movement* in Twayne's Masterwork Studies series. His articles on Beckett have appeared in *Modern Fiction Studies, College Literature, Southern Humanities Review,* and the *Journal of Beckett Studies.*

S. E. Gontarski is professor of English at Florida State University. He has published widely on modern literature, theater, and theory. Among his publications are *Samuel Beckett's "Happy Days": A Manuscript Study; The Intent of Undoing in Samuel Beckett's Dramatic Texts;* and *On Beckett: Essays and Criticism.* He has recently edited two volumes in *The Theatrical Notebooks of Samuel Beckett* series and is currently editor of the *Journal of Beckett Studies.*

James Hansford teaches English at the Royal Grammar School, Guildford.

Katherine Kelly is associate professor of English at Texas A & M University. She has written *Tom Stoppard and the Craft of Comedy* (1991) and essays on George Bernard Shaw, Tom Stoppard, T. S. Eliot, and Samuel Beckett. She is currently at work on a study of the Actresses' Franchise League, an Edwardian suffragist organization.

Jeri Kroll has taught at Flinders and Adelaide universities, both in Australia, and is currently a free-lance writer. She has published four children's books, four volumes of poetry, the most recent of which are *Monster Love* and *House Arrest,* and a collection of fiction entitled *The Electrolux Man and Other Stories.*

Paul Lawley is senior lecturer in English at the University of Plymouth (Exmouth campus), England. His essays on Beckett's work have appeared in *Modern Drama, Modern Fiction Studies,* the *Journal of Beckett Studies,* and the collection *"Make Sense Who May": Essays on Samuel Beckett's Later Works.*

Heath Lees is professor of music in the School of Music at the University of Auckland, New Zealand. In addition to writing principally on musicological subjects, he is interested in the place of music in twentieth-century literature, and he has also written "The Introduction to 'Sirens' and the *Fuga per Canonem*" for the *James Joyce Quarterly.*

Ileana Marcoulesco has recently retired from teaching in the Graduate Philosophy program at the University of St. Thomas, Houston, Texas. She has coedited *Contemplation and Action in World Religions* and edits *Krisis,* the journal of the Circle for Research and Philosophy, which she founded in 1981.

Anne C. Murch has taught in the French Department of Monash University, Australia, and currently works for the Australian Nouveau Theatre.

J. D. O'Hara is professor of English at the University of Connecticut, Storrs. He has edited *Twentieth Century Interpretations of "Molloy," "Malone Dies," "The Unnamable"* and is currently completing a book-length study of Beckett's early fiction.

John Pilling is reader in English at the University of Reading and associate director of the Beckett International Foundation. He is the author of *Samuel Beckett;* with James Knowlson, *Frescoes of the Skull: The Later Prose and Drama of Samuel Beckett; A Reader's Guide to Fifty Modern European Poets;* and *Autobiography and Imagination: Studies in Self-Scrutiny.* Recently he has edited, with Mary Bryden, *the ideal core of the onion: reading beckett archive* and a special Samuel Beckett number of the French journal *Europe.* He is also former editor of the *Journal of Beckett Studies.*

Index

Brater, Enoch, 2; "The Absurd' Actor in the Theatre of Samuel Beckett," 128n; *Beckett at 80/Beckett in Context*, 7
Brecht, Bertolt, 199
Brienza, Susan: *Samuel Beckett's New Worlds: Style in Metafiction*, 226
Brod, Max, 117
Bruno, Giordano, 160
Butler, Lance St. John: *"Make Sense Who May": Essays on Samuel Beckett's Later Work*, 34n; *Samuel Beckett and the Meaning of Being: A Study in Ontological Parable*, 34n
Buxtehude, Dietrich, 176–78

Calder, John, 2
Calderón de la Barca, Pedro, 12
Camus, Albert, 4, 32
Carr, H. W., 91n
Cervantes, Miguel de, 201
Chopin, Frederic, 95
Cioran, E. M.: "Encounters with Beckett," 77n
Cocteau, Jean, 12, 17
Coe, Richard, 84, 94; *Beckett*, 92n, 117n
Coetzee, J. M., 177–78; "The Manuscript Revisions of Beckett's *Watt*," 185n
Cohn, Ruby, 29, 88, 90, 116; *Back to Beckett*, 128n; "Beckett for Comparatists," 26n; "Beckett's German *Godot*," 2; *Casebook On "Waiting for Godot"*, 34n; *Disjecta: Miscellaneous Writings and a Dramatic Fragment*, 63n, 120n, 143, 145, 211n, 212n, 213n; *Just Play: Beckett's Theater*, 2, 226; *Samuel Beckett: A Collection of Critical Essays*, 117n, 166n; *Samuel Beckett: The Comic Gamut*, 33n, 92n, 120n
Columbus, Christopher, 48, 61n
Connor, Steven: *Samuel Beckett: Theory, Repetition and Text*, 226
Constant, 12
Cousin, 199
Cousineau, Thomas J., 4, 7, 8n, 64–77
Croker's Acres, 123–24, 127

Crusoe, Robinson, 48–49, 61n
Cunard, Nancy, 8n

Dante Alighieri, 35, 57, 79, 139, 144; *The Divine Comedy*, 82; *Purgatorio*, 136
Davis, Robin J.: *"Make Sense Who May": Essays on Samuel Beckett's Later Work*, 34n
Dearlove, J. E.: *Accommodating the Chaos: Samuel Beckett's Nonrelational Art*, 226; "Last Images: Samuel Beckett's Residual Fiction," 166n; "The Voice and Its Words: *How It Is* in Beckett's Canon," 164n
Dedalus, Stephen, 33, 63n, 98
Defoe, Daniel, 48
Derrida, Jacques, 1, 223; "Meaning and Representation," 165n; "The Retrait of Metaphor," 164n; "Signs and the Blink of an Eye," 165n; *Speech and Phenomena and Other Essays on Husserl's Theory of Signs*, 165n
Descartes, Réné, 6, 25, 46, 57, 63n, 143, 168, 171, 215–16
Devlin, Denis, 113; *Intercessions*, 210
Dickens, Charles: *David Copperfield*, 89, 93n
Doctor Faustus (Thomas Mann), 129
Doll, Mary: *Beckett and Myth: An Archetypal Approach*, 226
Donato, E.: "The Ruins of Memory: Archeological Fragments and Textual Artifacts," 165n
Dostoyevsky, Fyodor, 33
Driver, Tom: "Beckett by the Madeleine," 166n
Duckworth, Colin: *En attendant Godot: Pièce en deux acts*, 34n
Ducrot, O.: *Dictionnaire encyclopédique des sciences du langage*, 201n
Duthuit, Georges, 127
"The Dying of the Light," 118n

Ehrenzweig, Anton, 108; *The Hidden Order of Art: A Study in the Psychology of Artistic Imagination*, 119n
Eisenstein, Sergei, 92n